I'M COMING TO TAKE YOU

TO LUNCH

SIMON NAPIER-BELL

EBURY
PRESS

First published in Great Britain in 2005
This edition published in 2006

1 3 5 7 9 10 8 6 4 2

Text © Simon Napier Bell 2005

Simon Napier Bell has asserted his right to be identified as the author
of this work under the Copyright, Designs and Patents Act 1988.

First published by
Ebury Press
Random House, 20 Vauxhall Bridge Road, London SW1V 2SA

Random House Australia (Pty) Limited
20 Alfred Street, Milsons Point, Sydney, New South Wales 2061, Australia

Random House New Zealand Limited
18 Poland Road, Glenfield, Auckland 10, New Zealand

Random House South Africa (Pty) Limited
Isle of Houghton, Corner Boundary Road & Carse O'Gowrie,
Hoghton, 2198 South Africa

The Random House Group Limited Reg. No. 954009

www.randomhouse.co.uk

A CIP catalogue record for this book is available from the British Library.

Cover Design by Two Associates
Interior by seagulls.net

ISBN 9780091897628 (from Jan 2007)
ISBN 0091897629

Papers used by Ebury Press are natural, recyclable products
made from wood grown in sustainable forests.

Printed and bound in Great Britain by Bookmarque Ltd, Croydon, Surrey

CONTENTS

FOREWORD

All the people in this book are named and described as they really were except for Professor Rolf Neuber, whose name and appearance has been adjusted slightly, together with the names of his four friends – Lek, Manolo, Shin and Johnny Milano.

Of the other people in the book, I hope no-one takes offence. It's true that on occasion people's bad points seem to surface rather glaringly but hopefully each bad point is later redressed by some sort of balancing good point. One person, though, seems to have been presented with very few redeeming features – the Chinese gentleman who was most instrumental in Wham! playing their concert in Beijing – Mr Zhou Renkai. Consequently I decided to look him up before the book came out and see if meeting him again would make me feel different about anything I'd written. So in July of this year I flew to Beijing for the first time in nineteen years.

It was extraordinary. The grim, never-ending drabness I knew so well had completely disappeared. Beijing looked like Tokyo or Singapore. Everything that was old and grubby and depressing had been torn down and replaced with things that were tall and shiny and gleaming.

At the time Wham! went to China, Beijing had just one modern hotel – the Great Wall Hotel. Colin Thubron, in his book *Behind the Wall*, described it as a space capsule, lying on the outskirts of the city as if it had been 'discharged from another planet', with a lobby in which 'neon-lit elevators glided like glass beetles'. It was, he said, as if 'Beijing and the hotel were severed from each other'.

In 1984, Beijing and the Great Wall Hotel were indeed like two different worlds – but today it's the world of the hotel that has triumphed.

The Great Wall Hotel is now simply one of thousands of glittering steel and glass buildings.

Even more surprising are the countless districts dedicated to night life – bars, discos, restaurants and clubs of all types from grunge rock to gay. The change in just twenty years is as great as the change that has taken place in most Western cities in sixty or seventy years. Wide avenues, once empty except for a single clattering lane of bicycles, are now jammed to a standstill across all five lanes with Audis, Volkswagens, Mercedes, BMWs and Nissans.

I stayed in the Peninsula, right downtown, brashly modern and extravagant – a marbled mezzanine, a French restaurant, plasma TVs all over the place, fashion shops by Gucci, Armani, Louis Vuitton, Ralph Lauren – just like five-star hotels anywhere else in the world. The road outside the hotel was a pedestrian street with outside eating places, beer bars and street entertainers. Teenagers dressed from Next or Giordano zoomed by on skateboards or mountain bikes, as hip and rowdy as kids in New York or London. In the mid-eighties it would have been unlit and deserted, with only a nervous late-night cyclist flitting home in the dark before the secret police set off for their round of midnight arrests. Now it's no longer surly men in uniform who accost passers-by; it's pretty girls.

'Do you want sex?'

The girl spoke in excellent English and was dressed like an air-stewardess, with wide-open innocent eyes.

'D'you mean with you?' I asked.

She giggled. 'Oh no. I'm still at university. This is my part-time job. I find customers for a bar where girls give you sex. They're very well trained. You'd enjoy it. Can I take you?'

I shook my head. 'What are you studying?'

'Traditional Chinese music and dance. I'm at the University of Classic Arts and Sciences.'

'Do you play an instrument?' I asked.

'A *guzheng*,' she explained. 'It's a classical instrument that was once played for the emperors in court. I play with a traditional Chinese orchestra.'

'And do you like Western music too? Do you listen to pop?'

She pulled an iPod from her pocket and waved it at me, grinning. 'Linkin' Park, I'm mad about them. I listen to them non-stop, and Usher too. Everybody at school is cr-a-a-a-a-zy about Usher!'

*

Despite these extraordinary changes, when I tried to contact Zhou Renkai I encountered something of the Beijing I'd known from the 1980s. At that time Mr Zhou had been the head of the All-China Youth Federation (a vast organisation that co-ordinated the activities of every youth organisation in China), so I now went along to their new offices, a forty-storey skyscraper.

When I asked if anyone knew where I might find him, I was guided to the personnel department. 'He was head of the All-China Youth Federation in 1985,' I explained. 'I believe he was the very top person, the number one man.'

The woman in charge looked at me with great mistrust. 'I've worked here for thirty years,' she told me coldly. 'I've never heard of anyone called this. Why do you want to contact him?'

I told her about Wham!'s concert in China in 1985. She said she knew nothing about it and went away to check.

When she came back she told me, 'We can concede there was a concert by your group but not that there was anyone called Zhou Renkai.'

'I have his name card,' I assured her. 'It says he was head of the All-China Youth Federation. And I have press cuttings from Chinese newspapers at the time. They also confirm it.'

'Your information is false,' she said with great finality. 'I can assure you, we've checked out records. No-one of that name ever had anything to do with this organisation.'

Mr Zhou had been erased from their records – who knows for what reason.

'Never mind,' I said. 'Perhaps you can check with a few other people and tomorrow I'll phone you to see if you've had any luck. Can you give me your name card?'

She did so, grudgingly, but the next morning when I called her back she sounded even more severe than previously. 'I've told you already. No-one of that name ever worked here. I suggest you stop trying to find him.'

So underneath all the glitz and money and Westernisation, Beijing was really still the same old place – bureaucratic, communist, mysterious and dangerous – a breeding ground for falsehood and intrigue. To find again the Beijing I'd known previously was somehow comforting. It gave me a sense of continuity, of stability. In the end I decided I liked it better that way.

As for Mr Zhou, despite his obliteration from the organisation's official history, in my book at least he's been allowed to keep the position he held twenty years ago – head of the All-China Youth Federation.

It was April 1985 when it happened. After two years and seventeen visits to China, I was amazed to find that I'd somehow pulled off the impossible. Wham!, the hottest pop act in the world, were going to be the first ever Western group to play in communist China.

Simon Napier-Bell
Thailand
September 2004

PART I
APRIL 1983

1 HAPPY BIRTHDAY

Allan was Chinese; Donavon was black. Most of the time they fought tooth and nail and refused to sit in the same room together. Other times they dressed up to the nines and went out on the town with each other, the best of friends.

Allan was my ex-boyfriend and Donavon the boyfriend who'd replaced him. Both of them ran their own businesses – Allan, a hairdressing salon in Knightsbridge, Donavon, a small independent record company – and the three of us lived together in a large house in Bryanston Square, just round the corner from Marble Arch, with tall plane trees and a private park in the centre of the square for residents.

There was also a Filipino cleaning lady who sat in the kitchen every afternoon, drinking tea and consuming food from the fridge.

Into this happy world, on the morning of my forty-fourth birthday, came Jazz Summers, not as another resident but as a knock on the door.

I'd been persuaded to meet him by a mutual friend, but when I opened the door and saw him I was taken aback. Jazz looked so completely different from anyone I might get on with. Thin and wiry with receding hair and a touch of acne, he was aggressively straight and spoke in a deliberately down-market manner. On the other hand, he had a sparkle in his eye and was completely unfazed by my strange household.

Over a Chinese lunch round the corner, he told me about himself. For the last few years he'd been managing both a pop group and a folk singer. Before that he'd been in the army, stationed in South East Asia, drumming with a rock band that played gigs on off-days from Saigon to Jakarta.

Since the Far East was a passion of mine we found some common ground.

'Let's form a management company,' he suggested.

'But I want to give up being a manager.'

'With your history of success, why would you want to give it up? Surely you need money to keep your household going?'

'I'm not sure I want to keep it going. I want to make a change in my life. I'm thinking of moving to South East Asia and doing something new.'

Jazz didn't understand. To him, like most people, pop success looked alluring, but I was tired of it.

'Don't be silly,' Jazz persisted. 'I know an act who've had a couple of hits but don't have a manager. With your name we could sign them up. I'll do the work – you provide the credibility.'

I sighed, my decisiveness slipping away, my vision of living as a writer in the Far East receding. I told him, 'It wouldn't work. As soon as we'd signed them I'd feel responsible. I'd end up working just as hard as you.'

Jazz looked delighted. 'Well, that would be perfect.'

He took a piece of paper from his jacket pocket and handed it to me – a press cutting about two young guys, George Michael and Andrew Ridgeley, the hottest new act of the year and already on their third hit single. I'd seen them recently on *Top Of The Pops*. They'd sung and danced with an extraordinary macho exuberance yet there seemed to be a strange intimacy flowing between them.

They called themselves Wham!

Dick Leahy and Bryan Morrison were Wham!'s publishers. Jazz had already met with them and suggested himself as manager but they'd thought him too inexperienced. Now we went together to meet them again.

Dick and Bryan were as oddly matched as me and Jazz. They both wore sharp suits and smoked Havana cigars, but while Bryan talked loudly in a don't-give-a-toss cockney accent, Dick was smoothly ingratiating, speaking softly like an army chaplain and sometimes coming too close as he did so.

'If you want to manage these two lads,' he purred, 'you must understand they have a unique talent and need careful nurturing.'

'Bugger that,' Bryan butted in. 'Just get them into the charts.'

Either way, these two knew they had a hit act on their hands and could see that Jazz and I would make a good management team. So they helped us fix a meeting.

A few days later, George Michael and Andrew Ridgeley came to 29 Bryanston Square. On *Top Of The Pops*, they'd come across as lookalikes

– two fun-loving teenagers – a matching pair. In person, they seemed complete opposites.

Andrew chose the longest settee in my sitting-room and draped himself along it lengthways. 'Nice pad,' he said, throwing his eyes around the room. 'Great for pulling.'

George chose an armchair and sat on the edge of it, eager to get down to business. 'Who've you managed before?' he asked brusquely.

Andrew remained stretched out. From the coffee-table he picked up a book – something I'd written about the music business in the sixties – and started browsing through it.

George remained suspicious. 'We won't want you looking after our money,' he said. 'We'll be appointing accountants.'

'Fantastic, man,' Andrew commented a couple of times from his reclined position with the book, then turned to George. 'Seems like Simon spent most of the sixties either drunk or having sex. He sounds just the right person for us.'

George ignored him. 'What guarantees can you give us? We won't want to give you a contract unless we have guarantees.'

Their different personalities complemented each other well; more important, though, was the quality of the three records they'd released – 'Wham Rap', 'Young Guns' and 'Bad Boys' – all with extraordinary vitality and super-sharp lyrics. If I was going to go back to managing a pop group, at least these two guys were talented and well-spoken. And they had a wonderful image – pure Hollywood – 'Butch Cassidy and the Sundance Kid', or 'Starsky & Hutch'.

As they left, the other members of my domestic entourage peered down at them from the top of the stairs.

'They're gorgeous,' the Filipino cleaning lady told me, which was the first time she'd shown appreciation for anything in the house other than the food in the fridge.

'It's a pity they're not blond,' drooled Donavon.

'I'll fix it,' Allan suggested. 'Send them to the salon.'

2 CHERRY BLOSSOM

Sometimes my life seems to have been one long ramble of rootless hedonism. Not that I've made it a frantic search for illicit pleasure; it's been more aimless than that, which is why I call it a ramble.

I left school with no desire to do anything more than wander round the world and see what was going on. I hitchhiked round America, played the trumpet in strip-joints in Canada, sold magazines door-to-door in Mexico City and finally came back to London to work as a film editor. It was only then that I found something that suited my talents.

Having got enough money together to make a down payment on an American convertible, I drove it one night to the Ad Lib Club (a sixties joint that throbbed with music and alcohol and sexually provocative people). My arrival was seen by an aspiring pop group who so coveted my car that they approached me (well after midnight, when I was sitting in a corner of the club with my eyes half-closed nodding vacantly to 'Gloria' by Them), to ask if I would be their manager. Only vaguely aware of their presence and unable to hear a word they said, I continued to nod to the beat, which they took to mean 'yes'.

That first group was not too successful but by the time the second and third came along I'd got the hang of it and we were getting hits. Aspiring pop stars, it seemed, while knowing where they wanted to go, had little idea of how to get there. All that was needed was some common sense to point them in the right direction. It was like riding a horse in a race – the artist did the running, the manager did the riding and together we ended up at the finishing post. Not only did I get an enjoyable ride round the course, I also collected twenty per cent of their winnings.

Surprisingly, social commentators of the day viewed the management of pop singers as a profession of some importance and having made myself vaguely competent at it I found myself being written about and even admired. Although I found this rather silly I saw no reason not to take advantage of it, so for the next eight years I lived in style, travelled around Europe and America, ate in the best restaurants, put money in the bank, managed a pop group here and there, and had lots of sex.

Well, who wouldn't?

Then I developed a dangerous passion – it was Kit Lambert's fault, The Who's manager, an old friend of mine.

One sharply cold April morning in 1972, in search of coffee and a chat, I dropped in to see him at his house in Egerton Crescent where the trees had just burst into flower.

'Isn't the cherry blossom marvellous,' I commented.

Kit, in a strangely one-uppish mood, was rather snooty. 'The only place worth looking at cherry blossom is Japan.'

It rankled. He'd made me realise – despite having enjoyed a decade of living it up in the music business, swinging my way round America and Europe, feasting and boozing and finding new partners to take to bed every night – there was still an enormous hole in my education: I'd never been to the Far East.

I heard myself saying, 'In that case, I'll go there at once,' and that very same evening I was on a plane to Tokyo.

I didn't really care about cherry blossom, it was just an excuse; I'd reached a moment in life when the excesses of the rock business were boring me. My mind was ready for something new and in Tokyo I found it. It wasn't just the people or the signboards or the architecture, it was *everything*. You could feel it in the air.

Outwardly, most things looked much the same – the buildings, the clothes, the cars – but this familiar topping was resting on a perversely different cultural base. Like flicking through one of those children's books that put the face of one person on the body of another, the results were endlessly strange and seductive. A Harley Davidson whizzed past. On the pillion seat was a Buddhist monk dressed in saffron robes wearing a crash helmet.

'Why you come to Japan?' the taxi driver asked me.

'To see your wonderful cherry blossom,' I said, intending to flatter him, but I'd picked the wrong man. It was his obsession.

'Aah so. In Japan we have chelly brossom many type! Chelly brossom Someiyoshino, chelly brossom Oshima, chelly brossom Edohigan, chelly ...'

He insisted on making a special detour to drive me round the perimeter of the royal gardens, turning to talk to me in the back seat, pointing out every individual tree, naming its species and telling me on which day of the week it had blossomed. By the time we arrived at the hotel I felt my enthusiasm for Tokyo flagging, but when I walked into the lobby it was instantly revitalised. I was in the five-star equivalent of a tropical street market.

In Japan it was the custom not to invite foreign visitors to a company's offices but to go instead to their hotels. Here, among gleaming mirrors and pink marble floors, over coffee and patisserie served by doll-like waitresses and impeccable waiters in bow-tie and tails, Japanese businessmen sat listening impassively as visiting foreigners pitched their deals. Silk-shirted Filipinos, dark-suited Taiwanese, clove-smoking Indonesians, soft-smiling Thais – this lobby was not just Japan, it was the whole of South East Asia. I remembered all the books I'd read about it by Maugham and Greene and Conrad and Clavell. Why on earth had it taken me so long to get here?

Seduced in an instant, I stayed for a year. For the next twelve months, with guidebooks and language cassettes, I travelled to every country represented in that lobby. But my new-found addiction gave me a dilemma.

The sixties had introduced me to pop management which gave me money and success, but it had come entirely from working in Europe and America. Now I would have to choose – was it to be the music industry or the Far East? It was like a happily married man falling for an unsuitable mistress and I did what most men do in that situation – cheated on both.

Throughout the rest of the seventies I flew from West to East and back again, trying to find business projects that could tie the two together. I wrote songs in Indonesia, produced records in London, opened a publishing company in Hong Kong and managed a singer in Spain who was also a Filipino film star. Towards the end of the decade, someone in London introduced me to Japan, a new group searching for success.

In the middle of the punk era, when everyone else was walking round London in black leather and safety pins, the lead singer came to see me wearing full make-up and pretty clothes. Presuming he'd received advance warning of a new fashion trend, I rushed to sign his group. But I was wrong. He had no insider knowledge of things to come and when I launched the group Japan in the UK they flopped miserably. However, when their records were released in the country whose name they'd adopted, Japan became huge. Japanese teenagers liked the idea of a group named after their country, and unlike their British counterparts they didn't like pop stars in grubby punk fashions; they wanted their young men clean and neatly dressed. And if a little make-up was added, well, why not? Like Kabuki theatre, it was a part of Japanese culture.

With success in South East Asia, my life should have been perfect but Japan had little interest in being big in the Far East, they wanted to be big in Britain. Ever dutiful, I spent more time in London working on the British market and by the time the eighties rolled round they'd started getting hits.

Their success in Britain trapped me in London. Not that it was particularly dreadful. This was 1983, the punk era was over and the capital had developed a swing not seen since the sixties. Making money was respectable again. Expensive new bars and restaurants were opening all over town; designer clothes were the new fashion and the car to be seen in was a Porsche.

Getting by with a Bentley, I was back in the thick of it all. Like everyone else in London's inner circle, I ate out every night, discoed till dawn and jumped on planes at a moment's notice to go to the sun, or America, or anywhere else that took my fancy. But when the bass-player's girlfriend moved in with the lead singer, Japan broke up.

It was then that I got a niggling feeling I should be doing more with my life than managing groups. I was tired of being tied to prima donna pop stars; I felt the time had come for me finally to give up the music business and move to South East Asia – Hong Kong, perhaps, or Singapore – to start a new business or write books.

But before I could do so, Jazz Summers turned up on my doorstep and persuaded me we should manage Wham!.

3

SUCH A REMNANT

'**D**ahlink, you're looking w-u-u-n-derful.'

Connie was an Australian-Italian with an accent to match – the publicist for Allan's hairdressing salon, she was a genius at getting newspaper coverage. Glamorous, gregarious and flirtatious, she loved to flatter everyone outrageously. Whenever I went into her office she would scream with delight. 'Dahlink, what have you done to yourself? You're looking magn-i-i-i-ficent. Like a sex-god.'

To walk into Connie's room with a bad hangover and be told I looked like a sex-god was most revitalising; she made it sound so believable. The first time it happened I even went to the bathroom to check in the mirror. Well, maybe she's right, I thought, there is something rather handsome about the wasted look in my face. I should get hangovers more often.

Then from upstairs I heard it again. 'You're looking w-u-u-n-derful. What have you done with yourself?'

I went to see who was stealing my compliment – a famous footballer perhaps, or a visiting film star? No, it was our aging brown-toothed cleaning lady.

And then the hideous spotty boy from the sandwich shop arrived with lunch.

'Dahlink ...'

Our offices were in a house in Gosfield Street, a quiet side road near Oxford Circus. Connie shared her office with Richard Chadwick, with whom I'd started a music publishing company some six years earlier. Before he started working with me, Richard had been a civil servant and something of that profession had stayed with him. He was the sort of person who enjoyed making a good job of a VAT return. He did all the company accounts and already, in the early eighties, had mastered computers, which in those days meant working with an impossible system called DOS. For me, uninterested in the detail of day-to-day administration, he was a perfect partner, though I had to admit he could sometimes be a little prickly.

One day I stood behind him at the computer while he tried to show me how a spreadsheet worked. Try as I might I couldn't relate the movements of his hands on the keyboard to what was appearing on the screen.

'I'm sorry,' I told him. 'I simply don't understand.'

'Because you don't want to!' he snapped, exasperated.

He may have been right. But to be scolded by Richard now and again was a small price to pay for the benefits of having him around.

On the floor below Connie and Richard was an office meant for me, but I'd never used it. Since everyone else had offices, whenever I needed to talk to them I could use theirs. On a typical day I would go to the gym, visit Allan's salon, play squash and have a long lunch. That didn't leave much time for sitting in offices, so I gave mine to Jazz.

George and Andrew seemed to enjoy their visits to our offices. They enjoyed looking through their fan mail in the reception area and progressing upwards to the first floor where Donavon worked on a host of mysterious projects with his two secretaries. Dressed for work as other people dress for parties, he would flash a blinding white smile and jig infectiously as they passed.

One floor further and they would pass Jazz's office, usually without saying much, for Jazz would be busy on the phone berating people. Then to the top floor and Connie.

'Dahlinks, hullo – my two wonderful sex gods.'

Wham!'s self-made image of happy-go-lucky, good-looking best friends was the simple truth, but it soon became clear that in George's case the image hid a complex character full of angst and self-doubt.

Andrew brimmed with natural self-confidence; as a child he must have been given nothing but love and encouragement. George, I decided, some time in his childhood, must have been let down badly by someone in whom he'd put faith. He could shoot mistrust from his eyes like fire from a flamethrower. One moment you would be discussing a routine piece of business, the next you were enveloped in burning suspicion.

Jazz and I went with them to meet their new lawyer, Tony Russell. He had a reputation as the toughest in the business but he was a most benign person – slightly portly with owl-like glasses, always good-natured and polite. His bills were said to be as big as his reputation, but there was no sign of any lavish spending in his offices. They were small and cramped.

'I think it's best to tell you straight off,' I said, 'there'll be no money to pay you with for quite some time.'

He smiled. 'No problem. Dick Leahy says these two boys are going to be huge. I trust him. I'll wait till they get some money in before I start charging.'

It was difficult not to warm to someone so charitable. The four of us accepted his offer of tea and crowded into his small office to get started.

George had a point of view on every subject that came up. Andrew was more relaxed, accepting George's opinion on most matters as their joint one. At one point I suggested, when they started to earn money, Wham! should put their accounts with Wilson Wright, a well-known city accounting firm.

'Why them?' George snapped back.

It had been an innocent enough suggestion but the fire in his eyes accused me of being in league with Wilson Wright up to my neck. We were obviously planning to plunder Wham! for every penny they earned.

I shrugged. 'They're supposed to be the best, but there are others.' I looked at Tony for more ideas. 'What d'you think?'

Tony's suggestion received a slightly lesser blast of fire and George was quiet for a moment. 'Anyway, I want two firms, not one.'

We seemed to be living in a world of double-acts. There was George and Andrew, Jazz and Simon, Dick and Bryan, and now two separate companies to do the accounts.

'Why two?' Tony asked.

George sighed heavily, as if we were all as thick as thatched roofs. 'So one lot can keep an eye on the others, that's why.'

All this talk about money and accountants was premature – George and Andrew were flat broke.

They were signed to Innervision – a small company financed and distributed by CBS – which consisted of just four people, Mark Dean, its young owner, and his three assistants. And Innervision had signed Wham! to an unusually awful recording contract.

Before they'd signed it, George and Andrew had consulted a lawyer who'd told them not to – the terms of the contract were dreadful. But desperate to get started on their career as superstars, they'd signed anyway.

Jazz and I fixed a meeting at Bryanston Square with this previous lawyer. When we met him we understood at once why George and Andrew had paid no attention to his advice; he put his feet on the glass coffee table, drank straight from the large bottle of Evian I'd put on a tray with glasses for five people, and burped.

Andrew took me aside and apologised. 'Such a remnant. I don't know how we ever got involved with him.'

However, with the lawyer's input, Jazz and I began to unravel the various problems we had to deal with.

Wham!'s royalties were half the industry norm, the advance had been just five hundred pounds, the group were tied up for eight albums, and like all record deals the cost of making their album plus a part of the cost of making their videos was to be deducted from any royalties which became due to them. With an album already recorded and videos having been made for the first three singles, it would be years before Wham! saw any money. It was depressing stuff and when we'd finished finding out about it we realised that we were going to have to get them out of the Innervision contract.

No-one with experience of the music business could possibly think it a good idea to disrupt the smoothly advancing career of a new group by launching a court case against their record company, yet it was inevitable. If Wham! were ever going to make money, they would have to take legal action. But who was going to pay for it?

Wham! didn't have a bean.

If Wham! were doing badly money-wise, their new managers were doing even worse. It seemed I'd not only blown my chance of giving up London for the Far East, I'd done it without any financial compensation. By persuading me to continue with management, Jazz had effectively ensured I would also continue with my extravagant domestic life. And there was more to pay for than just household expenses – both Allan and Donavon's businesses needed subsidising.

Most people thought Allan's salon was a roaring success, and in terms of publicity it was. Financially, though, it wasn't. The salon was so full of film stars and footballers having their hair done for nothing that there was scarcely room for paying customers. But since it was building Allan's name, with which we intended eventually to market hair products, I persuaded myself that each week's loss was a sound investment. Allan, fully approving of this approach, drove a Rolls-Royce.

Seeing how well Allan was looked after, Donavon expected even better. He decided a new sports car might create the right image for success and a few days later he was whizzing round town in a red Mercedes. He was not only running his own record label but also trying to arrange a festival of black music at Wembley Arena which for some unknown reason required his secretary to tour London each day in the back of a chauffeur-driven car.

The bills for these things landed on my desk each month and although the break-up of Japan had given me the opportunity to escape them by moving to the Far East, I'd failed to take it.

It felt like I'd made a mistake. Our percentage from Wham! amounted to absolutely nothing, which was what we had to run our business on. And it was going to get worse. Some time in the near future we would have to make plans for getting them out of their terrible record contract.

I grumbled a little at Jazz for persuading me back into management, but not too much. Unlike me, he didn't have a house in Bryanston Square or money in the bank yet he was still managing to survive; it would have been uncharitable to complain too much. But there was another reason why I didn't grumble: I thought I'd found a way of freeing myself from the group's day-to-day management.

It had happened at our first management meeting – at the Bombay Brasserie, the best Indian in town, with a white cocktail piano and a glassed-in conservatory. Over lamb pasanda and spiced sea-bass, George and Andrew told us they wanted to be the biggest group in the world.

Jazz explained about his group Blue Zoo. 'Three years to crack the charts; then they broke up.'

'Same with Japan,' I added. 'Six years to get to the top and they broke up too. You wouldn't do that, would you?'

They laughed. 'Us? Break up? Impossible! Make us into the biggest group in the world and we'll go on forever. But we can't wait five years. You'll have to do it in two.'

That was scarcely possible.

'Especially in the States,' I emphasised. 'There's no national press, no quick way to spread the word through the *Sun* or the *Mirror*.'

'There's more than four thousand radio stations,' Jazz added. 'It means endless cosying up to DJs, hanging out with them in the evenings, taking photos with their wives and girlfriends.'

George and Andrew looked less than impressed.

'We won't do that,' George insisted. 'You'll have to find another way.'

But what? Jazz and I finished our meal in silence; the plates were cleared, the wine drunk, the menus brought for dessert. Across the room the cocktail pianist tinkled annoyingly.

Then Jazz came up with an idea. 'Maybe you could be the first group ever to play in communist China.'

There was a moment of silence as the idea sank in.

'Like when Elton played in Russia,' Jazz added.

'Only bigger,' I said. 'Because China is even more of a closed society.'

George and Andrew looked doubtful.

'You'd get every headline,' Jazz insisted. 'You'd be on TV news around the world. It'd be sensational.'

I suddenly realised I was being given the perfect excuse for travelling to the Far East while still being a pop manager in London. 'I should go to China at once,' I suggested. 'And start working on it.'

And like hearing my lottery number come up a winner, George nodded. 'Sure – go ahead. Fix it!'

4

FRESH AS DAISIES

I am the total opposite of a control freak.

If other people want to put their fingers in the pie and keep them there night and day, I'm happy to let them do so. Management is the art of taking credit for other people's work and the biggest mistake is to do too much of the work yourself. I'm prepared to put complete trust in anyone who wants to do something I would otherwise have to do myself, and in Jazz I had someone who was capable of doing everything connected with Wham!'s day-to-day management as well or better than I could. Moreover, he actually *wanted* to do it. So while Jazz worked in London, I would head for the Far East and get permission for Wham! to play a concert in China. It was the perfect arrangement.

A phone call to the Chinese consulate provided me with my first obstacle: a recorded message. 'There are no visas for private tourists. You must travel in an official tour group. If it's business, we need a formal letter of invitation from the Chinese company you are visiting. It will take a minimum of three months to come through.'

I was disappointed. London was feeling claustrophobic and I was wound up and ready to travel. I didn't feel like putting it off so I simply told Jazz there was a change of destination. 'More urgent than China, I should go and talk to Sony in Tokyo. Japan were huge there. If I could do the same with Wham! we could sell a million albums in Japan alone.'

Jazz agreed at once. I was surprised. I'd thought he might not want me leaving London when there were so many things to do, but he seemed to like the idea of being left in charge.

Since Wham! had no money, I would have to fund the trip myself. I knew a travel agent in an untidy attic in Oxford Street who could get remarkable deals. He offered me a first-class seat at a surprising discount, the snag being that it was with Pakistan airways. But the travel agent,

17

himself a Pakistani, was very reassuring. 'You will find, sir, that while people in economy get hot and crumpled, you, in your first-class cabin, will be as fresh as daisies.'

He was right. The next day, settled back in my first-class seat, I was indeed as fresh as daisies, but there was another snag – the flight was going by way of Islamabad. When we arrived there we were told to stay on the plane; the airport grounds were being used for a public execution. We peered through the windows and saw a vast crowd, three hundred yards away and stretching as far as the eye could see. Somewhere in the middle of it, I could see some sort of stage, but due to the distance and the fanciful nature of my own imagination, I wasn't sure what I could see on top of it. A gallows? A firing squad? An executioner with a scimitar? To be honest, I had no idea.

Probably because the airport officials didn't want us seeing too much of this, the plane took off ahead of schedule. But as we were hurtling along the tarmac I caught a glimpse of something far more disturbing than a public execution. In the middle of the tarmac, not thirty yards from us as we charged by, was a pile of luggage. And the suitcase on top was mine.

From the shouts of dismay emanating from the economy cabin, other people had spotted their cases too. The din of stewardesses' call buttons rang through the cabin like machines in a games arcade. 'Stay in your seats,' came the repeated announcement, 'the seat-belt sign is not yet turned off.'

The hoi-polloi from economy weren't up for such niceties; they came barging into first class demanding the pilot go back and a few minutes later the matter was resolved. The captain announced he'd received clearance to return to Islamabad and collect the luggage.

Half an hour later we took off again. I was fed an excellent curry and snoozed soundly until I was woken by an announcement. Below us were the Himalayas with Mount Everest strikingly visible, but the captain had some bad news: 'Because we were doing two take-offs instead of one we are not having enough fuel to reach Tokyo.'

I looked again at Mount Everest. To be flying above it on an empty fuel tank felt most exhilarating, but the pilot had other ideas. 'We will changing route at once and head for nearest big airport. Beijing.'

The moment the plane emerged from the clouds I was looking down eagerly on this forbidden world. China, according to all reports, was even now not fully recovered from the disastrous effects of the Cultural Revolution. As I'd found out from the consulate in London when I enquired about a visa, unless foreigners were on an official visit they were none too welcome.

At the airport the most visible thing was a signboard of Chairman Mao, forty foot high. There were guards all over the place in dingy blue uniforms but although they were carrying machine guns they looked bored rather than threatening. Still, it rather felt we might never be allowed to travel any further.

A staircase was wheeled out to the plane and an immigration official mounted it. From his briefcase he produced the most dazzlingly simple tool for processing two hundred unwanted passengers into a totalitarian country – an empty sack, which he shook open. As we passed by him, each of us tossed our passport into it. We then walked down the steps, across the tarmac, through the doors of the arrival hall and into China having given up the one thing we would most need if we were ever to leave again.

A couple of hundred of us found ourselves in an area which appeared to be outside of both immigration and customs. It was the general area in which the public milled around meeting or seeing off relatives and friends. Its air of normality surprised me, and its cleanliness too – two women mopped the stone floor endlessly from end to end and back again, trailing a smell of disinfectant – but there was not a drop of colour or excitement about the place – no advertisements, no welcoming signs, just the drab greyness of communism.

I saw our chief steward. 'How long will we be here?'

'Four or five hours, I'm afraid. They are not giving us any credit to buy fuel so we are having to have money wired from Pakistan.'

In a corner was a table where a uniformed girl sat on a folding chair. Behind her was a golden globe with arrows pointing around it but what caught my eye was a word I recognised in Russian – 'Intourist'.

I walked over to her. 'Do you speak English?'

'Russian better.'

'Sorry, I don't speak Russian. But I have a few hours free and I want to hire a car...' (I made steering-wheel movements) '... and a guide.' (For which I could think of no suitable mime.)

'Only if speak Russian.'

I shook my head. 'English, I'm afraid.'

'Cannot,' she said firmly. 'For tour you must understand what guide is speaking. Must be Russian or Chinese. If no speak, no tour.'

In the first-class cabin, apart from me there had been two other passengers. One of them, now sitting quietly at the end of the hall, was a handsome but elderly man with a high sweep of silver hair; not the dull grey hair that normally passes for silver, this was the real thing, like the metallic paintwork of a Mercedes. Although he'd spoken to the purser in English with a slight German accent, there was something vaguely oriental about his eyes, and I'd noticed him reading a book in Chinese.

I walked over to him. 'I'm sorry to butt in on your privacy, but do you speak Chinese?'

He stood up, fumbled in his pocket and with a slight bow held out both hands with a business card. He was a professor of languages from a German university – Professor Rolf Neuber.

'Look,' I told him, 'the cabin purser says we'll be here at least five hours and I've managed to hire a guide and a car to go into Beijing, but they refuse to take me unless I speak either Russian or Chinese. Would you like to go?'

The German man's face positively leapt with excitement. 'Beijing, well surely I would, sir. I haven't been here for three years, I'm on their unwanted list, I'm afraid. But this city, like so many others, is a passion of mine, and if we can get in without papers ...'

His accent and manner were strange – almost British public school but tinged unmistakably with German. It was only the merest hint, yet it was a disastrous accent for it was the accent used by Hollywood to portray gentlemen Nazis. And for me, that's what he immediately became.

In no time at all, the Nazi professor, the guide and I were sitting in the back of a ponderous black limousine, with net curtains and lace covers on the cushions, rolling along a country lane.

I couldn't believe this was the main road into Beijing – it was so rural, with fields on either side. When we'd arrived it had been drizzling; now the sun came out. The road gleamed like glass and the wet hedgerows flashed as if they were filled with sequins. Far from feeling like the ominous approach to an isolationist communist capital it felt like autumn in the English countryside.

Our guide started speaking but the Nazi professor ignored him completely and turned to me. 'Sir, let me tell you about the city you're about to see. When Mao Zedong entered Beijing in 1949 he ordered the city to be re-orientated. Instead of the north–south layout decreed by the ancient Emperors, Mao wanted to make the city politically meaningful and built wide boulevards running from East to West. Previously, visitors would approach from the south passing gates and arches that were built in magnificence to a grand finale at the Forbidden City. Now we must arrive from the east and you can see how drab it is – everything over-powered by the sheer size of these empty avenues.'

We were driving on a flat wide road, on each side of which were drab multi-storey concrete buildings. The professor had a camera but when he lifted it to take a picture the Chinese guide smacked his hand down and shook his head. I asked the professor why it was he could no longer come here officially.

He shook his head sadly. 'Oh – that's a long story. And there would be a better time than now to tell it.'

When we reached the empty vastness of Tiananmen Square, the guide encouraged us to get out of the car and have our photo taken by one of the Polaroid cameramen snapping tourists. In Chinese, the professor snapped bad-temperedly at him.

'I told him,' Professor Rolf explained, 'that I know the truth. Every ice-cream seller and Polaroid photographer in this square is a secret policeman, spying on tourists.'

Then the professor went back to his dissertation ...

'... they killed all the dogs too – clubbed them to death and took them away in carts. The Minister of Health said it was because America had used germ warfare in Korea and dogs were found to carry the diseases. But really it was so the secret police wouldn't be bothered by their bark-ing when they went round at night arresting people.'

Two hours later we were back at the airport. An hour after that, our pass-ports were returned to us and we reboarded the plane. The seat next to the professor was free and he suggested I join him.

I took out the business card he'd handed me at the airport – apart from naming him as Professor Rolf Neuber, it said he was from the Feldkirch International College of Languages. I asked him what languages he taught.

'I shouldn't really call myself a professor; I don't teach these days, I just organise things. I own a small language school in Berlin.'

'Your card makes it sound more than that.'

He shrugged.

'Why can't you go to China?' I asked.

He flicked his hand as if brushing the question away. 'Oh, it's just something political. I'm on one of their lists. I can still go if I use a different passport, but it's a bit risky.'

'And how come you speak Chinese?'

'And Japanese too,' he said with a smile, before telling me about his strange background.

His mother was German (from a German father and a Chinese mother); his father was Japanese (from a Japanese father and an English mother). They'd met in the overseas community in Shanghai in the 1920s, which is where their respective parents had also met some twenty-five years earlier. 'I was bought up speaking four languages,' the professor explained. 'Japanese, Chinese, German and English. The Eurasian community could be like that.'

'Which nationality do you feel most comfortable with?'

'German, undoubtedly. When I was ten, my father died in a motoring accident and my mother took me to live in Berlin, but then she died too. It was just before the war and I was sixteen. There was some family there from my mother's side – an uncle and aunt in Munich, very proper, with a son my age – my cousin Heinrich – already in the Hitler Youth. They didn't want a Eurasian half-caste to look after, though I admit they did offer.'

It must have been strange for him, a teenager alone in wartime Berlin with Japanese nationality and Teutonic blond hair.

'I was quite attractive,' he explained. 'Quite exotic. And that helped me stay out of the army. I found the right people to help me.'

He smiled conspiratorially. I decided he was letting me know he was gay, which I'd suspected from the beginning, and I suppose he'd guessed the same about me.

'I slept with the right people. I was seventeen and handsome and made use of it. On one occasion I even slept with Hess – they called him Fraulein Anna, you know – but in the end I settled for Herr Golsparn, a high up civil servant who'd been invalided out of the air force. He kept me out of the army and away from danger.'

'Were you studying? Or just being kept?'

'During the war, I was being kept, and in considerable style too. But when it finished Herr Golsparn disappeared and left me high and dry. Berlin was in such turmoil. Through contacts I managed to get a teaching degree without having to study for it. Looking back, it was a mistake, but that's another story. I moved to Bournemouth where I taught German and Japanese for ten years and eventually got a British passport.'

I was taking a great liking to Professor Rolf, his stories were fascinating. I'd not met anyone so interesting for years. I told him about Wham! and how I was going to try to get permission for them to play a concert in China.

'Is this for political purposes?' he asked. 'A germ of Western youth culture planted among their young people – a highly infectious virus.'

I laughed. 'Undermine communism? It's a nice concept! But it's nothing so serious. I just want to get publicity to help push them in America.'

'I can probably help you; I know lots of people in China. When are you planning to go?'

'I haven't even managed to get a visa.'

He took two passports from his jacket pocket, selected one and waved it in front of me. 'This is the secret – a British passport – I'm sure you've got one. There's a travel shop in Kowloon that has the right to issue visas for Hong Kong Chinese. They're actually called "visas for Hong Kong residents", but since all UK passport holders technically have the right to Hong Kong residence, for a few dollars they stretch the rules a bit. As a non-Chinese you shouldn't really be travelling in China on your own but in reality once you're in, if you keep your head down, no-one will ask questions. Just don't get yourself into trouble. If you want to call me in Tokyo I shall be there for three weeks – at the Okura Hotel. I shall enjoy getting involved in your project.'

I wasn't sure I wanted this stranger 'involved'; I was keen to do the whole thing on my own. If he had contacts though, perhaps I should accept some help from him. But only a little.

He put his passports on the armrest between us – one German, one British. I noticed that the German one spelt his name 'Neuber', while the British one spelt it 'Nueber'.

'Is that a mistake?'

'No. It keeps my name from coming up on annoying computer lists.'

I didn't call him while I was in Tokyo; I spent my evenings with friends from earlier visits and my daytimes in meetings with Sony, Wham!'s record company in Japan. When I got back to London I had good news for everyone. 'I think Japan will be huge for us – we could sell a million of each album.'

Sony had agreed to give Wham! their top promotion. But for George and Andrew I had even better news: 'I've made some money for you. You're going to do a TV advertisement.'

Sony had persuaded Maxwell Tapes that Wham! would soon be the biggest act in Japan and that they should use them in an advertisement. For George and Andrew it was good money – ten thousand dollars.

'And by the way,' I told Jazz, 'I've started on that Chinese idea. On the way to Tokyo I popped into Beijing to check it out.'

I returned to Tokyo almost immediately, this time sitting with George and Andrew in economy (economy tickets were all we'd been sent and I could hardly sit separately from them). I was looking forward to seeing their reactions to Japan and by co-incidence we'd been booked into the very same hotel that had first hooked me on the Far East eleven years earlier.

As we walked into the lobby it was still as wonderful as ever, but George and Andrew hardly seemed to notice. Moreover, all the way from the airport, a drive of more than two hours, George had sat reading a comic book. I found it amazing that someone so bright and interested in life could be so uninterested in the foreign culture passing him by on the other side of the window. But when a journalist came to interview them an hour after we'd arrived and asked what they thought of Japan, George's answer was perfect – relevant, observant and detailed.

Afterwards I asked him, 'How on earth could you know all that, seeing as you were reading a book all the way from the airport?'

George was nonchalant. 'While I was unpacking I turned on the TV.'

We had supper in the hotel coffee shop, George playing safe with a club sandwich and Andrew mildly adventurous with something Japanese. I didn't care either way so long as I got some wine, but none of it was any good; the coffee shop was a meeting place, not an eating place. We'd only gone there to grab something quick before going to bed early to recover from jetlag.

On the other side of the room I saw someone I knew from New York and went to say hello. When I came back George and Andrew were picking unenthusiastically at their food.

'Who was that?' Andrew asked.

'The head of a CBS label in New York.'

George didn't like where we were eating – it was meant to look like an

American coffee shop but the fluorescent chandeliers and over-fussy decor made it unmistakably Japanese, as did the bad Western food.

'Why would anyone in that position come and eat here?' George asked, nibbling the potato chips surrounding his sandwich.

'He's probably jetlagged and off to bed early like us. Besides he's just another record company crook – what would he know about good food?'

It was typical of the sort of remark I sometimes drop after a few glasses of wine and George jumped on it. 'What d'you mean, a crook? Why?'

'Anyone who works for a record company is a crook. All the major companies use sharp tricks to underpay their artists, everyone who works for them knows that.'

I'd asked for another carafe of wine but the waitress came with just a thimble-sized glass.

'My tempura's soggy,' Andrew told her. 'N-o-t c-r-i-s-p.'

He lifted the plate to show her and she solved the problem by walking away.

'Simon – about these sharp tricks ...' George fixed me with accusing eyes – he wasn't going to let the subject drop. 'How can you say *anyone* who works for a record company is a crook? Do you think a secretary in the promotion department is a crook too?'

My thimble-size glass of wine went in a gulp. I had nothing left to help me through the argument. 'What I meant was ... since everyone knows what record companies are up to, if you go and work for one you're condoning it.'

'That's such a sweeping statement. How can a secretary working in the promotion department be called a crook? You're a manager. You negotiate a contract with a record company then tell the artist, "Go ahead and sign it, it's a good deal." Aren't you condoning it too? Doesn't that make you a crook too?'

I was a bit tipsy and I hadn't intended to be drawn into such a serious discussion. 'Yes!' I told him. 'That's the fundamental problem of working in the music business. It's so riddled with dishonesty that just by being in it you're tarred with the same brush.'

'Do you blame us for signing with Innervision?' Andrew asked.

'Not at all! Signing a bad contract is the normal initiation ceremony for an artist entering the business. But you have to admit – it's also like signing a disclaimer, like saying you accept the industry the way it is. You can't have it both ways.'

*

Next day the commercial was filmed and it was not an enjoyable experience. The advertisement was for blank cassette tapes but the plot required George and Andrew to be 'Supermen', flying over Tokyo.

They were hung horizontally by wires from the gantry of the film studio – strung up by their ankles, their knees, their chests and their necks – and would stay that way the whole day, uncomfortable, unhappy and unfed. It was the most undignified thing anyone could possibly do to them and they grumbled accordingly.

'I can't believe I'm doing this,' George complained, swinging horizontally three feet from the ground.

To be honest, nor could I.

I had to admit, I was ashamed of what I'd got them into; most artists would have taken one look and left. On the other hand, in another twelve hours they would each have five thousand dollars cash in their pockets.

'How much longer?' Andrew asked.

It was ten in the morning. They'd started at nine and were due to finish in seven hours' time at five in the evening but I couldn't bring myself to tell them. I gave them good news instead. 'There's a coffee break in an hour. They're planning to lower you to the floor so you can rest for a bit.'

Round midday, a trifle bored, I called the Okura Hotel to see if Professor Rolf might still be in Tokyo. Surprisingly, he was.

'Do you want lunch?' he asked. 'I've been attending a teaching conference but it finished yesterday. I'm leaving for the States later this afternoon so lunch is the only time I have free.'

'I'm with my group in a film studio. I shouldn't really go too far.'

He came to the studio and watched with interest as Wham! were filmed swinging around on their hooks. 'Is this normal for pop groups?' he asked.

'If they want to be stars they have to put up with it.'

'And what about managers? Do they have to put up with it too? Do you have to stay with them all day?'

I shook my head. 'No way!'

So he took me across the road to what looked like a private house but turned out to be a most exclusive restaurant.

From the modern Japan of TV studios, advertising agencies, complaining pop groups and hotel coffee shops, we moved to another age – quiet and intimate – and for the first time I heard the professor speak Japanese. When he did so, he immediately stopped looking German and became a prosperous, confident Japanese businessman – his whole face seemed to change shape.

We were taken to a private room where Rolf showed me how to sit cross-legged on the floor. 'This is one of the best tempura places in town. Each tiny fried shrimp or piece of aubergine is a miniature work of art.'

We were attended by traditionally dressed girls who brought endless pieces of deep-fried food, the batter so thin it was almost invisible. 'Just to seal the flavour and make the food crisp,' Rolf explained. 'We should really be drinking a different sake with each dish but we'd end up far too drunk.'

Instead, we stuck to beer, eating in relative silence, Rolf telling me what each thing was as it came. 'A slice of young abalone – the claw of a freshwater prawn – a crab's egg – a shrimp's eye.'

'Don't joke – tell me what it really is.'

'To tell the truth, I haven't a clue. When it comes to food I'm much more German than Japanese – I'd rather have a litre of beer with sausages and sauerkraut. If I spend too long in a Japanese environment, it drives me mad. I can fake it for a while – the Chinese thing too – but my stomach stays predominantly European.'

It's little wonder I found him so fascinating. His personality was a mix of British humour, European manners and everything Far Eastern. 'Rolf, I'm jealous of the way you slide so easily into any one of four different cultures.'

'That's just *your* perception. To me, I'm a misfit in all four of them. I feel more at home when I'm somewhere totally foreign and nothing's expected of me. Like Mexico, or Thailand. I have houses in both, you know.'

When we'd finished eating we stretched back against cushions and let girls with cool towels bathe our feet while we sipped green tea. 'In the right environment, the bathing continues further up the legs,' Rolf explained. 'But *those* sorts of places no longer serve the best food.'

When the bill came, it was a piece of calligraphy – *kanji*, written with a brush by the cashier, an artistic feature of the restaurant presumably intended to soften bad news. It sent Rolf off on one of his short dissertations.

'The single thing that made the deepest impact on Japanese culture was the difficulty of writing. The way something is written – the weight and balance of the brush strokes, its beauty on paper – takes precedence over the idea being expressed. This filters through into ordinary life – the manner in which somebody speaks can take precedence over what is actually said. A foreigner might think he's hearing the word "yes" but that's because he's listening only to words. A Japanese would know from the way the words were spoken that the real meaning is, "I don't want to offend you but my answer *cannot* be yes."'

I asked, 'What does the bill say – "We don't want to offend you but three hundred dollars"?'

'Not exactly. It says, "Food is a life-zone of knowledge and understanding – seventy-five thousand yen."'

That evening, with Rolf departed, I had a rather different meal. At the end of their long day's uncomfortable filming, the key people from the record company turned up to take George and Andrew (and me) to dinner and asked if we wanted Japanese or European. George and Andrew told them European so they took us to the best French restaurant in Tokyo where George instantly ordered Beluga caviar. I was shocked. I thought he should at least have said, 'Would you mind if ...' or something like that. But he just did it.

In the taxi on the way back to the hotel I brought it up. 'Don't you think it was a bit rude ordering caviar? It must have cost as much as all the rest of the meal put together.'

He was staggered at my propriety. 'Well, that's rich, coming from you who says record companies are crooks. Why shouldn't I make them pay for caviar?'

George always had impeccable logic but there was something I'd forgotten to tell him: despite the underlying dishonesty of record company contracts, except during legal disputes, it was normal for artists and record companies to observe a truce and abide by normal good manners.

Later though, when I thought about all the underpaid royalty statements I'd seen in my life, I came to the conclusion that George, as usual, was right. Besides, we were about to embark on a legal battle that would make CBS and its licensees our mortal enemies. I should have ordered caviar too, and stuffed myself with every mouthful I could get hold of.

5 A BIT STEEP

At school, when I was fourteen, pupils and staff had to congregate in the main hall every morning while prayers were said. Seated in rows, everyone had to bow their head and close their eyes. But *I* didn't. I sat bolt upright and looked straight in front of me.

Eventually I was called to see the headmaster. 'You don't close your eyes during prayers,' he snapped.

'Nor, apparently, do you,' I replied.

For that, I was sent to London to see a psychiatrist. When I explained the reason I was there, he asked, 'Why do you do it? Why not just close your eyes like they want you to?'

'It's a matter of principle,' I told him.

'It's not,' he said, 'you're mistaken.' But he was a pleasant man, and realising how ridiculous it was for me to have been sent to see him, he stopped the consultation and gave me five shillings to go to a movie to pass the time till I caught the train back to school.

As he was seeing me out, he said, 'You're wrong, you know. You must never mistake your emotions or ambitions for principles.'

At the time I wasn't sure what he meant, but his remark came clearly into focus when George told me, 'Suing Innervision is a matter of principle.'

Principle, it was *not*.

Getting Wham! out of their contract with Innervision was primarily to do with emotion (George and Andrew not liking to think they'd been conned) and ambition (wanting a deal that would help take them further and earn them more), but unless they'd been planning to leave the music business altogether it could never be considered a matter of principle.

In the music business you don't get out of an unfair contract to get into a fair one; you get out of one unfair contract with bad terms to get into another unfair contract with slightly better terms. As you climb the pop hierarchy you get better contractual conditions as you go, moving from a bottom-rung deal where you're ripped off by every technique a record company knows, to a higher-rung deal where you're ripped off with greater subtlety. That's the fun of the music business; it's like Monopoly, or one of those other board games that make wet winter afternoons so enjoyable.

* * *

When we sat down with Tony Russell to make plans to get the group out of their record contract it wasn't only legal matters we discussed: there was also management strategy. The first thing would be to establish that Innervision had refused to renegotiate voluntarily.

If Innervision were to stand up in court and say, 'If only they'd come and asked us, we would have compromised,' the judge would throw out the case. So Tony's first advice was to approach them and try once more to reach an amicable settlement.

George and Andrew were convinced they wouldn't.

'We've already tried.'

'Over and over again.'

'They wouldn't even buy us a couple of new shirts for *Top Of The Pops*.'

Because it would go against us in court if we were unable to show we'd tried, later that afternoon I called Mark Dean, Innervision's young owner, and told him the changes we wanted in his contract. To make sure I got some sort of result from my phone call I added a few detrimental remarks about his personal morality in making such a bad deal, and to make *absolutely* sure, I added a few more about his personal hygiene.

It was Wimbledon week. Having made the call I settled down to watch some tennis on TV, but just as I was enjoying John McEnroe haranguing the umpire, the crowd, and the world in general, I was interrupted by the arrival of a motorcycle messenger. It was a letter from Mark Dean – not a nice one – more in the mood of McEnroe's threatening tirade on the Centre Court.

Perfect – just what we needed! I put it in the safe and went back to the tennis.

The following month Innervision released Wham!'s first album and it went straight to Number One. That same night I took Donavon to Provans and bumped into Obie (Maurice Oberstein, the head of CBS, the man who'd given Innvervision their deal); someone who revelled in projecting himself as grumpy and belligerent.

Provans was an odd restaurant – up a staircase to a first floor the size and shape of a railway dining car with a row of tables for four on each side of a centre aisle. Obie was five or six tables away, so half expecting to be thrown off balance by the sway of a train, I walked down the narrow passage to talk to him.

'Obie, this Wham! thing is about to get out of hand. You gave Innervision a terrible deal, and they gave Wham! an even worse one. Why don't you just refinance Innervision so they can make a better deal with Wham!? That way the unpleasantness could be avoided.'

He looked at me as if I'd broken his strictest code of conduct. 'I can't talk about that. You're taking advantage of your friendship with me. If you want to talk with me, speak about something else. Who's that nice black boy you're with?'

I ignored the question and pursued the original subject. 'Obie, don't be so stupid about this Wham! thing. Their album's just gone to Number One – surely it's worth sorting it out amicably. Why can't we talk about it?'

Obie turned his attention back to his plate. 'If you won't introduce me to your nice black boy, there's nothing more to talk about. Send me a letter.'

He forked some food into his mouth and turned his head away, determined to talk no further.

I swayed back to my seat. Obie, it seemed, actually *wanted* us to go to court. Was it possible he'd planned this whole thing from the beginning? Had he intentionally engineered Innervision into an impossible position so he could step forwards at the last minute and sign Wham! directly to CBS?

Perhaps he was even on our side!

* * *

Almost as soon as we met, George told me, 'I've never done anything I could regret later.'

Well, nor had I, but for quite different reasons. George avoided the possibility of regret by being cautious; I avoided it by banishing regret from my emotional vocabulary; that way I could rush headlong into whatever took my fancy. For me, the game was everything while the result was of less consequence. Even Jazz, who was always desperate to win, was happier taking chances than taking care.

Andrew liked our attitudes, but for someone as serious about his career as George we must have looked dangerous (and it was him rather than Andrew who counted in these matters). He usually sought advice from Dick Leahy, one of the two cigar-smoking publishers.

For me this was simply one more piece of delegation. Dick – always planning, always cautious – was the sharpest of all the people around Wham!; the one person who'd seen from the start that Wham!'s image was not as real as people thought it was. It wasn't really George and Andrew; it was Andrew (the real person), and Andrew (the copycat version played by George). 'Wham! is George writing for Andrew and a friend,' Dick explained to me. 'George just happens to be the friend.'

When George went in a wrong direction, Dick could usually edge him back in the right one. Like when Wham! initially refused to do a children's TV show because they thought it wasn't cool; or when George buried the master tapes for their album in his garden and refused to give them to Innervision until they came up with some money.

Had it been me talking to George, I might have walked away from the argument or told him he was acting like a fool. Jazz might have picked him up and shaken him, even banged him against the wall. But Dick could be relied on to come to the rescue, talking in his soft, persuasive, chaplain-like voice and eventually getting his own way (which was usually our way too).

When it came to taking legal action against the record company we thought Dick's caution might kill the idea; the case could take a full year and even then we might lose. Moreover, during that year no new songs would be recorded nor records released; the group's career would not move forward one inch. We were sure Dick would initially counsel against it; so when he called us, having spoken to George, and said go ahead, we knew it was really on.

But before we could send Innervision a letter announcing legal action we had to make sure Wham! were truly the biggest act in the UK. Innervision had already released the album which had gone to Number One; now we had to arrange a nationwide tour to coincide with the start of our legal action. The tour would give us money to pay our legal costs and provide a basis for hyping the media, but to do this it needed kudos. And big money!

*

Harvey Goldsmith was Britain's top rock promoter; he put on shows by superstars – big names who'd been around a decade or more – but he never promoted new groups. He was more used to promoting gigs at Wembley Stadium than at Hammersmith Odeon or Glasgow Apollo. But if Harvey's name was attached to Wham!'s first tour it would make the industry sit up and notice. Harvey was class and we wanted him.

'No way,' he said down the phone. 'I don't promote beginners.' But Jazz worked on him and persuaded him at least to come round and talk about it.

Harvey was a roly-poly man, almost as wide as he was tall, and he enjoyed it. His company logo was a small silhouette of his rotund body. His face was also round, much of it covered with a thick black beard. He enjoyed his unmistakable Jewishness – he could equally well have been a New York jeweller or a wholesaler of Kosher meat.

At Bryanston Square he parked himself in an armchair and accepted a cup of coffee. Our plan was to ask him for an amount of money well in excess of what most new groups would get for their first tour and Jazz was the first to speak.

'Wham! are the biggest new act to come out of Britain in a decade. A year from now they'll be the biggest act in America too. If you agree to promote them in the UK, we'll let you handle them in Europe too, but we want a minimum guaranteed fee of one hundred and ten thousand pounds.'

Harvey was astounded. He wanted to leave but felt trapped; he thought he was with madmen. 'I've hardly heard of them,' he gasped. 'Who's going to go and see them? Have they got any fans?'

'Don't you read *Music Week* or *Melody Maker*?' I asked. 'Their album's at Number One and their latest single's at Number Four.'

'What's it called?' he gasped disbelievingly.

'"Club Tropicana" – how could you be in the music business and not know an act which is having its fourth Top Ten record?'

Harvey glanced around him as if he wanted to escape. 'Where's the loo?'

He needed a break; we were pressuring him too much. And when he reappeared, he didn't go back to his seat, but stayed standing, ready to leave.

'Look,' he said hesitantly, rather embarrassed, 'you don't seem to understand. I'm busy promoting big acts – I mean *really* big ones – Queen, Crosby Stills & Nash, the Rolling Stones, Aerosmith. I'm sorry I don't know more about your group but I haven't got time to dig around in the music press reading about every little British act that comes along.'

Jazz was outraged. 'How dare you call Wham! a little act. Haven't you got children? Aren't you interested in what their tastes are?'

Harvey looked offended. 'I've got a teenage daughter, but she has classy taste. She wouldn't know about an act like this.'

'Ring her up and ask her,' I suggested. 'Ask her, should you promote Wham! or not.'

So Harvey rang home and asked his wife to put their daughter on the line. While he waited he said, 'You know, you guys need a smaller promoter for this. As for the money ...' He shook his head in disbelief.

Then his daughter came on the phone. 'Have you heard of Wham!?' he asked her. 'Should I promote their concerts?'

He never got a reply; instead we watched as he wrenched the handset away from his ear, recoiling from his daughter's shrieks.

After a moment he replaced the receiver and rubbed the palm of his hand thoughtfully over his chin. 'You know guys – I still think the money's a bit steep.'

6

SO YOUNG

Allan loved to laugh. He spent his evenings watching old American movies, revelling in the bitchy dialogue of Lana Turner or Bette Davis, choosing lines to try out the next day on his clients. He had an extraordinary ability to get jokes wrong. If I told him one he would retell it with the punch line as the build-up and the build-up as the punch line. At the end he would laugh so uproariously that everyone else laughed too. 'You see,' he insisted, 'I make them funnier than you.'

One day Connie announced, 'Dahlink, Allan is going to give a special tea party at his house.'

'*His* house?' I said. 'I thought it was mine.'

'Well dahlink, just for the afternoon it will be *his* house.' She closed her eyes and spoke the headline she was imagining for the article. 'The magnificent residence of London's most celebrated hairdresser.'

She was right about it being a fine residence – 29 Bryanston Square was impressive, though most people didn't realise it was only half of what it had once been. The curved staircase from the hall to the chandeliered first floor actually led to nowhere but a mid-floor landing. The first floor and the floors above it had been donated to the house next door to be turned into apartments. Even so, what was left was exceedingly spacious. On the ground floor was a magnificent drawing room with thick white carpets and ceiling fans; the room next door to it was a wood-panelled library; downstairs was a kitchen and dining room leading onto a patio garden; and we each had our own bedroom suite.

Connie explained, 'Allan's inviting all his special clients. And I've given the *Evening Standard* the exclusive. I've told them he does this once a month for just a few of his celebrity clients and that he's never before allowed a journalist to be present.'

This sort of thing was Connie's forte. Every day she had a new idea, a new angle, a new headline for the tabloids. She would work furiously to get a newspaper or magazine to show interest in some imaginary event that she'd thought up, then work even harder to make the event actually happen.

Originally Connie had been introduced to me by Richard as someone who could answer the phones.

She'd only lasted an hour. She buzzed and said I had a call on '2' but when I picked it up there was no-one there, so I picked up '3' which was flashing, but that was a call for Richard in the other room and, of course, my call had been put through to him. When she tried to straighten the calls out, she lost them all. When the callers called back she got confused and lost them again.

I told her, 'Sorry, there's no job,' and she burst into tears.

'Couldn't I do publicity?' she begged.

'Have you done it before?'

'Never! But I'd be good, I'm sure. Let me get some publicity on that group of yours, Japan.'

At that time Japan were completely unknown; no-one could get publicity on them (God knows, I'd tried!), so there was nothing to lose in letting her have a go. At midday Connie went off with a folder of photographs; at five o'clock she came back to say we were going to have a five-page spread in the *Sunday Times* Magazine.

I was flabbergasted. 'How did you do it?'

Connie undid the zip of her silver track suit, threw the folder of photographs onto the floor and lay down next to them. She squirmed amongst the pictures, spreading them around her on the carpet so that I found myself looking down at a collage of sensuality: silver track suit, photos, boobs, more photos, blonde hair, yet more photos, Connie's pouting lips – all converging into one image.

'The editor just loved them,' she told me. 'He's promised me a five-page spread.'

And we got it.

From then on Connie was a publicist. Apart from the outrageous use of her own beauty, it was her persistence that was so special. When she called a journalist to get a story in the paper she was like a terrier tugging at a man's trouser leg. She shook and shook and wouldn't let go, never nasty, but quite annoying nevertheless, and in the end, nearly every single time, she ended up with a piece going into the paper. Then she would be so effusive with her thanks that the journalist felt like a saint.

'Dahlink, you're so wonderful. I adore you. You're my sex god.'

But with Wham!, it was Jazz and me who dealt with the media. And when I was doing publicity I could neither be as tenacious as Connie nor as grateful. For me to niggle away at the man from the *Mirror* the way Connie did would be just too annoying; and to thank him afterwards the way she did might be misinterpreted – especially from someone openly gay, like me. I preferred to rely on the old-fashioned method of a newsworthy story and a good lunch to go with it. And one afternoon, having given such a lunch to a journalist from the *Daily Express*, I arrived home slightly sozzled.

In search of an hour's snooze on the sofa I barged in on a strange bunch of people taking afternoon tea in my drawing-room. I'd interrupted Connie's tea-party stunt for Allan. It looked more like a union meeting for minor celebrities – actress Sarah Miles, transvestite pop singer Marilyn, someone from Tears for Fears, rock guitarist Gary Moore, and a lady who had a cooking programme on TV – all with cups of Earl Grey balanced on their laps and cakes from Fortnum & Mason.

In the middle of the room was Allan, keeping everyone in stitches with his muddled up jokes and hilarious laughter. And slinking silently round with a camera was a photographer from the *Evening Standard* taking 'candid' shots.

I made my excuses and went downstairs. In the kitchen I found two swishy blonds (boys not girls) preparing dinner for eight. A lot of chopping and cutting was going on and things were being stirred in pots. The dining table had already been laid with decorative settings and place markers.

'Isn't tea and cakes enough?' I asked. 'Do we have to feed those people dinner as well?'

The swishy blonds looked blank. 'This food's nothing to do with Allan,' one of them said. 'It's Donavon's. He's giving a special dinner for Jermaine Stewart.'

Donavon had an enormous aptitude for socialising and regularly filled the house with guests, many of them celebrities, some quite bizarre. They came in an endless stream, for meetings, or drinks, or dinner. But he and Allan were highly competitive. Now, because Allan had a room full of celebrities upstairs for a tea-party, Donavon felt the need to have a similar bunch of people for dinner.

'When do I get a chance to live quietly in my own house?' I grumbled.

I opened the fridge to get out a can of Coke but the drinks had disappeared. In their place were eight plates of prawns and things in shells.

'The starters,' one of the swishes shouted. 'Don't touch.'

He rushed to the fridge and pushed the door shut.

'I only wanted a diet Coke,' I told him.

'We took out all the cans. There wasn't room. They're under the sink.'

I walked across to take one but it was warm and undrinkable.

'Can I have some ice?' I asked.

'Sorry we're using the freezer to make an icebox cheesecake.'

Sometimes, it didn't seem worth coming home at all. The place had been turned into a celebrity doss-house. My monthly housekeeping bill paid for these parties and I didn't even get invited.

'Who else is coming to dinner?' I asked. 'Is there a place for me?'

The blonds looked at each other. 'Donavon didn't mention that. He said there'd just be eight.'

I walked into the dining room and looked at the place markings round the table – Bertice Redding, John Moulder-Brown, Angie Best, Leee John, Sinitta …

'Couldn't you fit in one more?'

I didn't really want to eat dinner with them, I was just feeling ratty.

'We could call and ask Donavon,' swish Number 1 suggested.

'Perhaps he could put you on the waiting list,' said swish Number 2. 'Then if someone cancelled …'

I left the room. My house had been taken over. I was an outcast. No wonder the Far East looked so inviting.

* * *

I was also managing Diana Dors, more as a friend than a business manager, for her career had come down to chat shows and supermarket openings.

To the British people, Diana had become something of a reserve Queen Mother – she had mystique and a glamorous past. And now, with a little age on her, she had a rather grand image – blonde, big-breasted and beautifully buttocked.

In the 1950s Diana had been Britain's answer to Marilyn Monroe, appearing in thirty or so British movies. Then she'd gone to Hollywood where she'd married and divorced with the frequency expected of a big star and also suffered suitable financial ups and downs. Back in Britain she'd finally made one truly great movie, then settled down to being a retired show-business icon.

I saw her in an Adam Ant video and it gave me the idea to make a record with her. It flopped – Diana's fans were not teenagers who bought records; moreover, on Radio Two it was being played five times a day. Rather than buy it, whenever they wanted to hear it, Diana's fans just turned on and listened.

Hit or not, from then on I was Diana's honorary manager and a friend of the family. They were delightful.

Alan Lake, her third husband, had once been a hell-raising alcoholic actor, the best friend of Oliver Reed. Now, his alcoholism cured, he lived the life of a well-kept poodle, for without alcohol he simply wasn't the actor he had been. And there were two children: Gary, from Diana's second marriage, who was eighteen, and young Jason from her marriage with Alan.

The evening of Donavon's dinner for Jermaine Stewart, I gave Diana a call and she invited me over for dinner. She had a marvellous house in the Surrey countryside decorated in 1950s glitz, like the Mayfair pad of a gangster in an old British 'B' picture – the sort of place he would take his moll – just the sort of part Diana used to play in those days. Her idea of what was glamorous must have stuck in her mind ever since.

Before we ate she took me aside to give me some bad news. The previous year she'd had cancer. After treatment, she and her doctors thought they'd beaten it, but it had come back again. The doctors said the chances of getting rid of it were negligible yet she was as bright and full of life as ever.

'I've come to terms with it, dear. The only difference between having it and not having it is, unlike everyone else, I more or less know when I'm going to die. Which is good! It means I can make plans I might otherwise not have made. Apart than that, I'm going to enjoy life to the full.'

And she did.

That night Lionel Bart came over too and in the middle of dinner told a bawdy joke that involved the word masturbation.

Ten-year-old Jason piped up, 'Mummy, what's masturbation?'

'Wanking, darling!' Diana told him curtly.

After dinner she took me aside again. 'What I really can't stand about this cancer thing is everybody knowing. I've only told one or two people – people I can trust to keep it secret. My biggest worry is that it's making me lose weight. People are going to see me wasting away and I just can't stand it. I don't want to sound nasty, but I simply don't want their sympathy.'

I understood completely. How would she be able to live normally and enjoy herself if the press got wind of it and people started writing letters of condolence by the thousand?

I had an idea. 'Diana. You're beautiful but you're biggish. You don't really have to worry that losing weight will make you look unwell. You could lose masses of weight and still be more buxom than Joan Collins. Why don't you do a diet column in the tabloids – the Diana Dors diet. You could write your own recipes each week, have a full page in the *Sun* or the *Mirror*, get publicity and make money. You'd lose weight with the whole of England watching and no-one would have the slightest suspicion it was due to bad health.'

She said nothing, leaving me with no idea as to whether she liked my idea or not.

Later we drank coffee sitting round the indoor pool then smoked some pot before we had a swim. Young Jason enjoyed having me swing him round in circles before letting him go flying into the pool the fifth or sixth time around. I don't know how many times he came back for more but finally the alcohol, the marijuana and the slippery floor ganged up on me and I accidentally let him go a little early and he went flying into the wall.

It was one of my less successful nights at Diana's. I left at one in the morning, head bowed in shame as the ambulance came up the driveway.

But Diana was forever forgiving, and anyway Jason was back at school the next morning, so just two days later when she did a chat show for the BBC, we were friends again and I went with her to Television Centre.

After the show I saw her off back home in the Rolls with her new chauffeur, rather good-looking I thought. I called Alan, her husband, to say Diana was on the way but two hours later he called back worried that she hadn't arrived.

'Perhaps I got it wrong,' I told him. 'Maybe she was going off to have dinner with someone in town.'

Later I asked Diana what happened.

'Well, it was the new chauffeur, dear, just too tempting.'

'Where did you do it?'

She was too well-known to go anywhere without being instantly recognised, especially with a young man in tow.

She winked. 'In the back of the car, dear. It made me feel so young.'

7 MUSCLE SHOALS

You could be travelling with George and Andrew in a limo, or a train, or a band bus; they might be in the seats behind you and you would hear this endless chattering, whispering and giggling. They would burst into hysterical laughter and bang each other on the knees then go back to nattering like monkeys. They got off on everything about each other – together, they were in a world of their own – utterly private and intensely annoying.

Sometimes, when something had to be done or said, it was difficult to bring them back to reality. 'OK,' I might tell them, arriving at Heathrow to take a flight to Paris, 'we're here. Get out of the car quickly and into the VIP lounge. Let's go.'

Chatter – giggle – chatter – giggle. There was nothing to show I'd even been heard.

'Come on – let's go.'

If I spoke loudly enough, one of them might look up. 'Oh, you mean us?'

'Well, who else is there in this damned car?'

They were like eight-year-olds, always presuming that any talking they heard in the background was something to do with adults, not them.

Pushed hard enough, they might, with a pout, turn momentarily into normal people and follow me into the airport, but even before we'd gone through the doors I would hear them behind me returning to their inevitable monkey-talk. It was like travelling with a different species. But the strange thing about their impenetrable two-man world was that as soon as they were apart they were both perfectly reasonable people.

Before I could set off on my first proper trip to China, I had to travel with George to America to record 'Careless Whisper', which everyone believed would one day be Wham!'s biggest hit.

I'd had the idea of using the great sixties soul producer Jerry Wexler to produce the record for us. I'd sent him the song and he loved it; then he suggested, 'Let's record it at Muscle Shoals.'

Muscle Shoals is a small town on the Tennessee River in Alabama. In 1921, auto tycoon Henry Ford went there with a vision: to employ one million workers and build a city seventy-five miles long.

Ford's plan hit the headlines and speculators bought land like crazy, parcelling it into thirty foot lots ready for resale and putting in sidewalks and street lighting. A little later Ford changed his mind but his plan had helped lay the foundations of the city.

The next time people heard about the place was in the sixties when Fame Recording Studios opened. Suddenly, artists as diverse as Aretha Franklin, The Osmonds and Paul Simon were heading there to record. More studios opened and session musicians started moving in from Nashville and New York to make it their new home. Soon the town had become a legend in the world of music, particularly soul music.

I'd never been to Muscle Shoals, so when Jerry suggested recording there I liked the idea. Not only would it give the resulting record extra credibility and class, but also I was interested in seeing the place.

George and I flew to New York and then to Nashville, where I hired a car and drove to Muscle Shoals, sixty miles down the freeway. We met Jerry Wexler, and George charmed him with his nice manners and respect. It was difficult to be anything *but* respectful to Jerry, a man who'd produced literally hundreds of the greatest soul records ever made, the entire output of Atlantic Records in the sixties and seventies.

For us, he'd assembled a typically top-notch crew of Muscle Shoals session musicians and they made a backing track as perfect as one had come to expect from them. When it was done, Jerry worked on George's voice while I wandered off and explored the town a little.

I stood on the banks of the Tennessee River trying to drum up historical images of Red Indians and the Civil War yet somehow the images wouldn't come. The Tennessee River was still there, but if you turned the other way you could see Burger King, Pizza Hut, Kentucky Fried Chicken, Pancake House and Wendys, all looking exactly like they did in every state, county, city and town in the USA. That's the trouble with so much of American history – it lies like a thin bottom crust of pastry covered with a topping of chicken nuggets, frankfurters, melted mozzarella and four types of dressing.

*

The next morning, with the backing track done and George's vocal recorded, Jerry had booked the top sax player in LA to fly in and do the solo. He arrived at eleven and should have been gone by twelve. Instead, after two hours, he was still there while everyone in the studio shuddered with embarrassment. He just couldn't play the riff the way George wanted it, the way it had been on the demo. But that had been made two years earlier with a friend round the corner who played sax for fun in the pub.

The saxophonist from LA appeared to be playing the part perfectly over and over again but each time he did so George told him, 'No, it's still not right, you see ...'

And he would lower his head patiently to the talkback microphone and hum the part to him yet again. 'It has to twitch upwards a little just there! See ...? Not there, but here! And not too much.'

Unable to take any more I wandered off to the studio's poolroom and idly knocked coloured balls around the table. Then Jerry joined me. 'What d'you think?' I asked. 'Is there really something George wants that's different from what the sax player is playing?'

Jerry thought so. 'Definitely! I've seen things like this before. There's some tiny nuance that the sax player is somehow not getting right. Although you and I can't hear what it is, it may be the very thing that will make the record a hit. The success of pop records is so ephemeral, so unbelievably unpredictable, we just can't take the risk of being impatient.'

He joined me in an idle game of pool, banging the balls around the table without any great seriousness, then suddenly said, 'You know – the sax player's not going to get it. Whatever it is George wants, he just can't convey it to him. We'll have to get someone else. It's a bit embarrassing though – this guy's the best session sax player in LA.'

He put down his cue and left the room. A few minutes later I went back to the studio to see the sax player packing up his sax, ashen faced, feeling humiliated. And I don't think George felt any better either.

A few hours later George must have felt even worse. Another sax player had arrived, this time from New York, and again George had lowered his head to the talkback, hummed the piece through and given the same instructions. 'Twitch upwards there! Not here! And not too much.'

And the same thing had happened – another hour of horrible embarrassment.

Eventually, two months later in London, George's amateur player from North London would get it right in just one take. Perhaps he played

43

the sax with an incorrect technique, using wrong fingering that made him unable to play the phrase smoothly thus putting into it the quirkiness George was searching for. These two American guys were too good to get it, but there was more than that wrong with the recording.

When the record was finished George and I listened to it with objectivity and found that the unidentifiable 'something' that was missing from the sax solo was also missing from the backing track. It had no kick to it; no balls.

We flew back to England wanting to be pleased with it but unable to be; we both knew it would eventually have to be recorded again. It sounded too much like standard Muscle Shoals product; slick and correct in the accepted manner, but no more than that either – just another piece of replicated Americana – like a Big Mac or a Wendyburger or a chocolate chip milkshake at the Muscle Shoals Pancake House.

8 MESSING ABOUT IN ASIA

I called Professor Neuber in Berlin. Someone at his language school told me he was away travelling, why didn't I leave my number? Within an hour he'd called me back from his house in Mexico. I asked him for the name of the travel shop in Hong Kong that could get me a visa for China.

'Of course. And where exactly are you going? Beijing?'

'No, I'm going to start with Canton. Just to get a feel of what China's about.'

'Well, don't forget to call it Guangzhou. The authorities don't like people who use the name Canton – it's considered subversive. And while you're there, you must look up Charlie Goh, he's very influential. He might be able to help you. Give me your telex number and I'll send you all the details.'

In Hong Kong, I took a taxi straight from the airport to the travel shop in Kowloon, on the fourth floor of Harbour City Shopping Plaza.

'Professor Neuber said you could get quick visas for Hong Kong residents. I'm hoping to go to Canton this afternoon. Is it possible?'

'Professor Neuber? Of course. He used to come here a lot. We haven't seen him for ages.'

Even though I paid through the nose it was cheaper than the visa would have been in London. And instead of waiting six months and having to get invitations and documents and guarantees, I simply passed a couple of hours over coffee in the lobby of the Regent Hotel. What a pleasure, sitting there with a freshly made cup of coffee and a view across the harbour, contemplating one of the world's greatest cities.

I could never really decide what gave Hong Kong its overpowering sense of excitement. Perhaps it was simply the two halves of the city being separated by sea, so that wherever you were you could look across the water to see another city even more alluring than the one you were in. Or maybe it was just the calm twenty minutes it took to cross from one half to the other by the green ferry boats. Or the conflicting mix of Chinese and European culture – the restaurants, the food on the streets, the madness of neon everywhere, or simply the feeling of *not* being in Britain. Or was it sex – overt or hidden, implicit or given – that gave the city its magnetism?

While I had coffee I pondered on something else too. In his telex Rolf Neuber had told me, if I was nervous about the visa it would be better to go by train. If they didn't let me in, I would still be on the border of Hong Kong and could easily go back again. But if I landed at a Chinese airport and they didn't like my visa, they could put me in jail. I wondered whether this caution was really applicable to me or was the professor being over-cautious as a result of whatever trouble he'd previously got himself into?

Two hours later I had a single entry visa, not as a stamp in my passport but as a folded piece of paper slipped inside it. I couldn't see why the Chinese embassy in London should demand so much paperwork and waiting-time before issuing a visa when somewhere else in the world the very same authorities allowed the same person to get a visa in a couple of hours with no paperwork whatsoever – anyway, I had one now and that was all that mattered.

That afternoon I took the train into China. It was packed with people visiting relatives in Canton, overdressed, as if they were off to a party – the men in their best sports shirts with well-pressed trousers, the women in dresses far too fancy for sitting on a train. Next to me a man said he was going back to visit his wife.

'Why didn't you bring her with you to Hong Kong when you left?' I asked.

The question seemed to astonish him. 'Why bring wife to Hong Kong? Hong Kong is freedom. Wife is not freedom.'

Nevertheless, like everyone else, he'd dressed for the occasion which suggested he still cared for her in some way, as did the pile of gift-wrapped packages on his knee. But then everyone had those; the carriage was jammed with them. Boxes and packages, cartons and carrier bags – TV sets, stereo machines, microwaves, pedal cars – treasure from Hong Kong for the poor relatives who waited in droves on the platform at Canton dressed in dingy clothes and flip-flops.

*

I had no idea who I'd come to see. I could have gone to any of the major record companies in Hong Kong and asked the people working there for contacts in Canton, but I didn't want other people in the record industry helping me. I wanted to do this whole thing my own way.

From a store in London's Chinatown I'd bought thirty music cassettes which a waiter at my local Chinese restaurant had gone through, identifying ones produced in Canton and translating the phone numbers and addresses of the companies. And that's all I'd brought with me to Canton; plus some albums and videos of Wham!.

My hotel was the White Swan on an island in the middle of the Pearl River – Shamian Island, where life had once been one hundred per cent European. In the days when the British and French were granted trade concessions, they'd turned the island into a haven of peace, away from the crowded slums and open sewers of the city. In his twenties, my father had worked there for Shell Oil and many times I'd looked through his photo albums of the place. There were villas, churches, parks and tennis courts; Europeans in white linen suits and Chinese servants in pyjamas or *cheong sam*.

Shamian Island had changed. It looked nothing like the sepia snaps my father had taken sixty years earlier. It was now an adjunct of China's new tourist industry. The White Swan was Canton's first five-star hotel and had only been open a month. Vast, modern and pristine clean, the lobby had an ornamental temple, a waterfall, pools full of carp and a shopping arcade selling thousand-dollar perfumes. At weekends, ordinary townspeople from across the river flocked to gawp at it in wonder.

My first evening, I went to the old quarter of Canton and wandered through alleyways of restaurants and neon signs – smoke, steam, noise and bawdy good humour. This was more like the pictures in my father's photo album but it bore no relationship to any communist city I'd ever been to. The place had an absolute obsession with food; it was a city of gluttons. Through open doors and windows I could see restaurants that were distinctly dirty. Even when they were four storeys high and had gold statues in the reception areas, the ceilings were still covered with cobwebs and there was muck on the floor. Mostly they were filled with parties of ten or more, sitting round large wooden tables; spitting, slurping, burping and shouting.

I chose to eat alone at a neon-lit outside restaurant where the waitress spoke a little English. 'How about dog meat cook at the table in clay pot?'

I chose something more digestible – baby steamed ribs with plain rice. Later she came back and asked if I'd enjoyed it.

'Yes', I told her. 'It was delicious.'

'You see, I knew you like dog meat. Everyone like it.'

Dog meat, I realised, was the only thing they served.

Simply in terms of meeting people, my trip was successful. In two days I visited five record companies and was introduced to a concert promoter and a local politician. But I soon found out that in China there was really only one record company – China Records, owned by the state. Every local record company was simply some sort of subsidiary to the one monolithic organisation. Some were partnerships with local government, some with educational organisations, some with sports committees or children's charities. None of them had the right to act truly independently; they could only release records made or approved by China Records, which meant the government.

At Long-Long Records I met Mr Lee. 'What you think of Canton?' he asked.

'I'm enjoying it.'

'Of course – everyone enjoy Canton. Here we have freedom a little. In Beijing people are not allowed to think – down here we can have our own thoughts.'

'But can you act on them?' I wanted to know. 'Or are they just for thinking?'

The question went unanswered; probably not understood.

I opened my briefcase and took out a copy of Wham!'s album. Before I could hand it to him he stepped across the room and pulled it out of my hand like a customs officer grabbing contraband. 'What's this?'

'I manage a pop group in England – Wham!. I want them to play a concert in China.'

'I never hear of Wham!. How about The Beatles? I think The Beatles would be better concert.'

'They broke up.'

'Oh really?' He seemed genuinely surprised. 'I thought Beatles is very good for England. Why the government let them break up?'

I laughed. 'In England people can do as they want. How could a government keep a pop group together if they wanted to break up?'

'Maybe put them in jail?' Mr Lee suggested.

It was a sharp reminder that the slight glow of capitalism that pervaded Canton was just a veneer created by the proximity of Hong Kong and all those relatives bringing in Western goods. Beneath it the acceptance of state control seemed as strong as ever.

By phone I made an appointment with Golden Emperor Records and was told I would be meeting with Mr Boon and Mr Bee. I half expected them to be characters from a children's TV show, probably living in flowerpots, but they turned out to be two sharply dressed businessmen.

Mr Boon offered me fortune cookies left over from his sister's wedding; Mr Bee showed me videos of the company's artists – the backing tracks were disco, the songs were 1930s kitsch, the voices were high and girlish.

'Have you ever heard of Wham!?' I asked.

Mr Boon laughed, showing off two gold teeth. 'What's Wham?'

'It's a pop group in Britain. I want to bring them to China for a concert.'

'Do they sing in Cantonese or Mandarin?' Mr Bee asked.

'In English.'

Messrs Bee and Boon shook their heads at the hopelessness of the task.

'Better play in Hong Kong,' suggested Mr Boon.

'Better teach them Chinese,' said Mr Bee.

Charlie Goh was in local government. Rolf's telex had given me two numbers for him, one of them with the extra information – 'answered in English'. I dialled it and was greeted with an accent half Brooklyn half Chinatown. 'Hi, this is Charrie.'

'Rolf Neuber gave me your number. I'm here on business, he said you might be able to help me.'

Half an hour later he was at my hotel promising to show me the whole of Canton. I hoped he wouldn't; I disliked him at once. He had the appearance of a cheap gangster – rough-mannered and bullying, bulbous and bristly, like a wild boar. I wished he hadn't come but now he was here there would be no escaping him.

'How do you know Rolf Neuber?' he asked.

'I met him in Beijing.'

'I thought he couldn't go there.'

I smiled. Charlie was such an obvious bully, I wanted to make him unsure of whom I might be. 'I managed to get him in. I pulled a few strings.'

He looked surprised. 'Rolf and I used to do business together. Are you in the same business?'

I shook my head. I wasn't sure what business he was talking about but I was pretty certain I wasn't in it.

Outside the hotel Charlie's driver waited for us in a VIP limo, huge, heavy and black, with net curtains and lace cushions. By Chinese standards these things were posh; anywhere else in the world they would be laughed at.

We drove along the waterfront, the Pearl River, a highway of thick brown water alive with tugs, barges and ferry boats. Charlie wanted to show me the docks. They were vast – hundreds of boats, thousands of cranes, tens of thousands of dock-workers. But among the noise of whining machinery, clanging hammers and loaded pallets swinging through the air, there was something else most surprising. All round the docks were loudspeakers, all screeching with overloud music. It wasn't the Chinese pop music I would have expected – it was Wagner.

Charlie told me, 'You like the music I choose? All this is belong to me. Charrie in charge of everything.'

I thought I was beginning to understand. He was the local union official – the party man who controlled the docks. In port cities all over the world, that was the ultimate seat of power. Control the stevedores and you control the town.

For lunch I was taken to eat snake at a restaurant where the windows were filled with glass cabinets of writhing serpents. Charlie spent a while choosing the right one and it was bought to our table hanging from the upheld hand of the headwaiter, four foot long and wriggling. Charlie nodded his approval and another waiter produced a knife and peeled off its skin which fell to the floor like a discarded lady's stocking. The snake turned into a giant wiggling worm.

'How do we eat it?' I asked the headwaiter.

'Make soup. Special for Mr Charrie. Dericious.'

The soup was indeed delicious – strangely warming, like drinking brandy. 'Good for coughs and sneezes,' Charlie explained. 'What's your business in Canton?'

I'd already decided he wasn't a person I wanted to deal with but he had power and in the end I would need someone like that, so I told him.

He wasn't impressed. 'I never heard of Wham! I don't think anyone in China ever heard of Wham! Why do you want to play a concert here?'

I explained it was for promotion; it would publicise the group all over the world; it wasn't meant for the Chinese, it was meant for the Western media.

'You want your group play China? Easy. Play in Canton. I fix everything. You don't have to ask anyone else. Charrie do it for you.'

'Who would go and see them?' I asked.

'Easy. I play their record at the docks. Soon everyone know it. Then they go and see concert.'

I could just imagine George and Andrew's reaction if they turned up in China to find an audience of dockworkers. Anyway, I'd already decided Canton wasn't the place for Wham! to play – at least, not the place they should play first. This wasn't the seat of government or communist ideology. This was just the fringe. If Wham! were going to be invited to play in China it should be at the invitation of the orthodox bureaucrats of Beijing, the central committee, not a corrupt docker in Canton.

'It's Beijing where the group have to play,' I explained. 'Not here.'

Charlie snorted disdainfully. 'Beijing's full of communists.'

I decided I'd had enough of him and wanted to get away. I stood up, ready to leave. 'I'm sorry, I have another meeting. You must excuse me, I'll be late.'

He was having none of it. 'More meetings not necessary. Charrie can fix everything.' He waved his hand, motioning me to sit down again.

'It's personal,' I explained. 'A friend in London asked me to go and see his mother.'

'I'll send my driver. Tell her to come here and have snake soup with Mr Charrie.' It was more like an order than a request – there was no pleasantness in his voice.

'She can't. She's bedridden. She's had a stroke.'

He patted his hand impatiently on the chair I'd been sitting on, like telling a dog to sit, trying to get me back to the table.

I shook my head. 'I'm sorry, Charlie, I have to go.'

Without looking back, I left quickly and turned into a maze of alleyways, afraid he might follow me in his limousine and insist on giving me a lift back to the hotel.

*

That evening I flew back to Hong Kong, I thought it would be quicker than by train, but I made a mistake. There was a heavy mist and flights were delayed several hours. Most people must have known in advance for there weren't many waiting passengers. The ones who turned up waited like me in the bar area on the mezzanine floor, looking down onto the empty arrival area below, deserted except for an elderly man collecting luggage carts and turning them into a silver snake.

I was starving. There was a food stall serving noodle soup but it looked too grubby. At the bar there was a cake covered with caraway seeds which looked quite nice. When I told the barman he clapped his hands above it and the caraway seeds lifted into the air – a small cloud of flies. The cake's real topping was a layer of jam.

My stomach stayed empty, but it didn't matter, the trip had been a success. Even so, I realised there was no point coming back to Canton. Next time it had to be Beijing.

And there was something else that occurred to me. At last I'd found a way of combining the music business and the Far East. From now on I could spend half my time in London being a pop manager and the other half doing what I'd always enjoyed best ...

Messing about in Asia.

9 BELLY DANCING

Because Wham! were broke, Connie was not yet their publicist. To get the headlines we wanted from their tour, Jazz and I were going to have to make deals with the show business editors of all the tabloids. Since that would mean eating lots of lunches, I volunteered.

Our idea was to create Whamania and to do that we would need centre-page spreads and front-page headlines. If all the deals worked out right, one week into the tour teenage Britain would be in the grip of media-manipulated hysteria. If we could pull it off, the tour would earn enough money to pay for the group's upcoming legal battle. And with Whamania sweeping Britain, CBS would surely be persuaded to make Wham! a direct signing and force Innervision to let them go.

One by one I lunched with show business editors and offered them deals. In exchange for headlines they could have competition prizes – items of clothing from the boys, an intimate dinner with Andrew, a day at home with George – anything I could think of to secure the promise of column inches.

In the bar of Au Jardin de Gourmets the man from the principal Scottish tabloid scoured the wine list over pre-lunch Campari and nuts and commented on the fact that it was the first time he'd seen a wine list with pre-phyloxera wines, which meant they dated back to the 1880s.

I told him, 'With this Wham! tour we want to create Whamania. The boys are up to it, the fans are primed, everything's ready to explode. We just need the press to spread the word, preferably from the front pages.'

'Of course.' He nodded sagely and put his finger to the place on the wine list where he'd spotted the pre-phyloxera wine. 'A bottle of this would really be quite an experience, don't you think?'

In general I got on well with journalists; I liked their enquiring minds, though it was vital to remember that anything, once said, would end up in print. At Shalloos, an upmarket Indian joint in Knightsbridge,

I ate with a show business editor from the *Evening Standard*. He seemed almost uncaring about my request for help in creating Whamania. 'Of course, old boy, whatever you want. Delighted to help.'

We chatted about other things and he told me about a party he'd been to the night before where he'd seen George and Andrew with the two girls who did their backing singing, Dee and Shirley. 'Who sleeps with who?' he asked.

'Shirley used to be Andrew's girlfriend,' I told him. 'But that's long over.'

He knew about that; it wasn't news.

'But ...' I added, remembering something else, '... when we went to Ibiza to shoot the video for Club Tropicana last month, the hotel had reserved a suite each for George and Andrew and another for Dee and Shirley. But George insisted they all move in together in one suite. Who knows what went on!'

'Can I use that?'

Too late, I realised it would have been better left unsaid. 'I'd rather you didn't.'

But ninety minutes later, when we left the restaurant, the *Evening Standard* billboards at Knightsbridge tube station were screaming, 'Wham! Orgy!'

I bought the paper to look. It was a sentence, nothing more, in the showbiz gossip column – 'We hear the boys from Wham! and their two girl backing singers shared a room together on a recent trip to the sin island of Ibiza' – of absolutely no consequence, but enough to allow them to run a billboard flyer that sold newspapers. When the journalist had gone to the loo during lunch, he'd also been on the phone. Never mind – it was cheaper than pre-phyloxera wine!

Slowly but surely, I got each one of these show-business editors to agree to help us with Whamania, but it took plenty of food and wine. The man from the *Express* chose Dom Perignon to go with his lunch at Inigo Jones; the *Sun* went Italian and demanded Cecconis, and the man from the *Mirror* requested Simpsons in the Strand and brought with him a substantially constructed female who demolished an entire shoulder of lamb from the carvery trolley.

Not that any of this worried me. Some people ate lunches like this in order to do deals; for me it had always been the other way round. I did deals in order to justify eating lunches. But to make myself feel better about the cost (for it was me who had to pay since no-one else connected with Wham! had any money) I also included a little PR for Allan's salon and got some additional benefits – promises of half-page spreads for his latest hair shows.

Allan was frequently being asked to perform at hair shows. These were usually big two-day events at which all the leading hair salons in Britain would do a forty-five minute show. Our purpose in doing them was to get pictures in the paper and continue to build Allan's name. So while other salons settled for technical demonstrations and dull displays on the catwalk, we approached our shows in a more showbiz manner.

This made them pricey – sometimes as much as ten thousand pounds each – but I enjoyed being involved in them. It was creative and fun – a change from being target-practice for a pop stars flame-thrower eyes.

Sometimes Connie persuaded pop stars to appear and lipsync a couple of songs with a special hairstyle which Allan would invent for them. Many of these were his clients, getting their hair done free several times a week, unable to refuse under the pressure of Connie's persuasion. But mostly we hired professionals – conjurers, dancers, circus-people and the like – to whom Allan gave extraordinary hairstyles. For a show at Grosvenor House we had fire-eaters and Chinese acrobats. At the Barbican we had the Queen's double and dancers from Top Of The Pops. And for three weeks before a show at the Hippodrome, Allan trained as an illusionist so he could pick hairbrushes and combs from thin air, produce girls with surprising hairstyles from an empty cabinet and change one of his models into a gorilla that chased him offstage.

'Who's the Chinese magician?' an American in the audience asked. 'It's a great act. I'd like to book him for Vegas.'

I took his card but never called him back. I simply couldn't see an upside to turning Allan into a cabaret star.

Unsurprisingly, knowing the competitiveness between them, Allan's success stimulated Donavon to get in on the act. He decided to run an annual Black Hair festival called Afrodizziac. His panache was impressive. One minute he had the idea, the next minute it was happening – a convention for black hairdressers and manufacturers at Wembley Arena, no less – with every conceivable black hair product sold from stalls while on a central stage the

UK's major black salons turned out to do shows. Moreover, Donavon got stars to come too – Jocelyn Brown, Amazulu, Eartha Kitt.

But despite its apparent success, just like Allan's salon, Donavon's Afrodizziac hair convention didn't quite manage to cover its costs.

* * *

Connie was always getting invitations for receptions and when she received one for the opening of a new club in Baker Street she told me, 'Dahlink – tell your two sex gods to go and do some self-promotion. *Everyone* will be there.'

George wasn't interested but Andrew wanted to go, so I went with him. He was a good person to go out with – sharp-witted with no axes to grind and always amusing.

Connie was wrong about the party – *no-one* was there – it was a small room with an even smaller crowd. Andrew and I used it to provide us with some early evening drinks then moved on to dinner at the Caprice, driving there in my Bentley.

In 1983, the Caprice was edging Langans aside as the best place in town. It was more refined and usually escaped the gang of paparazzi at the front door. Here, Roger Moore might be at the next table to Joan Collins, or Melvin Bragg could be seen discussing the next episode of the *South Bank Show* with David Frost.

Well-known customers were greeted by London's most ingratiating head waiter, French and almost completely circular, his dinner jacket looking like something zipped round a giant football. But such charm!

'Oh Mr Napier-Bell. How simply wonderful to have you back again so soon. We have your favourite table waiting. Oh – and your guest tonight – what a famous face.'

Andrew liked the Caprice at once, as other stars had done for five decades. Opened in the twenties, it had quickly become the home of London's theatre crowd – red velvet seats, mirrored walls and autographed pictures of the stars. It glittered with the celebrity world that surrounded the lives of those in the theatre. But in the seventies, as theatre life had faded so the Caprice had faded with it.

In the eighties, though, it found new owners who refurbished it and brought it brilliantly back to life. It was now the restaurant everyone wanted to go to; London's buzz-zone. And pretty soon, over sautéed foie gras and Sancerre, Andrew was buzzing.

He talked mainly about sex. He seemed to think I fancied him but he couldn't have been more wrong; he was too tall and too obviously heterosexual for me to find sexually attractive. But his self-confident chatter was enjoyable and I could see what a good foil he was to George, so innately serious and self-questioning.

While Andrew rambled, I knocked back the best part of two bottles of wine, far too much because it left me unable to recall most of what he told me. But with a pleasant feeling of camaraderie we moved on to the Hippodrome, a vast noise-filled discotheque for young trendies.

In the VIP bar we found ourselves seated next to David Steele, the Leader of the Liberal Party, presumably thinking his presence would build credibility with young voters.

'Is there a photographer around?' David asked. (A photo with one of Wham! at the Hippodrome was just the sort of thing he needed to woo young voters.)

'Not allowed in the VIP bar,' I explained. 'This is the place where stars relax.'

David was prepared to go outside to get the right picture but Andrew wanted none of it. Then Allan and Donavon turned up in competing outfits; Donavon in a Jesus-like Japanese robe, Allan in something tight-fitting and Italian. Trying to win David two more votes, I introduced them to him.

'Come to the salon,' Allan suggested. 'I'll get rid of your grey bits.'

'D'you want to dance?' Donavon asked.

David did *not*. A photo like that would be the last thing he needed.

Allan and Donavon waltzed off together and I poured in more alcohol. For the next hour or so Andrew kept talking, people flowed in and out of the bar and my brain floated in and out of focus. During an in-focus period I heard him mention that his father came from Egypt.

'There's an Egyptian nightclub in Queensway,' I told him. 'Drinks and belly-dancers till four in the morning. Let's go!'

I recall nothing of the drive (my Bentley must have found its own way), but I clearly remember around three in the morning being seated twelve inches away from a mesmerising belly button set in a plump Egyptian tummy.

'She's a bit fat,' Andrew grumbled.

I agreed, and pointed it out to the waiter. 'Complaints aren't allowed after midnight,' he told us, which at the time seemed entirely reasonable.

We drank a bottle of champagne and ordered a second, but realising we'd now drunk enough, Andrew picked up the bottle and poured half of it over my head. 'Time to wake up,' he told me.

I grabbed the bottle and returned the compliment with the other half. It felt good – some sort of artist-manager bonding ritual.

We were then confronted with the difficulty of getting home. Too drunk to wave for a cab, and too dishevelled to be accepted by one, I thought perhaps we should sleep in my Bentley, but as soon as we got into it the engine somehow started and it moved off.

'You're drunk,' Andrew told me. 'You'd better drive on the pavement. It'll be safer.'

It sounded logical; there would certainly be less traffic.

Surprisingly, it was only after we'd reached Bryanston Square and I was negotiating a zebra crossing, trying to reach the pavement on the other side, that sirens wailed and blue lights appeared. Andrew opened the front passenger door and fled. I sank deep into the front seat.

At Paddington Police Station I was fingerprinted.

'Sit down,' I was told. And when I did so, 'Stand up!'

I stood up and was pushed back down again. 'Are you trying to cause trouble?'

I wasn't, so they gave me a tube to blow through. 'Stand up and blow,' they ordered. But when I did so the two officers pushed me back down again and held me in the chair. 'He's causing trouble,' one told the other. 'We'll have to keep him in overnight.'

His companion agreed. 'Blow – you bastard,' he shouted. And I blew.

Then they dragged me away to a cell.

I woke to find myself in the company of a stone floor and a porcelain toilet. There were three walls of brick and one with bars, and from outside I could hear the distant sounds of daytime – telephones ringing, people talking, buses passing, that sort of thing.

First I was sick; then I was bored. On the floor was what looked like the printout from a cashier's till. Not being familiar with this sort of accommodation I wondered if it might be the bill for my room. But it looked like it had come from the machine I'd blown into the night before and had various numbers on it.

Some hours later an exceptionally polite policeman came and told me I could go home, but without the car because I still had too much alcohol in my blood to drive. A few days later I was delivered a notice of prosecution that charged me with driving over the limit. I asked a lawyer to represent me and sent him the bit of paper that had been dropped through the bars of my cell. By the time the case came to court he'd found a technicality; the paper from the breathalyser should have been in duplicate. The machine was meant to print out three copies – one for the police and two for me – that was the law.

In court the police claimed all had been as it should have been and that I was given two copies. The magistrate questioned me about what happened in the police station. 'Why did they keep you in overnight?'

'I don't know. I thought that's what happened to everyone.'

'Not normally,' he explained to me. 'Only if you cause trouble. Did you?'

'Not at all.'

The magistrate turned to the single policeman attending court to give evidence. 'What sort of trouble did he cause?'

'He threatened us.'

'Is that true?' the magistrate asked me.

I explained how I'd repeatedly been made to stand up and sit down.

'And what about the printouts from the machine? Are you sure you weren't given two copies?'

I told him, 'I admit I was drunk and I admit I drove the car. It was grossly irresponsible of me and I apologise to the court. I'm prepared to accept any sentence you give me, but I can promise you there was only one bit of paper in my cell. I was very bored and there was nothing to do. I read it ten or twenty times to pass the time. If there'd been a second piece of paper, I would have noticed it. It would have been something else to read.'

My lawyer handed the magistrate the copy of the printout I'd been given in my cell. 'You'll notice,' he pointed out, 'there are red lines on it which suggest it was coming to the end of the roll. I propose to you that it had reached the point where one of the three layers of paper had expired and the machine therefore only printed two copies.'

The magistrate stared at the small piece of paper and glared sourly at the policeman. 'Case dismissed.'

I'd been blind drunk and I'd got off. Afterwards, I asked my lawyer, 'If I'd been found guilty what would the penalty have been?'

He told me two hundred pounds and a two-year ban, so I went straight home, donated two hundred pounds to Oxfam and vowed not to drive again for two years. I then phoned my local garage and told them to fetch the car from the police station. 'Sell it. I have no more use for it.'

A week later I had to fly with George and Andrew to Norway where they were doing a TV show. Late in the evening we found ourselves in the rooftop restaurant of Oslo's top hotel accompanied by the head of the record company and some of his staff. Andrew related the story of our night out and George asked what had happened in court.

When I explained how I'd got off he was scandalised. 'It's immoral!'

'What is?'

'That you got off.'

'But I didn't lie. I admitted I did it.'

'But you used a lawyer who got you off. Why did you do that? You should have pleaded guilty and taken the punishment.'

George on a moral crusade was very unforgiving.

'Look – I paid two hundred pounds to Oxfam and vowed not to drive for two years.'

'That's not the point; you escaped punishment for doing something against the law. That's wrong.'

'And what if it had been a silly law – like something to do with Apartheid in South Africa, then would I have been wrong to break it?'

George sighed heavily, agitated by the puerile nature of my argument. 'Of course not – you must use your own judgements on these things. But you know perfectly well you shouldn't drive when you're drunk. It's a public danger. You should have let yourself be found guilty and suffered for it. You should have had your name in the newspaper, that sort of thing.'

I turned to Andrew for support but he was already floating in too-much-cocktail-land and hadn't heard a word we said. I turned to the people from the record company but they were chattering together in Norwegian. I was on my own.

And George, of course, was right. He could be very annoying like that.

10 BERLIN

David Sylvian, the lead singer of Japan (the person the bass-player's girlfriend moved in with), was in Berlin making his first solo album. I still hadn't decided whether to continue managing him or not, so when Allan and Donavon re-ignited their sporadic war one Sunday in September it seemed like a good time to fly to Germany and listen to what he was recording.

The music on David's new album was wonderful but uncommercial; dreamy rather than focused, with large periods of improvisation between rambling vocals. His songwriting had lost its previous discipline. On the other hand the music drifted into emotional areas it might not otherwise have reached.

When I got bored I wandered out of the studio to find I was in a dead-end street just fifteen yards from the Berlin wall. At the end of it, overlooking empty roads and deserted houses, was a fifteen foot wooden staircase and a small platform. On it, people stood gazing into the East as if they were star-ing into the Grand Canyon or a nature reserve in Yellowstone Park.

On the other side, although there was nothing to see, there was some-thing to sense – a mist of cruelty, corruption and fear. Or was it just in the mind of the viewer?

And there was a strange smell.

As I'd come up the stairs, I'd noticed at the bottom a man I thought might be a plain clothes policeman. I now realised he was selling drugs. Everyone on the platform was smoking, not normally but in a weird and private manner.

'Grass?' I asked one young man. 'Is it marijuana?'

'No!' he shook his head. 'Heroin. You want some?'

'No thanks.'

After that I paid more attention. I couldn't believe I'd missed it when I first came up the stairs. Some were smoking what looked like joints, presumably laced with heroin. Others sniffed smoke from powder placed on foil and heated with a match. Previously I'd been too intent on absorbing the atmosphere of the East to turn round and notice.

I asked one, 'Does it fit well – the view – the atmosphere – the heroin?'

'The people I love most are on the other side. It hurts to stand here and think of them so I smoke to find comfort.'

How bizarre!

This small viewing platform in a remote side-street of West Berlin had turned into a drug kiosk for escaped East Berliners – a perfect advertisement, really, for the freedoms of the West.

By the time I got back to the recording studio I'd made up my mind – David Sylvian's new album was too uncommercial – I would give up managing him. It was a hard decision because over the previous seven years we'd been through a lot together.

Japan had been signed to a Berlin-based record company. As a result we'd been to the city many times, usually just David and me doing promotion without the rest of the band. One time, on the eve of an international soccer match, we'd arrived without a hotel reservation. Everywhere was booked and the town was jammed with Scottish football fans so we started asking for rooms at hotels in the back streets.

I knew it was going to be tough because David, as always, was plastered with make-up. I could never understand why. He wasn't gay, he wasn't even effeminate. 'Why d'you have to wear that bloody stuff?' I asked him.

'It's important,' he said, which wasn't much of an answer.

With David lipsticked and pansticked to the hilt, his hair rising above his head in a two-tone bouffant of blond and squirrel, we pushed through crowds of noisy Scots drinking on the pavement.

'Tell us me lovelies, who takes the high road and who takes the low?'

It was amazing what a bit of lipstick on a bloke could drag from the lips of a Scottish soccer fan.

'Och, the turd burglars are a-passing.'

We trudged from hotel to hotel, asking without much hope, 'Any chance of a couple of rooms?'

Berlin was not the tolerant place it was to become twenty years later. At each place, as soon as the reception clerk saw us come through the door, he decided in the negative. After the fourth or fifth hotel I began suggesting, 'Just one room, perhaps? Just one bed?'

And by the sixth, 'Maybe you could put a mattress on the floor behind the bar?'

Eventually someone mistook David for Quentin Crisp about whom a docudrama had recently been shown on TV. The power of celebrity won. We were in.

But that had been two years ago, and now we were about to separate. It was strange – while I'd never complained about any of the problems David's make-up had caused, I wasn't prepared to stay with him through one uncommercial album. But there was more to it than that. He'd told me, 'In future I want to be thought of like a minor Left Bank poet in post-war Paris – a celebrity but not famous.'

I didn't want to be a minor Left Bank manager. Management wasn't a love affair; it wasn't about sticking with each other through thick and thin. Even when you liked each other, the job was still about business.

* * *

I had something else to do while I was in Berlin – I wanted to call Professor Rolf Neuber – my friend from the Pakistan Airways flight to Tokyo. He seemed pleased to hear from me and invited me to dinner.

I was waiting outside the hotel when he arrived in the back of a black-windowed Mercedes. 'My dear chap,' he shouted excitedly, 'so good to see you.' And he shook my hand up and down enthusiastically, using his left hand to clasp my arm. It was most surprising after the formality and reserve he'd shown in China and Japan.

'My Berlin personality,' he explained, seeing my surprise. 'I'm such a chameleon.'

In the car there was a young man behind the wheel. 'This is Karl,' the professor told me.

Karl was a casually dressed youth with something uncomfortably tough about him. His name suited his hard look, but when Rolf spoke to him in German he called him 'Bubi', which didn't.

Speaking in German, Professor Rolf seemed not quite the same person I'd met in Beijing; he was less softly spoken, more overtly in charge. He took me to a Mexican restaurant where he appeared to be the best-known customer. At the bar he clicked his fingers to call for a drink, a brash slightly-rude gesture, rather Germanic. Yet in English his manners were impeccable.

'What about your pop group?' he asked with a solicitous smile. 'Have you started trying to get them into China yet?'

'There's too much else to do for the moment. I'm here in Berlin with another artist I manage.'

The drinks came and he raised his to mine. 'Did you meet Charlie Goh when you were in Canton?'

'I did. But Canton isn't the place to do Wham!'s concert, it will have to be Beijing.'

'Well don't forget to tell me when you're going. I'll give you some contacts. Remember, we're in this project together.' He stared at me hard as if we were entering into a serious mutual arrangement. Then he loosened up again and smiled. 'What music was Charlie playing at the docks?'

'Wagner.'

Rolf laughed. 'It's absurd isn't it? He just loves classical music.'

With an unusual degree of deference a waiter led us to a table already laid with a banquet of Mexican food. 'I'm a part-owner,' the professor explained. 'They know my taste backwards. I hope you can find something among all this you'll enjoy.'

I couldn't – the food was awful, but when the wine arrived it was wonderful, so I drank rather than ate.

'Perhaps I should have taken you somewhere better,' he said. 'But I had some business here to attend to.'

I was interested to learn more about his businesses. 'Tell me about your work – what did you do with Charlie Goh?'

'Oh things, you know?'

'Your card says you're a "Professor of Languages".'

'I told you, I shouldn't really call myself that. I don't teach; I just own a language school. Do you have your passport with you?'

I pulled it out of my pocket.

'Good! There's a bar I want you to see in East Berlin.'

When we'd finished eating we got into the back of the Mercedes and Karl drove us to Checkpoint Charlie where Professor Rolf handed our passports to the border guard who gave them the most cursory of glances.

'They seem to know you.'

'Of course.'

We drove down the main avenue and into a weave of small streets and alleys. 'Do you like photography?' he asked. 'It's another of my hobbies. The club I'm taking you to is decorated with my pictures. When I travel

I take pictures wherever I go, especially of young men. Maybe I should photograph your pop group for you.'

I wasn't sure that the professor's ideas on photographing young men would fit with Wham!'s, and when we got to the bar I saw I was right. The walls were hung with black and white shots of gently muscled youths, naked or nearly so. The bar itself was dreadful – small, smoky and vaguely gay – half a dozen middle-aged customers and two young men behind the bar, both with bad skin, one with appalling black teeth.

'It's not much of a place, is it?' Rolf said, after we'd had one quick drink. 'I just wanted to show off my pictures.'

As we drove back I asked, 'Do you live in Berlin permanently?'

He smiled. 'Permanently sometimes! I think I told you, I also have houses in Mexico and Thailand with a boyfriend in each. I can tell you – nothing is more extravagant or complicated than having two boyfriends. They both want exactly what the other one is getting, and more.'

'You're describing my life exactly. Except in my case, instead of keeping them five thousand miles apart, all three of us live in the same house.'

Rolf was delighted that we'd found such clear common ground. 'Ah Simon – we're just like twins. I knew it as soon as you came and spoke to me at Beijing airport.'

At Checkpoint Charlie I noticed it was his British passport he proffered, not his German one. 'This may take a while,' he explained. 'Getting in is easy. Getting out is more difficult.'

It didn't appear to be true. The documents were checked with the same cursory glance as previously.

I was impressed. 'You seem to be very well known.'

Karl, the tough driver, turned round. 'Of course. In Berlin everyone knows the professor.'

I was surprised. I'd presumed he couldn't speak English.

The professor smiled. 'Don't forget,' he reminded me. 'I own a language school.'

11 SORE THROAT

In London in early October, George re-recorded 'Careless Whisper' with a flair so extraordinary that it hooked onto your ears from the first note and haunted you right to the last. A unique piece of brilliance that would surely sell millions – just the sort of confidence-giving material we needed in our hands before launching our legal action.

A few days later, on October 7th, Russells sent a letter to Innervision claiming that Wham!'s recording contract was unfair and unreasonable; that it had been signed under duress without proper legal representation; that George and Andrew's signatures had been obtained by fraudulent misrepresentation. Within hours we heard that Innervision had filed an injunction to restrain Wham! from leaving them and applied for a court hearing to settle the matter.

The following day Wham!'s tour started in Aberdeen. Just about everyone flew up to see the show – Jazz and me, Wham!'s parents, Wham!'s lawyers, even Mark Dean from Innervision.

There's something refreshing about Aberdeen. On Scotland's northern shoulder beside the North Sea, its old parts are clean and the new parts are thoroughly modern. It felt a good place to start a tour which was to take us through the oldest, most decrepit music-hall theatres of Britain. Starting the tour in Aberdeen was like starting the day with a cold shower. Equally invigorating was the reception George and Andrew got when they walked out onstage with their backing singers, Dee and Shirley. This was the first live show they'd ever played but from its slickness and dazzle you would have thought it was their hundredth. The audience was insanely noisy, obsessed with everything Wham!, and the encores went on till the theatre management ordered them stopped.

After the show everyone mingled happily in the hotel bar, even Mark Dean, who chatted amicably despite having sent me such a threatening letter some three months earlier.

'In your book,' he said, referring to the book I'd written about the sixties which Andrew had found on my coffee-table, 'you said "record companies are the enemy". Do you still believe that?'

'Of course.'

'The enemy of what, precisely?'

'Artistry, perhaps. Morality. An efficiently run music industry. Anything, really, that I can blame them for. The point is, to energise the process of promoting an artist, there needs to be polarisation, something to fight. And record companies seem as good a target as anything else.'

Mark grinned slyly. 'I think we'll use that in court.'

'You're welcome to,' I told him. 'But if you quote from the book remember to ask permission from the copyright owner.'

Later, Tony Russell took me aside and said, 'Be careful talking to him. You shouldn't have done that without me being around. You mustn't forget we are now in legal opposition to each other.'

I felt like a little boy who'd done something wrong being scolded by his mum and it made me feel nervous. But when I woke up next morning and saw the papers, the feeling was swept away. We'd got everything we wanted – every tabloid in Britain had Wham! spread across their front pages.

'Not since the Beatles ...' started one journalist. 'George and Andrew – the new John, Paul, George & Ringo,' said another. And from all of the tabloids – the *Express*, the *Mail*, the *Sun*, the *Mirror* and the *Star* – the word we'd so much wanted to see: 'Whamania.'

The lunches had paid off.

It was Whamania on the next night too, though at one stage I thought it might not be.

We were playing in a decrepit music-hall theatre from the last century – the Glasgow Apollo – jammed to the gills. I was standing by the stage, and as the group romped through 'Wham! Rap' and hit the chorus I saw the upper balcony fall down three feet in the middle, then spring up again.

Five hundred fans were standing on the balcony, stomping on the beat. I'd been at that venue many times before but never seen movement in the structure that great. It was swinging fit to snap. I called one of the theatre staff and pointed it out.

He shrugged. 'Yeah – that often happens – no problem.'

I couldn't believe that a structural engineer building a theatre over a hundred years ago in the mid-nineteenth century had allowed for the balcony to be filled with demented pop fans jumping up and down on the beat.

In the end, I couldn't bear to watch it.

The tour stormed on to Newcastle, where at breakfast (with an unforgiving hangover) I quarrelled with the waitress over flabby toast and hard fried eggs. The previous evening the radio mikes had gone wrong in the middle of a song and George had changed to a normal wired mike. After breakfast, in the car to the airport, George took it out on Jake Duncan, the tour manager.

'Are those the best radio mikes there are?'

'About second best. The best are almost twice the price, but they're not much better.'

George put on his coldest voice, the one that could burn like dry ice. 'Who told you to economise? From here onwards, don't ask – just get the best. Another thing, why do we have to get up at nine to catch an internal flight? In future make sure that Andrew and I never have to travel before midday.'

It was only the third night of the tour but he was already getting the hang of things.

As Whamania swept Britain, George and Andrew could smell the scent of approaching superstardom. Every day there was something new spread across the tabloids – sometimes the front page, sometimes Page Three, sometimes the centre pages. The more the press gave us, the greater Whamania grew, which gave the press an incentive to print even more. We had them on a roll.

But as the tour went on, George's throat started playing up. Finally, one night, a few hours before a show was due to start, he told Jazz, 'My throat's gone. I can't sing tonight. You'll have to cancel the show.'

The venue was sold out, the equipment was set up and hundreds of fans were already milling around. But for Jazz and me, what worried us most was that the tour was running on a very tight budget. Money was being eaten up, not only by normal touring costs but also by the court case. A glitch like this could be disastrous so we tried to persuade George it wasn't as bad as he thought.

'Look,' he said, croaking a bit and totally firm in his resolve, 'I'm not singing and that's that. If I tried to, I'd probably do myself some permanent harm.'

While Jazz called Harvey and told him the date had to be cancelled I called round radio stations and told them to announce that George had a severe throat infection and was unable to perform.

It caused a lot of bad feeling among the fans, many of whom had seen George at the venue earlier in the day looking OK, but then George compounded it further. He and Andrew drove back to London and went to see a movie at the Leicester Square Odeon.

The next day the tabloids had pictures of them leaving the cinema and ran a story saying they'd cancelled the gig to go to a movie. Fans were enraged and the tabloids, in typical fashion, took their side and riled against George.

I thought it had been a crazy thing to do. 'Why on earth did you go to a movie?' I wanted to know.

'I only had a sore throat,' he told me. 'Why shouldn't I go and see a film? I didn't have to use my voice sitting in a cinema.'

'Didn't you realise you'd get recognised, that it would get in the papers, that people who had tickets for the cancelled show would be furious?'

'Why should they?' George seemed genuinely surprised at the idea. 'I announced I had a sore throat and couldn't sing. Everyone knows that people can't sing with sore throats. And everyone knows it doesn't stop you going to see a movie.'

It just hadn't occurred to him that the general public might not think the same way he did. For George, a set of clear-cut facts could produce only one clear-cut conclusion. Anyone who didn't arrive at it was obviously not thinking properly. Anyway, when his throat got worse and the tour was put on hold for two weeks, the problems with the media cooled down – they could now see that he was suffering from something serious and their anger turned to sympathy.

For Jazz and me it was depressing. It looked like everything we'd engineered so skilfully – the opening of the court case, the tabloids, Whamania – was about to go wrong. But Harvey Goldsmith remained upbeat, and while Jazz filled up the insurance claim forms, Harvey re-arranged the remaining tour dates.

At Bryanston Square, Donavon and Allan were at war; perhaps Wham!'s battle with Innervision had permeated their mood. Donovan bought a brown leather Armani jacket, a snip at a thousand pounds, and Allan immediately went out and bought the very same thing in black. Things came to a head when they bumped into each other in the Star Bar in Heaven. I never heard the full details but at Bryanston Square communication between the Chinese and African factions was suspended, replaced by a silence so icy it hurt to enter the house.

Home wasn't the place to be that week, so while George's throat recovered I decided on another trip to China. This time to Beijing.

* * *

The weather was freezing and foolishly I'd arrived without a coat. I'd chosen the Holiday Inn, one of only two international hotels in Beijing, where the lobby was warm and the check-in girl had a nice smile. 'The bellboy will show you to your room.'

A young man wearing a padded donkey jacket over his uniform came to pick up my bags. It seemed strange he should wear a coat inside the hotel but I soon found out why. The Holiday Inn in Beijing was an economy model built with plans left over from a tropical nudist camp. The corridors were open-air, lined with occasional Greek pillars but no walls. When it rained, or snowed, or blew a howling gale, they were open to the elements. The temperature the day I arrived was ten below zero and my room was the furthest away possible. By the time we reached it I was a shivering wreck.

Once inside I told the bellboy, 'I want to buy your coat.'

It was a plastic jacket filled with foam padding, probably no more than two dollars in the market, but to keep myself warm during trips to the lobby I was happy to pay more.

'I'll give you twenty dollars for it,' I told him, and pulled a twenty dollar bill from my pocket.

'No, no, cannot!' he protested, then grabbed my twenty dollars and ran out of the room.

I couldn't be bothered to walk down the icy passageway to make a complaint at reception so I started unpacking my bag. Before I'd finished he was back with another coat and a fistful of Chinese money – twenty dollars worth, which he'd changed for me at the front desk.

'Here – this coat is fit you OK.' (It was bigger than his and looked brand new.) 'And you pay Rimimbi – no must pay dollar.'

I offered him the entire handful of Chinese money he'd brought me but he only took about a third of it.

'Is that enough?' I asked.

He pointed at what looked like a smoke-alarm in a corner of the ceiling then beckoned me to follow him outside into the cold.

71

'Now you can give me tip big dollar,' he explained. 'Speak inside no good.'

Beijing was miserable. It shared none of Canton's delight with food or fun. This was still the time of Mao jackets – men and women dressed alike in identical blue boiler suits, the girls with no make up, everyone wearing soft canvas slippers even in the coldest weather. And nobody smiling.

It was a city of streets rather than people – the most soulless place I'd ever been in. Professor Rolf had explained how the city's walls had been pulled down after the revolution. A city without walls, he'd said, was like a chicken without its skin. I remembered the snake Charlie Goh ordered for our dinner in Canton. As it was skinned, it turned from a proud green predator into a helpless wiggling worm. That's how Mao had tamed Beijing. Without its walls it lost its shape and definition and the people lost their pride in it. It became a vast camp of obedient workers – millions of them – riding their bicycles along uncrossably wide avenues, lined by continuous concrete buildings that turned the streets into endless miles of prison yard.

I went to Tiananmen Square, bleak and empty, the perfect centre for a city that consisted of roads rather than people. Sleet blew in my face and it was freezing cold. An official guide approached me, giving me facts and figures. 'The paving-slabs are painted with numbers for the organi-sation of our great people on joyous occasions. It can hold half a million – five hundred in each row. Shall I take a Polaroid of you?'

I remembered Professor Rolf saying these guides were secret police so I shook him off and went into the mausoleum. Mao looked dreadful – bad colour and shiny skin, as if he was made of cheap plastic. I left and walked two hundred yards to the other side of the square, the cold crawl-ing up my trouser legs, the wind cutting through the cheap coat I'd bought from the bellboy. Mao's REAL mausoleum, I decided, was Beijing itself – the whole city – as grey and dead as his own corpse.

My instant dislike of Beijing did nothing to change my opinion that Wham! should play their concert there. This was the capital and that's where they had to perform, which meant I would have to come to Beijing each time I visited China. The thought was unbearable.

I made a plan. I would come once a month on a trip that lasted ten days. I would spend three days in Beijing and the rest somewhere a lot nicer – Hong Kong, where I had to get my visas, or Bangkok. During my three days in Beijing I would phone twenty or so important people suggesting I bought them lunch. But I wouldn't sit around for a week waiting for them to call back; I would simply come back the next month and call them again. If they saw me coming often enough, offering them lunch yet apparently unconcerned when they refused it, they would presume that the *real* purpose of my visit was to see someone more important than themselves, which might goad them into replying to my calls. This, at least, was the theory.

At the 'Trade Desk' in the hotel lobby I found an English language phone book listing staff at all the important ministries. I spent the afternoon in my room struggling through phone calls, trying to make myself understood, telling secretaries, office workers, even cleaning ladies (anyone who spoke a few words of English) what it was I wanted and what number they could call me back on. 'Tell the minister, Simon Napier-Bell is in town and wants to take him to lunch.'

Amazingly, the very next morning I had my first taker – none other than the Under Minister for Energy, which was strange because I didn't remember calling him.

He turned up at the hotel on a bike wearing a regulation Mao suit and came into the lobby still wearing cycle clips.

'You Mr Simon?' he asked, proffering his hand for a shake. 'Very please to meet you. Very please to talk about coal.'

It was a puzzling introduction but it turned out he'd got my message muddled with someone else's. He thought I was from Norway and had come to buy Grade 2 coal from the mines in Jiangsu.

It would have been churlish of me not to take him to lunch so having informed him of his mistake I fed him anyway. And I was glad I did for by the end of it I'd realised the correctness of my technique.

He suggested I take him to the rooftop Chinese restaurant at the Great Wall Hotel, Beijing's other international hotel, recently opened by Sheraton. It was excellent; well up to Western standards with an atrium, glass lifts and blizzard proof corridors.

Over lunch the Under Minister told me, 'In Beijing, food in restaurants is terrible. But not here.'

Years of collective farming, he explained, had emptied the country of its great chefs – they'd all fled to Hong Kong, New York and London. But now five-star hotels like this one were opening for foreign businessmen, and these places had fine restaurants with good chefs. But they weren't open to ordinary people (not even members of the Central Committee). To the Chinese, the price of a meal was astronomical, especially when accompanied by French wine; moreover, meals had to be paid for in US dollars which it was forbidden to possess.

'I don't know about music,' he told me over a dessert of toffee banana and ice cream. 'But I know about people in government. They all love good food.'

I was pleased. It looked like my plan might just work.

12

BLACK FAIRIES

George's throat was better.

In late November the tour restarted at the Lyceum, one of London's more fun venues. Fears that Whamania might have suffered were quickly squashed. George and Andrew got it restarted by swapping hair colours – before the two-week break Andrew had been dark and George blond, now it was the other way round. The audience was besotted with them.

The Lyceum was mostly famous for the BBC's weekly programme, *Come Dancing*, a genteel competition for middle-aged practitioners of the waltz and the quickstep. But on nights when it was used for rock and pop concerts, there was often trouble. I'd once been there when the Sex Pistols played and the place was full of amphetamised punks and pill-takers, replete with knives and knuckle dusters.

With Wham! in residence, the mood was somewhere between the two. Their fans were a good deal noisier than the *Come Dancing* crowd, but positively meek compared with the excesses of a rock audience. The bouncers – who enjoyed themselves so much on the rougher nights, smashing kneecaps, poking eyes out and slinging people down the back steps onto the pavement – were positively scornful of the well-behaved teenagers who came to see Wham!.

'So boring,' one of them complained to me. 'Why don't you manage a group with some *proper* fans? I haven't had a decent dust up all evening.'

The court case moved slowly onwards. There was plenty of playing dirty. The book I'd written about the music business in the sixties, the very same one that had encouraged Andrew to think I was the right person to manage Wham!, was read out in court. They used the passage Mark Dean had asked me about in Aberdeen, about the record company being the enemy.

It was Innervision's lawyer who used the quote, not ours. He thought, if he could show that Wham! was managed by someone who's underlying philosophy was to dislike record companies, it might lessen the strength of Wham!'s case.

What effect the quote had on the judge, I had no idea, but as an author it was good to see my book being so widely read.

The court case was eating up money Wham! never had in the first place and with all the cancelled dates we were really short of funds. Jazz and I were anxious to make up the money they'd lost from their cancelled dates so I called TV producer Mike Mansfield and asked if he would film the last show of Wham!'s tour at Hammersmith Odeon.

'What's the point?' he asked. 'Surely the rights would belong to Innervision.'

Except they didn't. It was the one thing in the recording contract which worked in our favour. Somehow Innervision had forgotten to include the rights for the sale of videotapes. Mike agreed to finance it and split the profits fifty–fifty.

For a group as broke as Wham! it was an amazingly good deal and to thank him for it I took him to dinner at September. It was a strange place with the tables arranged around a glassed-in square of garden in the centre of the room. If it rained or snowed, the weather was there with you inside the restaurant which made it rather fun; however, the main attraction was September's clientele.

It was the haunt of well-heeled gays; a place they could feel relaxed dining with a boyfriend, rented or permanent. And September attracted celebrities too, lots of them. Sometimes this mix would make something quite innocent look much less so. The night I went with Mike we met David Steele, the Liberal Party leader I'd last seen at the Hippodrome when I was out with Andrew. He was seated at a table for two with a delicate-faced teenage lad.

'The son of a constituent,' David explained with all honesty.

But he'd chosen the wrong place for such a meeting. The photo journalists who hung around outside would never believe such innocent truth. Nor did Mike.

'Is David Steele gay?' he asked.

'No!' I explained. 'Just naive.'

His naiveté triggered an idea. The next morning I woke up pondering the extraordinary case of Jeremy Thorpe, the former leader of the Liberal Party. In 1979 he'd been found not guilty of conspiring to murder

Norman Scott, a male model with whom he'd had a fling. It had been alleged that friends of Thorpe had hired a hit-man to stalk Scott and shoot him, but in the end he'd only shot his dog.

I had an idea buzzing around in my head as to how this dismal old story could be brightened up – Thorpe's trial should be turned into a musical – a hilarious, glamorous colourful and very camp musical. Perhaps George and Andrew could write the music for it, but more important would be to come up with a script as good as the actual story. So I called Graham Chapman, one of the Monty Pythons.

'Lunch at Mario's,' he insisted.

Before becoming a comedy scriptwriter for the BBC, Graham had studied to be a doctor and could play the part to perfection. After we'd eaten, as we sat with our coffee, laughing over ideas for our musical, Graham called out to a woman at an adjacent table. 'Excuse me madam – do you know you're displaying symptoms.'

Surprisingly, she stepped across to us and stood meekly beside Graham who lit his pipe and drew on it with great sense of medical purpose. 'I'm afraid it might be Python's disease,' he told her. 'Absolutely incurable.'

Then he burst into a high camp voice and sang a chorus of 'I Will Survive'.

'Sing it three times a day after meals. It's a prophylactic. It'll keep the disease at bay.'

* * *

For twenty years, Hammersmith Odeon had been London's principal medium-size music venue. There was hardly a major pop artist in the world who hadn't played there and Mike Mansfield had filmed concerts there twenty times or more. Still, it seemed worth going there early to make sure he had no problems. Just a year before, when Japan were doing their final UK gig there, I'd arranged for David Bowie to see the show and come backstage afterwards, something Japan wanted very much. But when Bowie turned up in the back of a stretch limo and lowered the window he was confronted with a snarling security guard.

'Who d'you think *you* are?'

'I'm David Bowie,' said David Bowie.

'Well, I'm President Reagan,' the guard sneered scornfully. 'So you can piss off.'

And he did. Which left Japan quite upset.

*

At Wham!'s concert I wanted no such accidents. We needed a perfect last show for Mike's filming, a faultless finale for the tour that had created Whamania.

The audience was of the 'everyone-who's-anyone' variety – heads of record companies, that sort of thing. They'd come to check out a group that had a Number One album and four Top Ten singles yet was in dispute with its record label.

In the foyer at the end of the show, David Simone of Arista told me, 'They're fantastic. What are the chances of us signing them? Are you really going to get out of the CBS deal?'

I shook my head. 'On the contrary – the whole purpose of the legal action is to end up signing direct to CBS instead of Innervision.'

'If you change your mind,' he said persuasively, 'there's a million waiting for you at Arista.'

I walked outside with the departing crowd, then round to the back of the theatre. Here was Arista talking about a million pounds yet for the moment George and Andrew remained flat broke.

As I walked in through the stage door I bumped into Mike Mansfield. 'Fantastic!' he told me. 'What a great show. Such vibrance! And we've got it all on tape. Quite brilliant.'

I perked up – perhaps we could pick up a hundred thousand or so for the rights to this video. But when I went into the dressing-room George was not in the happy mood I thought he would be. Instead of chattering cheerfully with Andrew as he usually did after a gig, he was sitting silently. And when I walked in the door he instantly told me, 'I don't want the video used.'

'Why? What happened? The show was terrific. Mike loved it.'

George, it seemed, had suffered an enormous moment of self-doubt. The tour had been subsidised by Fila, the sportswear company, who'd provided Wham! with as much Fila clothing as they wanted. To make use of it George and Andrew had decided to perform half the show in running shorts. Towards the end of the second half they stopped the music and played badminton at the front of the stage, producing shuttlecocks from their briefs. It was this little stunt that George disliked most.

'I hate it,' he told me. 'It's tacky crap – that dreadful thing we do with shuttlecocks down our pants. It can't go out.'

Like everything George ever made up his mind about, it was said with absolute finality.

Jazz had followed me into the room. 'But George – Mike just financed a five camera shoot. He paid the costs with his own money – thirty thousand pounds. How are we going to deal with that?'

George turned away, disinterested. 'I don't know. You're the manager.'

Jazz tried again, this time with Andrew. 'Come on – at least you could come to the truck and look at some of it.'

Andrew shrugged, not in charge of the situation, and George pouted. Eventually, though, we persuaded them to sit with Mike in the back of Harvey Goldsmith's limo in the car park and look at some unedited excerpts.

'I hate it,' George insisted. 'It can't go out. You can't use it.'

'I think it's great,' Mike told him.

'Because,' George explained, 'you're talking about lighting and camera coverage and sound quality. But I'm looking at something different. Simon and Jazz want to go into CBS offices all over the world and say, "Wham! is the greatest new act in a decade", right? But how can they possibly do that with a video of two silly schoolboys putting shuttlecocks down their trousers.'

'We could cut that out,' Mike suggested.

'No!' George insisted. 'It simply isn't good enough.'

Andrew was torn between both points of view. Like the rest of us, he wasn't too keen on losing money. 'What about the cost?'

'No! We have to get things right,' George insisted. 'We can't just think about money.'

Although it was an admirable sentiment there had to be *someone* thinking about money, presumably the managers. Mike said nothing but we knew he would want compensation for the money he'd spent and there wasn't a penny in the bank. We sat in the limo in horrible silence – Jazz, me, Andrew, George and Mike – a week before Christmas without an ounce of good cheer between us, and I couldn't help thinking about the million pounds waiting at Arista.

If only ...

At Bryanston Square, things were a touch better. Donavon and Allan had declared a truce for the Festive Season and the fighting had stopped. Competition between them was no longer being expressed with arguments and bad words but with trying to outdo each other in the dressing-up department.

Allan splashed out a few hundred on Issey Miyaki; Donavon found something flashier by Dolce & Gabbana. Each night the two of them set off together, doing the rounds of discos and clubs; dressed to kill.

It was all rather daft (and not without a downside on the bank-balance) but at least December '83 was a rare month of domestic peace. Donavon, who believed in a traditional Christmas, had bought a tree to put in the hall and it was flashing away nicely with a black fairy at the top.

Allan laughed at it and Donavon was hurt. 'Who says fairies can't be black?' he asked indignantly. Allan laughed louder.

Their peace-on-earth relationship looked too fragile to withstand the rigours of festive drinking so I decided against staying around. Instead, I settled on a quick trip to Beijing in the few days left before Christmas, then on to Thailand where I could meet up with Professor Rolf.

At Heathrow we took off through the drizzling gloominess of a British winter and flew straight into clouds which were even gloomier. It depressed me and set me wondering whether Wham! was a complete waste of time.

The group had a Number One album and four hit singles. Publicity-wise they were the biggest act in Britain yet they were locked in litigation and prevented from recording. The money from their tour had all gone on legal fees and my attempt to make them something extra by filming at Hammersmith had put them another thirty thousand pounds in debt because George didn't like their stage act.

Pop stars!!! I needed a drink.

But what had looked so gloomy a minute before looked a lot better when we emerged from the clouds and flew into sunshine. In a couple of months Wham! would win their case and be back in the charts. Money would pour in; the concert in China would be fixed and with the result-ing publicity Jazz and I would do as we promised and make them the biggest group in the world.

With the sun warm on my face and the drinks trolley approaching, I decided life wasn't so bad. I felt free and the future was promising.

As I leant across to take a glass of champagne from the stewardess I caught sight of the paper the man next to me was reading. It was a piece about Diana Dors. For the last six months she'd been doing as I'd suggested, following her own special diet, the X-cel diet. But she wasn't doing it for a newspaper, she was doing it on breakfast television –

weighing-in once a week on TVAM. And of course, she was losing weight like mad.

The sun went in again. It felt such a lonely thing for her to be doing – coping with cancer all on her own – pretending it wasn't happening.

I wished I'd never thought of the idea in the first place.

13

BROKEN GLASS

The drugstore at the Great Wall hotel was out of all toothpastes known to Western man. When I asked for Colgate they gave me 'Bright & Glorious'. It sounded more like propaganda than toothpaste but I bought it anyway, together with a phrase book.

Chinese in a day was hard-going. In the end I settled for learning just enough to deal with taxi drivers – the numbers 1 to 100, 'left', 'right' and 'how much'. Other than that, I stuck to my original plan and phoned the people I'd left messages for on my first trip – thirty-one of them. I also made calls to a new batch of people, another twenty-five.

I did OK. I got five takers for lunch at the Great Wall's rooftop restaurant and decided to put them together into one bumper banquet but it wasn't a great success. None of them spoke English and they each brought a translator, so it was lunch for eleven. When they were speaking together in Chinese it was like the chatter in a school dining-room, but when I spoke up and asked a question the atmosphere went as stiff as a board. Nevertheless, I told them what I was there for and asked them if they could help.

I was anxious not to ask a question to which anyone could answer, 'No! Wham! cannot come and play in China.' As long as no-one ever said that, I wouldn't lose my excuse for popping off to Asia every time I got bored with life in London, so I spoke instead in statements: 'I think it would be really nice if one day China and England could have a cultural exchange of popular music artists.'

If that statement went down alright, I would go a bit further. 'I manage an English pop band called Wham!. If one day there was a cultural exchange of pop artists it would be really nice if Wham! were one of them. Please give me your views on this.'

I looked round the table, waiting for their answers, but it was as if they hadn't even heard me speak. They were too involved in the special roast duck with tamarind sauce.

*

I'd now heard that the Beijing Hotel held a weekly disco on Wednesdays from eight to eleven.

The interior of the Beijing Hotel was olive green, the colour of government offices around the world, and the disco was held in a bleak meeting room, like a church hall, big and bare, hung with lines of small triangular flags. Yet it was packed with young people, many of them university students. The sound system was suitable only for a room a fifth its size but had been connected to another one which filled the room with a muffled throb of bass, giving people the tempo but none of the melody. Closer to the DJ you could make out what the records were – twenty-year-old Beatles, ten-year-old Boney M, current Michael Jackson.

I leant against the wall and watched the dancers. Their dancing had no recognisable form; they just lurched from side to side, occasionally hiccupping their bodies into the air, rarely in rhythm. There was no sexuality, just extrovert movement. But none of this mattered, for in that room I saw something I'd not seen during my previous visit to Beijing. Smiles! They burst out all over the place as people chattered or danced or just leant against the walls and listened.

Yet under this happy facade there was still no real freedom. Around the walls were 'prefects', young men with red armbands. If they saw something they didn't like – a hint of romance perhaps, or an over-raucous piece of dancing – they would step forward and calm things by laying their hands on the person's arm.

'Are you from America? I'm Zhang Jin.'

The speaker materialised from the dance floor – an earnest-looking male student.

'No. From England. I'm Simon.'

Zhang Jin had glasses, a white shirt, black jeans and clear well-spoken English. 'Do you like our disco?'

'In comparison with my hotel room, yes. In comparison with other discos, not much.'

He frowned, apparently not pleased with my reply. 'I could show you our disco at the university, then you might like this one better.'

'How could yours be worse than this one?'

'We have no sound system.'

I laughed. 'So how can it be a disco?'

'It can't be. Not any more. That's why the authorities took away the sound system.'

84

It was the sort of conversation about which a quick decision had to be made. Any minute now Zhang Jin would introduce me to his friends and I would be tied up in a serious student conversation about life in the West. If I didn't want to suffer it, I had to move away quickly, but I wasn't quick enough. A few moments later I was trapped in a small cafe round the corner – a grubby shack with noodles, pots of tea, plastic tables and three of Zhang Jin's friends – May Ling and Pang Yu (two tiny girls), and Chuen (a pipe-smoking male).

I asked. 'If we wanted to go to the best place in Beijing to have a meal and chat, where would that be?'

'Here,' said Zhang Jin. 'Everywhere else there are secret police. In the disco in the Beijing Hotel there are secret police. But not here.'

'Why not?'

May Ling giggled. 'The food's so bad they refuse to come.'

We sat there for two hours having a long earnest conversation about students, politics and pop culture, which to them meant dissident Chinese rock groups. I mentioned Wham! but they'd never heard of them.

'What about Culture Club?' I asked hopefully. 'Boy George? Queen? The Sex Pistols? Paul McCartney? John Lennon? The Beatles?'

Yes – Pang Yu knew The Beatles. 'My uncle had one of their records – "Bits and Pieces". During the Cultural Revolution he was reported by a neighbour for playing it and sent to the countryside to work in the fields for three months.'

'Bits and Pieces' was by the Dave Clark Five but it didn't seem worth telling her. A knowledge of pop music was just one more of the many things that Mao's Cultural Revolution government had erased from the minds of young people.

Later they called a taxi and sent me back to the hotel. I took their names and numbers, though for the moment I didn't plan to contact them again. There would be little benefit to me; only a possible downside for them. And to be honest, they were too earnest.

It was time for my Christmas break.

Late afternoon I arrived in Bangkok, checked into my hotel and showered and changed. At Professor Rolf's suggestion we'd agreed to meet at a bar called Gulasch, not the sort of place I would have expected him to suggest. It was almost empty and smelt of disinfectant. When I sat at the bar a girl appeared from nowhere and sat next to me. 'My name Pooki. You wanna buy me a drink?'

I ignored her. But at the other end of the bar there was a willowy boy who took my refusal to buy her a drink as a promising sign. He came and sat the other side of me. 'How about me? You wanna buy *me* a drink?'

Before I could answer Rolf breezed in dressed in an old-fashioned tropical suit, his sheaf of silver hair falling down over his forehead. 'Oh there you are, Simon. I see you've made yourself at home.' He pointed to the boy and girl on either side of me. 'Trying to make up your mind, are you?'

'Not at all,' I said firmly.

He flicked his fingers and they were gone – like a gamekeeper calling off the dogs.

It was the day before Christmas Eve; he was staying at the Regent and took me there for dinner. While we ate he explained about the Gulasch Club. He was the owner; it was a place he'd opened for German visitors 'of a certain type'.

'Mostly middle-aged,' he admitted, 'some of them quite important in business. It provides them with whatever they want – boys or girls. This gives me useful information. It can help me in business. Most of these people are not so open about their sexual tastes back home.'

I didn't know what to make of what he'd just said. It sounded like blackmail. 'How exactly do you use the information you get?'

Rolf smiled charmingly. 'Oh, I don't do anything awful. It's just good for leverage. It can help push a deal through. Now tell me, when are you planning to go to Beijing?'

I felt guilty that I'd been twice without letting him know I was going, so I lied a bit. 'I've just been there – for the first time. It was so dreary! With you and a limo it seemed fun. Alone, it's dreadful.'

'You should have told me earlier you were going, I know so many people you should meet. Have you made any progress?'

'I had dinner with the Under Minister for Energy.'

'Was it useful?'

'I don't think so. He wanted to sell me coal.'

Professor Rolf raised his glass. 'Well, here's to your project. I'll do all I can to help, but remember, everyone who helps you will be wanting to use it for their own ends.'

'Including you?'

He look bemused by the question. 'Of course. Why not?'

*

This man was fascinating. I hadn't worked out who he really was or what he did, but his life obviously skirted the fringes of legality. I'd noticed in Berlin, when he spoke in German he had a tendency to impatience, but in English his demeanour was as perfect as when we'd first met, the Hollywood portrayal of a gentleman Nazi. And he laughed a lot; he had a wonderful sense of humour.

When we got to Chiang Mai I found he also had a wonderful home. It was in the hills about one hour's drive from the city, more like Bavaria than Thailand – cool, green and forested – and the house was something between a dream and a joke, a Disneyland Bavarian castle.

He shared it with Lek, his Thai boyfriend, about thirty-five and well paunched. 'He was a slender teenager when we first met,' Rolf said, speaking in front of him. 'He's grown bulky on the generous allowance I give him. He buys the best designer clothes but as you can see, they cling in all the wrong places.'

Lek's answer to this embarrassing introduction was to light a cigarette, blow smoke in Rolf's face and leave the room.

The house was hung everywhere with Rolf's photographs of young men. It had several guest-rooms built round a central courtyard and a swimming pool. 'We built it in 1968,' Rolf said. 'Thailand was so wonderful then – so undiscovered – and Lek and I were so in love.'

He looked out of the window where Lek and his sagging stomach were resting themselves by the pool. 'All my friends came – from Germany, from Japan, from Mexico. But as Lek and I drifted apart, my friends stopped coming. He's getting hopeless now – beginning to drink too much and chasing young boys. It was my fault. I should have given him some training in something – given him a career.'

'You said you had a friend in Mexico too.'

'I do. He's so different. I sent him to college and he's got some real objectives in life.'

He took me down to the wine-cellar, beautiful in both style and content, with a strange musty smell but not unpleasant – like dried apples.

I spotted a half bottle of a vintage d'Yquem, 1937. 'I didn't know you could keep it that long,' I said, and bent over to study the label more closely.

'Mostly you can't, but 1937 was especially good. To revive it, it needs to be poured from a height.' He removed it from the wine rack. 'Would you like to try it?'

He took two large iced wine glasses from the freezer and poured the wine into them, holding the bottle three feet above the glasses.

'It revives it, splashing down from a height like that. I don't know why, it just does. But we need to drink it quickly while it's still fresh in the glass.'

It was like drinking some sort of nutty, dry-tasting, sweet cream, with a magically disappearing after-taste that lingered in the mind rather than the palate. Heaven.

'Looks like you're enjoying it,' Rolf commented.

'I am, I am. But enjoyment is too trivial a word.'

He searched in the rack and found another bottle. 'Good! After we've eaten we'll have another one.'

For dinner we celebrated Christmas Eve the German way – roast goose, venison, red cabbage and potato dumplings. Lek rejoined us and I asked him, 'How long did you say you'd been together?'

'Eighteen years,' he answered softly. 'But I'm afraid the glass is broken.'

'That's rather poetic isn't it?'

'It's an old Thai expression. We believe, once the glass is broken, it cannot be repaired.'

Rolf quickly changed the subject. 'That reminds me of a story ...'

He told us how he'd irrevocably fallen out with Heinrich, his cousin from Munich.

'In my house in Bournemouth I had a beautiful crystal vase. I also had an old-fashioned English butler who broke it when he was dusting. My cousin was getting married and I had to send him a wedding present so I told the butler, "Pack up all the pieces very beautifully in a gift box and send it by mail." It would arrive broken in the box. "Ach lieb! The post is so bad these days, things are handled so roughly." But my damned fool butler wrapped each piece of broken glass in a separate piece of tissue paper. My cousin received it two days later and has never spoken to me since.'

The thought of it made him giggle so much he got hiccups and went to bed.

The next morning I was up before him. Lek offered me breakfast then sat with me while I ate it. I asked him if he'd travelled at all with the professor.

He had, and hadn't enjoyed it. His dislike of the outside world was absolute. Professor Rolf had taken him to Germany where it was too cold, to England where the food was bad, to American where the waiters were rude, to Japan where the people thought Thais were inferior, and to Italy where Lek had thrown endless coins in the Trevi fountain without his wish being granted.

'What were you wishing for?'

'To come back to Thailand as quickly as possible.'

These depressing images of a marriage gone sour were interrupted by the professor coming into the room.

'Happy Christmas,' we said to each other simultaneously.

Things felt better with Rolf around, but although I liked him immensely I'd already decided I didn't want to spend too long amidst the dying embers of his relationship with Lek. Tomorrow I would leave for three weeks in Pattaya, a seaside town almost as decadent as the Berlin of the professor's youth.

'Why not join me for a few days?' I asked him. 'I'm sure you'd have fun.'

Professor Rolf shook his head. 'Too many Germans!' He pursed his lips disparagingly. 'You know ... the *new* type.'

14 SETTLEMENT

With Wham's career at a standstill, February in London dragged badly. The high spot was when Donavon brought Sharon Redd to the house to see me.

'I've been ripped off by everyone whoever touched me,' she told me. 'I never seem to get any royalties and Donavon said you might be able to help.'

Sharon had been a backing singer for Bette Middler before signing a record deal with a company backed by RCA in America in the same way that Wham!'s record company was backed by CBS. She was a black American in her late thirties with a compelling presence, her attractiveness coming more from her energy than her looks. Under her contract, she'd recorded three R&B albums which had sold poorly in the USA. But when the songs were remixed for the European club market, they'd taken off. She'd had several Top Ten dance hits but still had the same old complaint, 'All these hits and no money!'

I'd heard it so many times before; it was a repeat of the Wham! situation. Wham!'s contract allowed Innervision to pay them nothing for 12" singles. Although Wham!'s first two singles had sold three or four hundred thousand each in 12" format there'd been no royalties!

Sharon's contract had a different twist. Hidden away around page 30 or 40, there was a crucial sub-clause. 'No royalties will be paid until the costs of recording have been recouped *from sales in the USA.*'

Her records hadn't sold much in the USA and as long as they continued not to the record company could avoid paying royalties for sales in Europe.

I wasn't sure I wanted Donavon to manage Sharon. She'd admitted from the start she was a recovered junkie and it soon turned out she wasn't as recovered as she'd made out. Yet with regard to her contract I felt myself on a crusade. I hired an American attorney and we did some talking with the powers that be at RCA. We let them know I sometimes wrote for *The Times* and *Independent* in London and was currently writing a piece for the *New York Times* in which I might insinuate that RCA financed and shielded off-shoot record labels whose principal business was to rip off black artists.

In the USA, RCA held government licences for radio and TV stations. It was better for them not to be connected with such things.

Shortly after we spoke with them, they no longer were. Sharon was given a release from her contract.

It was just one more example of the many accounting tricks that appear in recording contracts. The artist's lawyer might persuade the record company to omit some of these clauses, but others will remain. And by agreeing to sign the contract, the artist (and his lawyer and manager) effectively condone the record company's dishonest approach. Which for a second time was what Wham! were about to do.

In March, Wham!'s legal case was settled out of court. CBS had played it tough. They'd set up Innervision in business and backed them to sign artists. But when Innervision had gone to court to keep one of those artists and found themselves short of money to fight the case, CBS hadn't helped. They'd waited until Innervision were on the verge of collapse, then stepped in with a substantial offer to sign Wham! direct.

This had been our plan from the beginning, so naturally we accepted.

Wham!'s new contract would mean better budgets for their albums and an advance of two hundred and fifty thousand pounds to help them enjoy life a little. But was it a good contract? Not at all. It was the same old stuff in a more attractive wrapping.

At least it was a settlement. It was now nine months since Jazz and I had started managing Wham!. We'd promised to make them the biggest group in the world in just two years and with the legal case settled we had just fifteen months left to do it. To pull it off we would want more than just hit records; we would need a huge piece of international publicity, something that could bring instant mega-success in America. The concert in China.

I was about to leave again for Beijing when Professor Rolf called to say he was coming to England for a couple of days.

'I have to go to Bournemouth – a reunion with some people I know – then I'll spend an evening with you in London.'

It seemed all wrong for Rolf to be in Britain, especially somewhere as mundane as Bournemouth; I'd come to connect him only with being abroad. On the other hand, he had a British passport so I could hardly begrudge him the occasional visit.

He called me two days later from the Connaught, which surprised me. 'Why stay *there*? It's ridiculously stuffy – you have to wear a tie just to walk through the lobby.'

He giggled. 'It makes me feel respectable.'

I wanted to show him where I lived and invited him over to the house for a drink. As he arrived Allan and Donavon were leaving for a fancy dress party; Allan, apparently, as some sort of pirate and Donavon in skin-tight head-to-toe black leather.

'An oil slick,' he explained before we could even ask.

'Quite a couple!' Rolf commented.

I'd planned to take him to The Ivy but he had other ideas. 'I've booked the Connaught for 9 p.m., so put on a jacket and tie. But first we have to go somewhere. I have some business to do.'

We took a taxi to a residential street just past the poshest part of Maida Vale where we were checked by a uniformed doorman before being led downstairs to a basement.

It could have been Bangkok or Manila – a darkened room, a bar, a small stage, a scantily dressed girl kneeling in front of a muscled young man.

The audience were men in suits. 'Mostly from overseas,' Rolf explained. 'Businessmen always feel safer going to these sort of places when they're travelling abroad. Like my little Gulasch Club in Bangkok.'

He waved me to a seat at the bar. 'Don't worry, Simon. We won't have to stay long.'

Onstage, the girl undid the man's zip. I was fascinated, not with the show or the sex, but with the fact that this was happening just down the road in London. It was naive of me really; I'd seen things like this all over the world but never thought of them happening right here on my doorstep.

A waiter put glasses of white wine in front of us and Rolf handed him an envelope, nodding towards someone, presumably the manager, on the other side of the room.

'Do you like oysters?' he asked me. 'At the moment, the Connaught has those beautiful big belons.'

The man's jeans fell to the floor revealing bulging underpants.

'Deliciously fresh. They come from Brittany every morning.'

The girl tugged at the man's briefs and his penis popped into full view.

'And the lamb is magnificent. Probably the best in the world.'

The waiter came back and nodded meaningfully.

Rolf tossed him some money for the drinks. 'Bottoms up! We're off.'

As we left, the couple onstage plunged into intercourse.

'So why did we have to go there?' I asked.

'Business! I told you already. Didn't you enjoy it?'

The Connaught required a tie. Normally I wouldn't wear one but for Rolf I bent my rules and sat through dinner feeling buttoned up and hot.

When we'd finished eating we went to the lounge for brandy and Rolf got out a piece of paper and handed it to me. 'Keep this phone number. Next time you go to Beijing make sure you meet this man – Mr Wu.'

'What does he do?'

'Works for the government.'

'For God's sake, Rolf, it's a communist country, everyone works for the government. What does he actually *do*?'

'He's a translator.'

I sipped my brandy and read the piece of paper Rolf had handed me. It was written in both English and Chinese. 'What makes this translator so special?'

'He's important. He's in charge of a government department, it's a sub-division of the department that bugs hotel rooms. When the hotel guests are foreigners, it's Mr Wu's department that translates what they say into Chinese and gives a transcript to the secret police.'

I was still puzzled. Mr Wu sounded more like someone to avoid than someone to contact. 'How can he help me?'

'Tell him what it is you want to do. He'll pass on the information. And remember, we're in this together.'

Now he was puzzling me even more. '*What* are we in together?'

He pulled a face. 'Who knows? Making history? Changing China? We'll have to wait and see.'

I was still mystified as to what he wanted. 'Rolf, apart from your language college in Berlin, what business are you actually in?'

He paused, apparently choosing his words carefully. 'I have contacts … all over the world … we *exchange* information.'

Going home in a taxi I decided Rolf must be some sort of inter-national gangster, Yakuza maybe, or Triad. Or since he was four nationalities rolled into one perhaps he was some sort of quadruple agent. But what was he up to at the sex show when he passed an envelope to the waiter? Surely it must have been drugs.

The next morning I saw how wrong I was. We'd arranged to meet for coffee in the lounge at the Connaught before he left for the airport. As I arrived he was coming out of the lift with the muscular young man from the sex show. So that's all it was – how stupid of me not to have realised.

The professor wasn't the slightest abashed. 'We had a midnight photo session. One of the horniest young men I've ever met.'

He ordered croissants and coffee and changed the subject. 'You know, as you proceed with what you're doing in China, there's going to be a lot of people interested. And they'll all want something different from it.'

'Like you, for instance?'

He dipped his croissant in his coffee, French style, then leant his head back to receive the soggy mess. 'Maybe. But I'm talking now about your idea of persuading the Chinese to let Wham! play a concert by telling them it will make the rest of the world believe China is opening up when in fact they'll keep the group's visit a virtual secret from their own population. There's a lot of people who would like to get your concert publicised inside China too. There's a great deal of effort being made by all sorts of people to destabilise the Chinese government and some of that comes from within the government's own ranks. There's a lot of factions there and you may have to play some of them off against each other.'

He sounded patronising, as if he was lecturing me. I frowned. 'I'm not that interested really. I just want to get Wham! into China for the sake of publicity in America.'

'But you're doing it by playing politics.'

'That's just it – I'm only *playing* – I'm not serious.'

He sighed impatiently, as if I was missing the point. 'Politics is something you can't play at. Everything is cause and effect. It gets out of control. You start with a little manipulation then things get a life of their own.'

On his way to the airport Rolf gave me a lift back to Bryanston Square, reminding me again about the person whose number he'd given me the previous evening. 'Don't forget to call Mr Wu. He's great at spreading the word. But be careful – there are lots of power games going on in China, and you, Simon, seem to be heading for the middle of them.'

PART II
APRIL 1984

15 HAPPY BIRTHDAY

I was woken by the fire alarm. It rang through my skull as if someone was drilling a hole in it. When I realised it was only the telephone I threw out my arm and knocked the receiver off the hook.

'Simon?'

It was hanging by its wire. I remembered now, I was back in Hong Kong and the previous evening had been my forty-fifth birthday.

'Simon? Are you there?'

I leant over and got hold of it but my vocal chords were dried to the back of my throat like cabbage to the bottom of a burned saucepan. When I tried to speak no sound emerged.

'Simon? It's Sam Jor.'

At the other end the receiver was replaced.

Sam Jor was a journalist – someone I'd known for some years. He'd interviewed Japan on several occasions and helped them to become big in the region. The previous evening I'd met him in Disco Disco, Hong Kong's meeting place for celebrities. When he'd heard what I was trying to do with Wham! he told me, 'You've got to meet Lew Mon Hung, he knows everyone in China.'

'Everyone?' I asked.

'Everyone who counts,' he insisted.

I'd agreed to meet for lunch, but having lunch was the last thing I now wanted. A Japanese gong band had infiltrated my skull and was playing a symphony in percussion.

But hangovers were nothing unusual and providing I worked at it I would cure this one in an hour. The secret was a run in the gym. Actually, I hated gyms. Whenever I was running all I could think of was something nicer to be doing – sitting down, reading a book, watching TV, daydreaming. But with a hangover I could do none of those things – I couldn't dream coherently or focus on a book or a TV screen, so I might just as well be running. And that's how I kept fit; hangovers got me to the gym; curing them forced me to take exercise. A substantial daily intake of alcohol was the perfect way to stay in shape.

Finished in the gym, I was ready for coffee. Finished with coffee, I went back to my room and noticed a red light flashing on my phone. Sam Jor had left his number and I called him back. Half an hour later he was introducing me to the person he'd said I should meet.

There was little about Lew Mon Hung to impress me. He spoke poor English, his skin was bad, his appearance was rough and his table manners had apparently been learned in a Cantonese restaurant. My first impression was that he should be working on a building site.

'Lew came from China ten years ago,' Sam explained. 'Now he's a businessman and an economist. He often lectures at universities.'

It seemed implausible; he just didn't look like an economics lecturer. I asked him, 'Since China switched to a market economy, which industries have benefited most?'

I shouldn't have. Once he was off and running there was no stopping him. 'Reforms were intend to give equal incentive for agriculture and heavy industry, but farmer, who is now three-quarter of China, is only get subsidy ten per cent because heavy industry is take forty-five per cent, and ...'

For ten minutes he hardly paused and I understood little of what he said. But by the time he'd finished I accepted he might possibly be some sort of economist though it was unlikely his lectures were delivered in English. 'Do you mean,' I asked, 'that heavy industry has benefited from the reforms?'

'No! I mean nothing is change much.'

I told him about Wham! and why I wanted them to play in China.

He claimed he knew all the right people in Beijing and would introduce them to me if I agreed to take him with me on my next trip. And my next trip was tomorrow.

It was a difficult decision. I'd contrived to get myself set up with a monthly trip to Asia during which time I was at the behest of no-one. I wanted to keep it that way but I already had Professor Rolf talking about Wham! going to China as being 'our project'. Now I was about to take another passenger on board, and unlike the professor, Lew was not particularly personable. It felt like a fundamentally bad idea.

On the other hand, it was only for one trip to Beijing, and since I hated the place anyway he probably wouldn't make too much difference to my enjoyment of it.

'OK!' I told him. 'You're on.'

On the plane he chattered in Chinglish and quite soon I'd got the hang of it myself. 'Lew,' I asked. 'How long live Hong Kong?'

'Nine year.'

He told me how he'd fallen out with the authorities during the cultural revolution and had been sent to do compulsory labour in the countryside where everyone lived in a cowshed – more than one hundred people sleeping on the concrete floor including disgraced party officials, scholars and professors. They were made to scrub the floor with their toothbrushes and learn the sayings of Chairman Mao by heart.

'Why were you sent there?'

'A friend report me to authorities. I had American watch – Timex – my grandfather give me but I never use.'

Later, Lew escaped. He walked (only by night and taking three months to do it) the entire length of the country, avoiding towns and villages and living off the land – edible shrubs and fruit – and when there was no fresh water to be found, drinking the small pool of liquid that sits atop a fresh cow-pat at dawn. Eventually he reached Canton and swam to Hong Kong.

'How come you can now go back to China?' I asked.

'Things is change. China now open for business, so I go do it.'

'And what business is it you do?' I asked.

'Doing-business business!' he explained succinctly.

In Beijing we checked into the Great Wall Hotel and he promised me lunch with someone interesting. He was right – it was the son of the Prime Minister, Zhao Ziyang.

Zhao junior was in his twenties. His English was good when he used it but he apparently preferred not to do so; instead he allowed Lew Mon Hung to do the translation. The Prime Minister's son had no hint of a Mao suit or bad teeth or a Chinese crew cut – he had a sharp Western suit, white sparkling teeth and a slick hairdo. He could have come from Hong Kong, whereas Lew Mon Hung, who now came from Hong Kong, looked like he still worked on a farm in China. I had no idea what the original contact between the two men was or if they were really friends or not.

Zhao junior had little to offer me other than the amusement of talking with the Prime Minister's son. He wanted to find overseas markets for various bits of small plunder he'd picked up through being who he was – industrial machinery, iron and steel products, cheaply made bulk clothing. The cut of his suit and the quality of his shirt suggested he was doing well, but he looked uninterested in the suggestion that he might help me get Wham! into China.

Although I couldn't understand what they were saying it was obvious that Lew Mon Hung was being pushy with him, persuading him he should at least pretend he would do something for me.

Lew, I decided, was simply a deal-broker – a wide-boy. I tried to compare him with Rolf. Were there similarities between getting by in the cultural revolution and getting by in wartime Germany?

I tried to believe Lew really was the economist and lecturer he said he was but when he turned and spoke to me at the end of lunch he seemed no more than a spiv. 'OK – your group come China – you pay, we fix.'

There was nothing I needed to do, he said, except pay for his trips to Beijing. My presence wouldn't be required.

I was non-committal. 'Maybe ...'

Because Lew was with me I didn't call the people I'd called on my previous trip when I was dishing out lunch appointments; I didn't want them coming to the hotel and Lew muscling in on them. But I did call the man Rolf had suggested I speak to, Mr Wu, who said he would meet me the next morning for coffee.

He turned up at eleven and talked for a few minutes in the lobby. 'Tell me what you're doing here, and how can I help?'

Mr Wu spoke in impeccable BBC English, which made his Chairman Mao outfit of blue overalls seem totally bizarre, like a wealthy industrialist pretending to be 'one of the boys' for an afternoon visit to the factory floor.

I told him, 'Rolf Neuber gave me your number. He said you'd be worth meeting. I'm trying to arrange for a British pop band to play a concert in Beijing.'

Mr Wu glanced round the lobby. 'Well let's not talk here. The whole place is bugged. I should know – it's my department that does the translations.'

While we drove into Beijing in an official car (presumably bugged too) he quizzed me about what I was doing there. Knowing what his job was, I thought whatever I told him might get back to the powers that be, so rather than be evasive I gave him the full hard sell ....

'The Chinese have billions of dollars flowing in from overseas investment, yet most of the world is still unconvinced about China opening up, especially in terms of political and personal freedoms. The Chinese government should do something that would let the whole world see they are genuine about opening up to Western ideas. If they did that, it would greatly help the inward flow of investment. If the government invited a famous pop group to play a concert in Beijing with an audience of young people and televised it to the world, it might help China enormously in both the political and economic fields.'

'Do you want to see a department store?' Mr Wu asked. 'I want to show you how China is opening up. Maybe we've already gone further than you think.'

He walked me round a dreary building full of counters stocked with nothing worth having until we reached a new cosmetics department. Women were clustered round an assistant who was demonstrating how to apply lipstick.

'But no-one is buying it,' I pointed out to him. 'And on the streets, there are still no women wearing it.'

'They will,' he assured me. 'The government has made cosmetic manufacture an industry approved for subsidy. There will soon be advertisements all over town with a new slogan – "to beautify yourself is glorious".'

Then he proudly showed me the electrical department, its shelves filled with Chinese-made television sets, cassette recorders and cumbersome hi-fis with vast speakers.

'You see – progress is being made.'

'My point is,' I explained, 'the outside world can't see all this. But by bringing a Western pop group here and televising it, there would be proof of the changes in government thinking.'

'And is it *your* group that you're suggesting we bring?' he asked.

I was still being careful to avoid saying anything that could get a negative response, so I shrugged. 'I'm talking theoretically. It's just an idea, that's all.'

*

When I got back to the hotel Lew Mon Hung was checking out, leaving for Hong Kong. His face looked particularly sour and when he saw me come in he strode across the lobby and spoke sharply. 'Not necessary you speak with Mr Wu. Lew can speak with Wu.'

Since I'd tried to keep my meeting with Mr Wu a secret, I was slightly abashed. 'I didn't know you knew Mr Wu?' I said. 'How did you know I spoke with him?'

Lew gestured round the spacious mezzanine lobby of the Great Wall Hotel – chrome pillars, thick carpets, comfortable settees, glass elevators speeding up and down its eighty-foot walls. 'Anything that happen in here is everybody know. Reception girl is secret police, boy carry bag is secret police, sound is bug, guest is made photo each one. This is place for secret police to watch foreigner. You didn't know?'

I remembered my bugged smoke alarm at the Holiday Inn, yet it was hard to believe that this place was bugged too. The lobby buzzed so nicely in the correct Western way; it could have been New York or Paris.

Lew picked up his bags and gave me the sort of withering glare a schoolmaster might give a child who had misbehaved in class. 'I'll be hearing from you, OK? Then Lew fix Wham! in China.'

16

QUITE EXCITED

I got home at ten in the morning. No-one else was in so I headed downstairs to the kitchen to make some breakfast and read the newspapers. While I was scrambling eggs, Dick Leahy's secretary called. 'The new song's finished. Dick's sending a taxi over to you with a copy.'

It was delivered ten minutes later while I was still eating. I ran upstairs to the front door, grabbed the package, threw it on a table next to all my accumulated mail and went back to my eggs. Some time later, when I'd finished reading the paper, I wandered back upstairs and noticed the envelope on the table where I'd left it. I took out the acetate, put it on the record player and started opening the stack of letters.

I was reading one of them when the song's intro started. There was a tension in the intro that grabbed me so completely that I couldn't let it continue. Instead, I dropped the letter, went back to the record player, put the record back to the beginning, turned up the volume and sat down in front of the speaker.

In the early days of Wham!, George had rhymed 'soul boy' with 'dole boy' and found a target market – unemployed sixteen to nineteen-year-old males with a distinct way of dressing.

'Soul Boys' were angry. They came from good families, good neighbourhoods, had completed their schooling and still couldn't find a job.

Wham!'s next two records had expanded this market to include teenagers of both sexes. Then they'd made 'Club Tropicana' – softer, less demanding, more fanciful. Mums and Dads could enjoy it and the video was of holidays, sunshine and fun.

Everyone involved with Wham! knew that one day 'Careless Whisper' would be the song to broaden the group's appeal to all ages. But because it was a ballad, we'd all decided we would first need a song that would smooth the transition. Moreover, Wham!'s first record after a six month absence caused by the court case simply *had* to be in the happy-go-lucky style that people connected with them.

'Wake Me Up Before You Go-Go' was the perfect answer. Bouncy, current and trendy, it also had jitterbug references and slow triplet brass runs that reeked of forties and fifties swing music. I must have played the record half a dozen times. It was mesmerising. As a piece of simple pop music it crossed all barriers, it was sheer perfection.

There was a forthcoming hair show at Grosvenor House; if Allan was to take part he would need a large subsidy. I'd been putting off making a decision about it, but when I'd finished listening to Wham!'s new record I called him to say go ahead.

Donavon too had been asking if there was any money available; he wanted to record a new rap group he'd found. I called him too to say yes.

I listened to the record yet again. From the first beat I knew this would be Number One, not just here but in America and around the world. When George's remake of 'Careless Whisper' had turned out so perfect, some of the people working with George had thought it a fluke. This record proved otherwise; George was turning into a pop genius.

Later that day I went to the office to see Connie. 'Dahlink, my sex god. Where have you been? You look wu-u-u-underful!'

'Beijing,' I answered shortly. 'Have you heard the new record?'

'Sheer brilliance,' she gushed. 'Jazz thinks so too, and so does everyone at CBS. That boy is a genius.'

Everyone seemed to be in agreement, except perhaps George himself.

While I was at the office he arrived with Andrew to do some press interviews and took me aside. 'Have you heard the new record yet? What d'you think?'

'It's good,' I told him. 'In fact, it's sheer bloody perfection.'

George pouted. He was always accusing me of being a cynic and he wasn't sure I was being straightforward with him. 'I'm not so sure,' he said, which was unusual because he was normally so certain about the quality of his work.

'Why are you unsure?' I asked. 'It's one of the most brilliant pop records I've ever heard.'

He shook his head. 'I'm afraid it's trivia.'

'But that's the definition of pop,' I told him. 'Selling trivia is what we both devote our lives to?'

He frowned. I was being cynical again.

*

At the beginning of May, almost nine months after her cancer came back, Diana Dors died. She'd lived with it without letting anyone know but her closest friends. The day before she died, she'd been on the phone from the hospital, as always interested in other people's lives rather than her own. I told her Wham! had won their court case and 'Go-Go' was their best record yet.

'How about the video?' she asked. 'You've got to get that right too. Give it lots of energy – that's what people want these days.'

And it's what they got.

As a visual creation the video turned out perfectly – immaculate pop art, as easily watchable as the record was listenable – it was Wham!'s stage persona captured to perfection.

The pseudo-intellectual critics hated it. 'A feeble ego-blast,' said Paul Morley. 'Insipid idiocy,' grumbled the music editor of the *Sunday Times*.

But the teen-papers loved it – *Smash Hits*, *Number One*, the *Mirror*, the *Sun* – they all revelled in it and raved accordingly. There was no doubt about it: 'Wake Me Up Before You Go-Go' was going straight to the top of the charts.

'Wham! Sh-bam! Britain's Number One Band.'

* * *

When Wham!'s new record hit Number One in the UK, Jazz and I headed for New York to sort out the next stage of their career. To make things happen there we would have to persuade Al Teller, the man who ran CBS's Epic label, to spend some big money on promotion. But Al had already made his mind up – Wham! were a peculiarly British phenomenon, the sort of thing that never sold well in the States. Jazz and I set up a meeting to see him.

George and Andrew, sensing there were difficulties, went with us to check out what we were doing. Until a few weeks earlier they'd been insisting on American managers for the States – Ron Weisner and Freddie DeMann, who managed Michael Jackson and Madonna – yet for all their status these two had achieved nothing for Wham! whatsoever. They'd been brought to a standstill by Al Teller's insistence that he would invest nothing more in British acts.

For Jazz and me, this was the big test. Could we really pull it off as American managers? Although 'Go-Go' had just got to Number One in the UK charts, the situation wasn't promising. Four weeks earlier I'd been in New York and had popped in to say hello to Clive Davis, the head of Arista, supposedly the man with the sharpest ears in the business.

'You can be the first person in the States to hear Wham!'s new record,' I told him. 'Next week this will be Number One in the UK.'

But when Clive put it on and played it his face went as blank as the top of his bald head. He didn't get halfway through it. 'A novelty song,' he said disparagingly. 'These things never work in the States. We like proper music.'

I thought of listing for him all the worst novelty records ever made, every one of them American, starting perhaps with 'How Much Is That Doggie In The Window'. Instead I held my tongue and told him, 'Just wait and see.'

Now as I headed off to see Al Teller, Clive's words were ringing in my ears. I told Jazz I'd been to see him.

'What did he say?' Jazz asked.

'A definite Number One. A dead cert!'

Jazz smiled confidently, encouraged; but he didn't really need encouragement, he was a warrior. Reports of Al Teller's indifference to Wham! had created in him a determination even greater than mine. He'd arranged for dance promoters to put the record into dance clubs in California and get it into the LA dance charts. This was the sort of work that Al Teller should have told his employees to organise, but he hadn't done. Jazz figured if we paid for it from the UK, Al Teller wouldn't know it had been done through promoters and would think the record was taking off by itself.

In New York, Jazz and I left George and Andrew in the hotel and went for our meeting at CBS where we were directed to the conference room. From the outset it looked like our meeting might be disastrous. In order to wipe us out quickly and persuade us to give up and go away, Al had herded his entire marketing and promotional staff into a conference room. When we arrived we were confronted with thirteen people. Al went round them individually, asking each person what they thought of the record, and all of them were against it.

'A novelty record.'

'Won't do well in America.'

'Wait until the next single.'

'The image isn't right.'

'Too British.'

The negatives were endless; and looking very pleased with what his staff had told us, Al turned to Jazz and me and said, 'You see, it just isn't worth our while to push it.'

The latest issue of *Billboard* was on the table. Jazz picked it up and folded it open at the regional dance charts. 'But we thought you *were* pushing it. If you're not, how come it's in all these California dance charts?'

He threw the *Billboard* on the table and everyone looked at it in surprise.

I told Al, 'You see! The record's a natural – it's happening on its own. You should give Wham! a major promotion campaign.'

'No way.'

Al said it loudly and firmly with obvious enjoyment, showing his staff the right way to deal with pushy British managers.

'That's disgusting,' I told him. 'CBS is an American company. If it signs artists in other countries who prove themselves in their own market, CBS has a duty to give them a shot at the US market. But if you don't want to do that, you should release Wham! from their contract for the USA and we'll take them to Arista. Clive Davis is dying to have them. He thinks the single's a definite US Number One. I played it to him last week.'

Al sat and glared at us, saying nothing. He was bored; wanted us to finish; couldn't wait to get back to his office and get on with the day.

Next, Jazz had a go. 'It's really sad, that people like you, whose job it is to sign and promote artists, haven't the slightest understanding of how artists think or feel. You build your corporation on their dreams and aspirations but you don't give a toss about them.'

Al was getting angry. He was shaking slightly. His twelve employees were becoming interested. Jazz and I caught each other's eye. In for a penny, in for a pound.

I went first. 'Listen Al ... during the court case in the UK, I watched the way CBS screwed Innervision, their own subsidiary, in order to grab Wham! for themselves. I'm nothing to do with Innervision, but even so, it showed a great lack of obligation and morality on behalf of CBS. The company now seems to be behaving with an equal lack of obligation to the very artist it fought so hard to get hold of. It doesn't make sense. Maybe you should get in some outside consultants to advise you how to do things better.'

Suddenly Al exploded with rage; he completely lost control of himself; he shouted, shook, banged his fist on the table and started to sweat. His employees were embarrassed; some even scared. Jazz and I looked at each other, not at all sure what we'd set in motion. Could this be the end of Wham! in America?

Surprisingly, Al calmed down quickly; he knew he'd made a fool of himself in front of his staff and he wanted the meeting finished as quickly as possible. He asked us, almost despairingly, 'What exactly do you two guys want?'

'We've already got it,' Jazz told him smartly. 'We just wanted your interest.'

'We'll do whatever you want,' Al said abruptly. 'Just tell us what you want us to do.'

'We don't want to tell you what to do,' Jazz said. 'You're the experts. Just give Wham! the promotion they deserve. We just wanted to make sure we'd drawn your attention to the matter?'

Al managed a wry smile. 'Deliver the album on September 1st and we'll give it the works.'

'And what about "Wake Me Up Before You Go-Go"?' I asked.

Al looked round the table at his staff. 'What d'you think guys? Can we launch the album with it?'

All of a sudden they were singing a new song.

'Why not?'

'It's a good record.'

'Doing well in California.'

'Could be a smash.'

When we got back to the hotel George and Andrew were waiting in the lobby. 'How did it go?' they asked.

'Al got really excited,' Jazz told them.

So did we.

Jazz and I had the feeling that CBS were really going to pull the stops out and make it happen, but later that evening, over an after-dinner drink in the hotel bar, George spoilt it. 'Some time soon we'll have to start thinking about me going solo.'

'But you've hardly started with Wham!,' Jazz replied, shocked.

'Have you forgotten?' I asked George. 'We were going to make you into the biggest group in the world?'

Jazz and I both had experience of groups who'd broken up just as things began to happen for them. We were well aware that the most important task a manager had was to keep his group together. The history of pop was riddled with instances of lead singers suddenly deciding they were more important than the rest of the group, but only after three or four years of being at the top. Wham! were still at the beginning of their career – they hadn't even had a hit in America. Hopefully, George's remark was just a passing case of 'lead-singeritis'.

Sure enough, as he was leaving the bar to collect Andrew for a night on the town, George softened a bit. 'I didn't mean right *now*. I meant – *some time*! Maybe after the third album.'

Jazz and I stayed behind in the bar. 'If he means it,' I said, 'three albums would mean a minimum of four years.'

Jazz agreed. 'So if we get them to the top in two years, like we said we would, there'll still be another two years to reap some reward from our work, touring them round the world.'

Looked at like that, it didn't seem too bad. Nevertheless – having created Whamania, having gone through litigation and won, having got ourselves a Number One single and album in the UK and a promise from CBS to promote Wham! to the full in America – George's intention to break up the group was not the sort of news we wanted.

'What should we do about it?' Jazz asked.

'Have another drink,' I suggested.

So we ordered two nightcaps and drank to success.

17 A PAINFULLY POINTLESS MEAL

From the front door to the armchair in the sitting-room, Eartha Kitt walked as if she was making an entrance onstage. People often referred to her as catlike and you could see what they meant; she walked like a perfectly groomed panther. On arrival at the armchair she sat so beautifully, and with such poise, that I expected her to launch into a monologue. But she didn't. She sat in silence, the air around her pervaded with a wonderful perfume, Chanel No. 9, I think.

A few nights before, Donavon and I had been to the Hilton to watch her in cabaret. Donavon wanted to manage her and had invited her to the house for tea. 'Eartha's just made a disco record,' he explained, 'with the producers of Village People. She thought perhaps I could manage her for disco work – singing in clubs and things. Maybe it would help bring her back to superstardom.'

There was a programme from Wham!'s first tour on the coffee-table and Eartha picked it up. 'I so much admire young people like Wham!' she said. 'So young, so successful, so much cleverer about business than we used to be. Getting rich at such an early age.'

I didn't bother telling her they'd only just got out of a court case that nearly killed their career stone dead. Instead I talked to her about performing in discos. 'They're raucous, dirty places full of disinterested teenagers. You have to sing at one in the morning. No changing rooms, no red carpet, just thousands of stoned kids putting up a communal moan when the DJ stops their dancing to announce "tonight's special guest".'

Wham! had already objected to doing this type of painful promotion yet here was a 60-year-old woman volunteering for the same thing, though I had to admit she was certainly fit enough. When we'd seen her at the Hilton she'd been as good as the first time I'd ever seen her twenty years earlier in Paris, and doing almost the same show – wonderful, wiry, sexy and vital.

113

I continued with my attempt to disillusion her about discos. 'After three songs and a thousand pounds cash shoved in your hand, there's a three-hour drive back to London down the motorway from Newcastle, or Manchester, or Cardiff – you get home tired and sweaty at four in the morning. No glory, no feeling of satisfaction, no achievement.'

And this for someone who could have an audience eating out of her hand in Las Vegas or Atlantic City.

Eartha looked disappointed at my lack of enthusiasm; Donavon even more so. I moved quickly to another subject. 'Eartha, I once heard you say – when you first became a star and heard people call "Eartha Kitt" a great artist, you couldn't recognise that person as *you*. You said "Eartha Kitt", the star onstage, was like a different person, a friend maybe, but not really you. You even felt guilty about benefiting from her success or buying things with the money she earned.'

Eartha's speaking voice was even sexier than her singing voice – like purring – she really was the cat they said she was. 'You see, Simon, I used to be Eartha May. That person onstage – Eartha Kitt – was just a role I was playing. But people thought it was the real me, so bit by bit I had to take my stage character, mix it together with the real me and make a new person. It took me many years to do it but eventually I managed to combine the two different personalities into one. Other people have gone mad trying to do it – especially when their stage image is *too* far from their real self.'

She left shortly after that, quite abruptly, as if she'd said enough for the day, or perhaps it was my negative attitude towards her proposed career as a disco diva. When she'd gone I found myself thinking about George and his insistence in New York that he wanted to finish Wham!. Was he having the same problem Eartha had described? Was he finding it too difficult to blend his stage persona with his real self? Was that why he was talking about going solo? And would going solo really help?

After all, he would then be George Michael, which was still a fake character, still not the real George Panayotiou; though perhaps it would be near enough to cope with.

'Careless Whisper' was his chance to find out. The record was to be put out under the name 'George Michael' and the making of the video would give him an opportunity to create a new public persona. It was to be shot in Miami and I went to watch, interested to see how he would approach the challenge of getting closer to his real self.

I arrived at midday. The filming was being done around Coconut Grove, among hotels and marinas and outside cafes. George was out on a speedboat with the film crew and since it was a blazing hot day, around 95 degrees, I went to the hotel bar.

I found Andrew checking out its range of malt whiskies. 'Are you going to be in the video?' I asked. 'I thought it was going to be just George.'

He laughed. 'I shall make a fleeting guest appearance. The time still hasn't come for me to be pushed aside completely.'

Later, George came back from his boat trip, happy with the day's filming. But the next morning when he looked at the rushes he flipped. 'It's my hair. It's dreadful. Too long. Too posey. Too poofy.'

His hair was as it had been for the last few photo sessions with Wham!. For his first record as George Michael he now decided he should look different – more mature. Having his hair cut and the filming redone would add almost fifty per cent to the total budget of the video, but when George was firm things were done. His sister Melanie was flown out to cut it and the next morning – with his hair restyled and the speedboat re-rented – the first day's filming was reshot.

I used the time to go to the local office of CBS and see what they were doing for Wham!. At the reception was a slender girl with short sun-bleached hair, deeply bronzed skin and almost no make-up; she was wearing cream shorts and a thin cotton blouse through which her nipples showed clearly. It gave me a shiver of apprehension. Normally I'm secure about my sexuality – I'm gay and that's that – but on this occasion I thought, 'Maybe I'll give up boys for a bit.'

Within seconds I'd invited her out to dinner, but she couldn't make it. 'How about lunch tomorrow?' she suggested. 'I've got the day off.'

Wham! were going to be in Miami for two more days so tomorrow was fine. I booked a table for 1 p.m. at a restaurant on the waterfront not too far from where we were filming.

The following day had been set aside for sex scenes. So while George stripped off to do his bit with a young actress in front of the camera-crew, I set off to meet the girl from CBS at the house in Coral Gables where she lived with her parents.

When I rang the bell she dashed downstairs, pulled open the front door and ran back upstairs to finish getting ready, leaving me standing at the bottom of the staircase. After a second she stuck her head over the top of the banisters and called out, 'Will you be wanting to fuck me after lunch?'

I was completely thrown. 'Well no, uh, of course not ... I just thought it would be nice to have a good meal.'

'Oh that's all right then,' she explained. 'You see, I've got to be somewhere at four so I thought, if you were expecting a fuck it might be better to get it out the way now.'

I should have either leapt up the stairs three at a time or turned round and walked out. Instead, in the most romantic of settings, overlooking glittering blue water and bobbing white yachts, I struggled through a painfully pointless meal.

That evening George filmed the most memorable scene in the video. Standing on the balcony of a penthouse overlooking night-time Miami he sang his greatest song with a passion that would sell it to the world.

With a competent director on hand, the manager's presence was superfluous. I absconded and headed for a disreputable bar in South Beach, all thoughts of girls dismissed from my mind for good.

From Miami, I was flying to Beijing, but Rolf called and persuaded me to make a stopover. 'I'm in Mexico City. Break your journey for twenty-four hours and I'll buy you dinner? It's literally on the way for you.'

I arrived in the early evening, the sun still shining brightly. Rolf met me in a hotel car. 'Before we go to the hotel, I'm taking you to the pyramids at Teotihuacan.'

'Why? I've seen them before.'

'Not with me, you haven't. And I'm sure, not at sunset in June. It's almost mid-summer's day, you know; the atmosphere at sunset is extraordinary.'

We reached them in an hour – a huge flat area with ten vast pyramids of different sizes, each of them built to be ascended by broad steps. With the sun getting low in the sky we climbed one of the tallest and looked out across the ancient city below.

Rolf was just as he had been in Beijing, the perfect tour guide, relating history and anecdote, snapping pictures as he spoke.

'That's the Avenue of the Dead,' he told me, pointing to the wide passageway that ran between the pyramids. 'We're on the Pyramid of the Moon, and that gloomy slag heap over there is the Pyramid of the Sun. There was no happiness in Aztec society. They would let blood from their genitals before leaving their house in case an offended god might cause a rock to fall out of the sky and kill them. They rubbed dead spiders on their skin, never bathed and kept their hair matted with blood. If they had spare money, they bought babies from their less well-off neighbours and gave them to priests to sacrifice by cutting their throats. They believed the universe was in complete chaos and even the sun's ability to rise each morning was in doubt.'

Rolf was such a pleasure to listen to. He had an enormous depth of knowledge but used it to amuse rather than show off; he had strong opinions but was never too pushy with them, and he was quite easy to interrupt. If his monologues carried on a bit too long it was because I was enjoying them, not because he was unstoppable.

'How on earth do you know all that?'

'I keep on telling you, I'm a collector of information.'

We climbed down the pyramid slowly, the steps downwards being tougher than the climb upwards, straining the sinews at the back of our knees. Then we drove back to the hotel.

On the way he asked out of the blue, 'This China thing! You're not using anyone else to help you other than me, are you, Simon?'

I don't know why, but I didn't want to mention Lew Mon Hung. Instead I said, 'Mostly I'm doing it by myself, meeting people in Beijing, that sort of thing, getting there slowly.'

He turned towards me. 'And what about Lew Mon Hung?'

I cursed myself for trying to hide it from him. It was probably to show he knew about Lew that he'd asked me to Mexico.

'Oh him,' I said, trying to sound as if it had slipped my mind. 'I suppose he could be helpful.'

18

A VERY BAD THING

I've often wondered why I should enjoy so much travel but the point is, the pressure to be working changes utterly when you're sitting in a plane, especially in first class. Five or six thousand miles to fly, ten or twelve hours in a big seat with food and drink – simply by travelling you're *doing* something, so any sense of unease or guilt at being inactive drifts away. As a result, you can relax in a way that's not possible at home or in the office. During a long flight life takes on a neat simplicity: you have no engagements, commitments, obligations or duties; the only thing of importance is whether to have a bit more sleep, a bit more wine, read another few pages of your book, or watch TV.

For me, travel was always an obsession, even when I was four or five. At that age I was sneaking out of the house at 5 a.m. on summer mornings to take what I called 'naughty bus-rides'.

I would remove a penny from the housekeeping jar on the kitchen sideboard, walk to the nearest bus stop and stand next to any friendly looking person, man or woman, until the first early morning bus came along at 5.00 a.m. Then I would climb on and sit next to them.

Early morning bus fares were one penny to go anywhere you wanted until 6.00 a.m. Children were half-price. For a halfpenny I could keep going on that bus till around 5.45. We lived in Ealing – a number 65 bus would take me as far as Leatherhead, though I only once dared stay on it for that long. Usually I would climb off at Richmond, cross the road and use my remaining halfpenny to take another bus back home to arrive around 7.00. If the family were already up, I told them, 'I've been playing in the garden.'

My trips to China had become the adult equivalent of my 'naughty bus rides'. To begin with, each time I set off for China, I was concerned about Jazz being left in London, doing Wham!'s day-to-day management. But I needn't have worried; Jazz loved it. With me away he was in sole charge; he had the power to himself, and if any glory came along he could have that too.

Jazz probably had no idea how indolent I really was. The inefficient communications of the early eighties kept my hedonist lifestyle under wraps. There were no mobile phones, no satellite links, no faxes. An overseas call had to be put through by the operator and anything written had to be sent by telex. When someone went on a trip to the other side of the world it was normal for them to be out of touch most of the time. And being out of touch was something I was getting very good at.

Each month of my life now contained everything I could possibly want – a few days with serious purpose dealing with Chinese politicians, seven or eight days holidaying in Hong Kong or Thailand, then back to London or New York to be a pop manager, annoying record company executives and finding the best restaurants to eat in each night. The only downside to all this was the time I had to spend sitting around in Beijing between meetings.

Two days after I'd left Mexico I found myself in just that position. Then I remembered the Chinese students from the disco at the Beijing Hotel. At the time I'd felt they were too dull, but to be alone in the Great Wall Hotel with nothing to do between lunch one day and lunch the next was enough to make their company appealing.

I sent a message to May Ling; would she and her friends like to come to the hotel for an evening meal? She called to say no, it was better for students not to be seen hanging around somewhere like that.

'I don't think anyone would notice you,' I said innocently.

May Ling laughed and told me what Lew had told me a few weeks earlier. 'Everyone working in the hotel is secret police. That's why the government allows these hotels to open – it's an open invitation to foreigners to come and spread useful information. Even this phone call – someone is listening.'

Even though Lew Mon Hung had said the same, I still couldn't tell if this was the truth or just a neurotic fear. Like most Westerners, I was endlessly naive about the extent of secret police involvement in everyday life.

At May Ling's suggestion I took a taxi to the Beijing Hotel where she walked me quickly to the cafe at which we'd talked previously, the one that served the worst noodles in town. She'd come with Zhang Jin on bicycles. She gave hers to me and got on the passenger seat of Zhang Jin's. Then we pedalled off into the dark.

Seeing how uncaringly I'd moved around Beijing previously, all this undercover stuff seemed unnecessary. But Zhang Jin and May Ling insisted it wasn't.

'Can never be too careful when students talk with foreigner,' Zhang Jin explained.

Fifteen minutes later we entered a room that could have been at any university in the world – a dozen or so young friends drinking coffee and tea, talking seriously about politics and art. They started asking me questions about everything from soccer to the behaviour of the British police. Was it possible, one of them asked, that Mrs Thatcher was really a CIA agent and that her return of Hong Kong to the Chinese was some sort of American plot to leave a Trojan Horse of capitalist values which would emerge one dark night and capture the hearts and minds of the Chinese?

I thought not, but admitted it was possible. And I told them about Wham!.

'Will bringing Western pop and rock into China be the same thing?' they wanted to know. 'Is it intended as Trojan Horse? Is that why you're doing it? To be subversive?'

'No', I explained, 'it's just for the worldwide publicity we'll get from TV and media.'

They couldn't believe I wasn't doing it for some sort of political purpose.

'Are you avoiding the truth?'

'Are you afraid to tell us?'

'What is Wham!'s message?'

This simply wasn't the right time to explain that Wham!'s entire success flowed from deliberately avoiding all serious and meaningful messages and that their only intention from the outset had been to enjoy themselves. Instead, I rather grandly told them, 'Wham! are for freedom of behaviour and thought.'

'Of course,' Chuen told me. 'Popular music must have a message these days.'

'And what about working people?' asked Pang Yu. 'What do your group think of them?'

I could feel myself getting into intellectual student mode. 'Wham! believe people should be allowed to work at whatever pleases them, not at what they're ordered to do. They think work should be an extension of thought.'

The students nodded appreciatively and offered me food – rice and beans with small bits of chicken. One by one they were turning their attention to the black and white TV in a corner of the room on which there appeared to be a talk show.

'Are they talking politics?' I asked.

A young man who'd been introduced as Wan Tey told me, 'No – much more interesting – it's about literature.' He waved a disparaging hand around his friends. 'The only thing my friends talk about is politics, but the real key to understanding is literature.'

As they watched the TV, Wan Tey translated some of what was being said on the screen. 'The man in the grey jacket has just come back from the USA where he studied in Wisconsin University. He says in America, if you write an essay, you must have a strong first paragraph. It must lay things out clearly before continuing. But in a Chinese essay we like to start with a nice atmosphere and let the reader just guess at what we're going to write about.'

After another ten minutes the talk show finished and Wan Tey explained its ending. 'They tell us that in the West the whole point of writing the essay is to have a firm conclusion – unequivocal – never have two possibilities to choose from, just one. But in China, it is essential never to do this. We must always end in an open way without directing the reader's mind to one single point.'

Chuen butted in. 'If you translate that into politics, you'll understand China much better.'

'You too,' I told him. 'If you made an effort to understand the differences in our approach, you'd understand the West better too.'

Wan Tey was delighted. 'You see – it's like I said – you will learn more from literature than you ever will from politics.'

'And from music too,' insisted Chuen. 'Listen to this – it's our new star – Cui Jian. Before, he was a trumpet player with the Beijing Philharmonic, now he has formed a rock band and is making his own album.'

The songs they played me sounded more like pop than rock.

'The authorities don't like him,' May Ling said, 'but we think he will be a big star. He's not afraid to sing about politics.'

'Or sex,' Wan Tey added.

May Ling handed me a T-shirt with some Chinese writing on the back – rather nice graphics – which I presumed were about Cui Jian, the rock star they'd just been talking about. Then I cycled back to the Beijing Hotel with her and Chuen.

The next morning I was up early and went for breakfast in the hotel coffee shop. I hadn't been there two minutes – sitting on a banquette seat against the wall, toying with bacon and eggs – when Lew Mon Hung walked in. I hadn't told him I was coming to Beijing but Lew didn't seem too surprised to see me.

'Why you no tell me you come Beijing?' he asked bossily.

I shrugged, devoid of an excuse.

He went on. 'Regarding, "Maybe-your-group-come-to-China" ... this will be *our* project – *together*. OK?'

'No!' I said instantly, but he didn't hear me, he'd gone to collect food from the buffet.

He came back with his breakfast and sat down. 'I have been meeting with people for Wham! come to China. Soon you must start pay me. This time I do free – next time you must give money. OK?'

I answered with a nod and left him finishing his breakfast.

As I walked away he glanced after me, then in an instant was by my side. 'You take off T-shirt *now*. At once.'

When I'd come down to breakfast, since I wasn't meeting anyone, I'd put on the T-shirt the university kids had given me. Something about it appeared to have upset Lew. He was now standing in front of me, looking over my shoulder towards the hotel lobby, a look of horror on his face. Then he pulled off his jacket and draped it round my shoulders just as the Prime Minister's son walked up beside us.

Lew held the jacket over my shoulders, covering the back side of the T-shirt. 'It's a very bad thing written on back of T-shirt,' he whispered harshly in my ear. 'Go to your room and take off, then bring back my jacket.'

I went up to my room, changed the T-shirt and went back downstairs to return Lew's jacket to him.

He was sitting with Zhao junior and took it from me with a nod. 'Don't wear T-shirt again in China,' he said curtly.

'What does it say?'

Lew looked embarrassed. He excused himself from Zhao and walked with me to the entrance of the coffee-shop. 'It's a poem. Student in Beijing begin to say this poem to each other and it is get very popular.

It sound very very nice – has very good rhythm but is very bad to say or wear on T-shirt. It say, "Mao Zedong's son went to the front. Zhao Ziyang's son speculates in colour TVs. Deng Xiaoping's son demands money from everyone.'"

On the way to the airport I thought about it. To be considered catchy, this poem must have sounded a whole lot better in Chinese than it did in English. But even though it didn't sound too shocking, I had to admit that a similar ditty in English would certainly fall foul of British libel laws. In China it would be a dangerous thing to be seen wearing, particularly for Lew who was doing business with the very man accused of speculating in colour TVs. And thinking about that led me to make a decision.

If Lew Mon Hung could give me access to the Prime Minister's son, why was I continually pushing him aside rather than bringing him in on the project? Especially as I'd now been to Beijing five times without making the slightest progress towards what I was meant to be achieving.

It suddenly dawned on me: I was going to make a monumental fool of myself if I didn't pull this thing off. It was time I started taking help from anyone who would give it to me.

19 THE TRUTH

With money in hand from their deal with CBS, Wham! could now afford Connie to do their PR. They also brought in a new backing singer, Pepsi, to replace Dee. And with our small percentage of the same money, Jazz and I could now hire someone first-rate to become a day-to-day contact with George and Andrew. Jazz chose Siobhan for the job, a real charmer, the most capable girl who ever worked in an office and, from her very first day, addicted to working for Wham!. It gave Jazz some of the same freedom I'd managed to get for myself twelve months earlier when I'd dumped the day-to-day work on his shoulders.

Not that it let him off the hook. Nor me either. George had a way of making anyone who worked for him feel permanently, underlyingly apprehensive. You didn't have to be at the same dinner table, or in the same office, or even on the same continent. Everyone who worked with him felt the same thing – a permanent frisson of tension in the air. No-one knew how he managed to project this feeling; it was like a shortwave radio signal letting you know, wherever you were, whatever you were doing, if it was something you were doing for yourself rather than for him, you shouldn't really be doing it.

More than anything else, this might have applied to the time I spent on Allan's hairdressing business, but it didn't. With that, George was particularly helpful.

My original intention had been to open the salon, make it profitable by making Allan famous, then sell products based on his name. For two years it had been hugely publicised and humming with business, yet it still wasn't profitable.

Apart from excellent hairdressing, one of the principal gimmicks of the salon was to give everyone a free glass of champagne. The problem was, after they'd been on shopping sprees in Harrods or Harvey Nichols, Allan's clients liked to drop by for a chat and a tipple whether they wanted their hair done or not.

Even so, it seemed impossible that the salon wouldn't eventually make money. Each time I thought up a new gimmick, Allan would turn it into a first-rate technique and Connie into a headline – 'Chopstick Perm', 'Chop Suey Hairweave', 'Dim Sum Steam and Set'. All these things went down a treat with his customers but unfortunately so did the champagne.

Wham!, like all the other stars who came to the salon, got their hair done for nothing. George asked if he could have some hair-care products to take away and use at home and when Allan asked him to pay for them he grumbled. The difficulty was, the products he'd asked for weren't ours, they were products we bought from a wholesaler.

In personal matters George was unusually generous but in business matters he could sometimes seem strangely mean. It wasn't about money; it was a fear of being taken advantage of. But once he realised the salon wasn't pulling in the profits he'd thought it was, he became exceptionally helpful and suggested his sister might make a good manager.

Melanie was already an accomplished hairdresser and had a natural talent for telling people what to do. She was a big girl and didn't suffer anyone messing her about, but her severe look hid a sharp sense of humour – when she wasn't frowning at people she was usually laughing.

When Melanie became manager the matter of giving George free products was solved at once. Given the job of making the salon profitable she refused point blank to give things away for nothing, whoever it was who wanted them. Even so, she managed to make George much more easy-going about having his name used in connection with publicity.

It was star names like George and Andrew that helped Connie get an endless chain of salon stories into the tabloids each day, and Connie was a great inventor. In a piece for the *Daily Mirror* she said, when George had turned up for a haircut, Linda, the new receptionist, had fainted.

Linda was embarrassed and went to Melanie complaining. Linda was ten years older than George; she'd never been a fan of Wham! and had never fainted in her life. She felt the article made a fool of her and was irate.

As Melanie was calming her down over a cup of coffee George turned up and told her, if *he* could put up with endless silly stories in the paper for the sake of publicising the salon, surely Linda could cope with just one of them.

Connie used George and Andrew's names quite shamelessly to publicise the salon and because Melanie now managed it George had dropped his usual objections to being taken advantage of and was helping as much as he could. So on reflection I told Melanie, 'You ought to give him free products after all.'

'Bollocks!' she said. 'You made me manager and I'll do it my way.'

She was brilliant. Just what the salon needed.

* * *

In Beijing I sometimes fooled myself I was doing something on a higher plane, something with broader implications – opening up communist society to Western youth culture. But that was baloney. Jazz and I had hit on the idea of making Wham! the first group to play in China purely as a publicity stunt – a way of cracking the American market a little more quickly than usual.

Baloney or not, dealing with Radio One and *Top Of The Pops*, or with the problems in Allan's hair salon, felt trivial in comparison to meeting politicians in Beijing. In England the nearest I ever got to politics was when Donavon made me go with him to the Greater London Council in search of grants to help finance his Black Music Festival.

The GLC was the home of London's far-left. It was housed in an echoing stone building by the Thames, full of earnest people battling social injustice. In the course of doing this they perpetrated quite a few social injustices of their own, one of which was to send innocent people to meet the woman to whom we were directed.

She had the glare of a cranky wildebeest. 'I don't take kindly to having my time wasted,' she snapped before we'd even spoken. 'What's this about?'

'It's a festival of black music,' Donavon told her. 'It's me who's promoting it – Simon's a partner in my company.'

His smile softened her slightly but the softening was *only* for him. This woman was a schizophrenic, I could see it at once. She had a totally sweet-and-sour demeanour – the sweet for Donavon, the sour for me.

'Is it anti-racist?' she asked him.

'Of course!'

Sweetnsour smiled. 'Good. Then we can offer you funds from "War on Racism".'

Despite my dislike of the woman I was pleased. The GLC's logo for War on Racism was a good thing to display on an event involving black music, and the subsidies the GLC gave for it were big enough to be helpful. But Sweetnsour wasn't finished yet.

'If you were to call it a "celebration" we might be able to contribute something from the "Parks and Parades" fund.'

'Absolutely,' Donavon agreed. 'We're fighting racism with a Celebration of Black Music.'

She smiled. 'Excellent! And if it aided minorities we might be able to come up with even more. Will there be any lesbians involved?'

'We're booking Amazulu,' Donavon told her, catching the mood nicely. 'They're well-known for not shaving their armpits.'

'Perfect!'

And so it went on. During the next half-hour Donavon and his new best friend searched through a treasure chest of minority grants and found subsidies galore.

'What about single mothers?' Donavon proposed. 'Perhaps we could provide nappy-changing facilities.'

Other than War on Racism these grants would provide very little money. Yet for each one accepted I could see additional interference coming from the GLC. 'Wouldn't it be better to go with War on Racism and forget the other minority grants,' I suggested, trying to keep things simple.

Sweetnsour's frown was like the closing of a portcullis. 'Why should we do that? I can see you're not at all like Donavon. He really cares – helping all these good causes.'

As far as I could see, it was the other way round – the good causes were helping Donavon.

Shortly afterwards, Graham Chapman phoned to say he was making progress with our Jeremy Thorpe show. 'I've got a first draft treatment but I'll only show it to you if you do a bungee jump.'

'What's a bungee jump?'

'It's a new sport. You go to the top of a tall building and jump off with rubber bands on your feet then bounce up in the air again just before you hit the ground. It's great for the adrenalin and makes the heart beat like mad – better then aerobics.'

'Not for me, thanks.'

Graham had already told me he'd joined something called the Dangerous Sports Club but I hadn't been sure what it required of him. Now he insisted on dragging me off to Fulham to meet the club's founder, a tubby, bearded fellow called David. 'Next summer we're doing

"Bareback across the Atlantic" – hot air balloons sculpted in the shape of horses with the riders sitting on them with no visible harness. If we catch a good wind it'll take seventy-two hours to get across. We want celebrities to compete. Would your Wham! boys be up for it?'

'If they get across in seventy-two hours,' I pointed out, 'it means the balloons will be travelling at forty miles an hour. How could anyone ride bareback?'

'Hmmm.' David looked thoughtful. 'How about this then? In December we're planning to put a grand piano on skis and send it down the slopes at St Moritz with someone sitting at it playing Chopin. Would Wham! agree to follow it down on a toboggan singing "Jingle Bells"?'

I thought not, and I finally dragged Graham away to Mario's for lunch. Over spinach fettucine he at last revealed his idea for our musical. 'I'm calling it "A Man, Another Man, and His Dog". It'll be an onstage re-enactment of the Jeremy Thorpe trial, but the catch is, it will be the Labour Party's Christmas pantomime.'

All the parts – the judge, Jeremy Thorpe, the top Liberals, the boyfriend, the hitman, even the dog – would be played by well-known members of past Labour Party cabinets – Harold Wilson, James Callaghan, Denis Healey and Barbara Castle – who themselves would be impersonated by actors.

As he related the idea, Graham impersonated each of the different labour politicians, themselves impersonating the characters in his play. I was still laughing ten minutes after he'd finished.

'I wish you'd done a bungee jump,' he said wistfully, tucking into his tiramisu, 'you've no idea what an appetite it gives you. You'd have enjoyed lunch so much more.'

He was wrong, of course. Lunch that day was as good as it gets.

* * *

In July, 'Careless Whisper' came out as George's first solo record and went straight to Number One. This was the beginning of the transition from Wham! to George Michael, but he still pretended to the press it was no such thing. 'Careless Whisper', he said, was only being issued as a solo record because it 'didn't fit' with the style of Wham!.

Then he spoilt it by telling them, 'Well, perhaps it *is* a sort of a spring-board for me.'

He was testing the waters; edging things towards the result he wanted. With Wham!'s new album not yet recorded he'd already told Jazz and me to take him seriously about an eventual break-up. With 'Careless Whisper' he was telling Andrew too.

As usual, Andrew took it in his stride, confident enough in himself not to worry. Besides, there was something else worrying him far more than a possible end to Wham!. His nose.

Slightly off centre as a result of a childhood accident, it gave Andrew's otherwise pretty face a bit of extra character. But he hated it. From the beginning, he'd told me, 'When I get enough money and spare time, I'm going to have it straightened.'

Finally the day came. Wham! had two weeks off while George was working in the studio on a new song.

My nice doctor, Barrington Cooper, guided Andrew to a suitable surgeon who sent him along to the Cromwell Clinic, a posh place in West London where the well-heeled could be unwell in comfort. Andrew went in on Monday morning and came out late the same afternoon with a heavily bandaged snout. What he shouldn't have done was go straight out clubbing.

It wasn't the actual activity that was the problem, nor the alcohol he drank while indulging in it, it was the paparazzi who spotted him and took pictures. In the middle of the night Connie was phoned by the show-business editors of all the main tabloids saying they had pictures of Andrew with his nose under wraps; what had happened?

Unprepared, and feeling it wouldn't be right to say outright, 'He's had a nose job,' she said instead, 'He got into a fight.'

'How?'

'With whom?'

'Who was it that hit him?'

Pushed into a corner, Connie invented, which she always did brilliantly. Andrew had been in a nightclub and got into an argument with a friend. They were a bit drunk, the argument got out of control and his friend threw an ice bucket which hit him on the nose. *Et voilà!*

The press seemed satisfied and Connie went back to sleep.

The next morning she arrived at the office to find the place besieged by journalists. Where was Andrew? Who was the person who threw the ice-bucket? Which club did it happen in? What did the doctor say? Would it stop him singing, talking, kissing, having sex?

When Connie opened the papers she found 'Andrew's Ice Bucket Injury' was the front-page headline in each one of them.

She called me at home in a panic. 'Dahlink, I just don't know what to do. I'm scared. This thing is getting out of control.'

By now it wasn't just the press, it was radio and television too. Capital Radio, Radio One, Radio Mersey, Piccadilly Radio in Manchester – over thirty radio stations had called asking for an interview with Andrew on air. And all the TV chat shows too. Connie felt out of her depth. 'So many journalists,' she wailed, 'and so aggressive.'

'Why not tell the truth?'

'I can't without asking Andrew first, and his phone's off the hook.'

As is normal when lies are told, more had to be invented to compound the first one. It had happened at Stringfellows and the friend who'd thrown the ice bucket was David Austin, George and Andrew's old school friend. The doctor, she added, had said everything would be OK in another four or five days – no permanent damage but the nose had been broken and was now reset.

The journalists spread out. Some went to Stringfellows, some to the hospital, some to Andrew's house to wait outside, some to David Austin's house. The next day the story made the tabloid headlines for the second time, this time with David Austin named. By mid-morning his house was surrounded by hundreds of Wham! fans eager to punch him up for the damage he'd done to their beloved Andrew.

Three days of headlines in all the tabloids should have been something of a windfall, but I could see this was going in the wrong direction. Now there were calls for the police to investigate with a view to charging David Austin with assault. The journalists had got hold of the story with a vengeance and were squeezing every last drop out of it.

David Austin called me, scared. What had he done to deserve this? Connie called me. Andrew called me. George called me. Jazz called me. 'We've got to *do* something!' they all insisted.

And the only thing to do was tell the truth.

'Andrew's had a nose job.'

20 BECAUSE YOU'RE DELICIOUS

Sometimes the truth was not so easy to tell.

If George had let the world know earlier about his gay tendencies everything might have turned out differently. But it would have been the wrong thing to do.

I'm gay, but it took me till I was forty to use the word easily about myself; not that I ever denied that I indulged in homosexual behaviour, I just found it difficult to use a word that would make my primary social identification a sexual one. I was English, middle class, public school educated, much travelled, born and brought up in a capital city. Put in a mixed group of people I wouldn't necessarily pick someone who was gay as a companion, I might prefer someone who mixed well with my other social qualifications. Because I fancied young men, it didn't mean I wanted to be lumped together with a hundred million homogenised homosexuals throughout the Western world, following gay fashion and adhering to gay political correctness. I wanted to be myself. And I'm sure George did too.

Of course, I'd heard rumours right from the beginning. Only a week after Jazz and I started to manage Wham!, someone called up and said, 'That new singer of yours – a friend of mine says he's gay.'

Until that moment I'd never thought of the possibility, but once it was mentioned I remembered that Dick Leahy, one of George and Andrew's two publishers, had been particularly helpful in making sure I became Wham!'s manager, very pointedly saying, 'I think you and George will be just the right combination.' And Boy George was always dropping hints about it to the press. Even so, my immediate reaction was to berate my friend for telling me such a thing.

'You're mistaken,' I told him. 'George is as straight as a die.'

And that was the line I always stuck to.

If George was aware he was gay and was covering it up, he was doing the right thing. The image of Wham! was an image of male friendship –

the image Hollywood had played on in endless films – two straight guys whose friendship with each other transcends all other things. At the beginning of the movie they arrive in town together, and at the end, despite having had hookers or girlfriends or wives, they go off into the sunset together. It was the image of Starsky and Hutch, or Butch Cassidy and the Sundance Kid, with the leading roles played as straight as a die. And since this was Wham!'s image, they too needed to play their roles dead straight.

George was right to take his time to come out. The world wanted a heterosexual duo and he made sure they got one (which turned out to be just as well, or they would never have gone to China).

In the basement of our building was a further office which we'd rented to an enterprising young Japanese man.

Kaz Utsonomiya acted as a London representative for Japanese record companies and artists. He also wrote articles about the London pop scene for Japanese music papers. His father was a diplomat and Kaz had come to London with him when he was eleven and gone to the Japanese school in Maida Vale. His English was excellent, slightly North London but still attractively Japanese. One day, when he'd just arrived from Tokyo, I asked him how it had been. 'Awful,' he told me, 'I had a most terrible fright.'

I thought he might have been mugged or attacked by rabid dogs, but he only meant his flight home had been badly delayed. And there was something else he wanted to tell me too.

Kaz had just heard that some Japanese filmmakers were making a huge war movie in China using tens of thousands of soldiers from the Chinese army as extras. 'They're spending billions of yen and Queen have asked them to use their contacts in China to arrange a concert in Beijing. From what I've heard, they've almost succeeded. You're about to be pipped at the post.'

I couldn't believe it. From London, I immediately called Lew Mon Hung and told him what I'd heard. 'Do you know anything about this?' I asked.

Lew was far too shrewd to say he *didn't* know about it – that would suggest he wasn't in the know. But to say he *did* might suggest he was two-timing me in some way. 'I've been working to solve it,' he told me. 'Leave to me. In the end, Wham! will go China. Don't worry.'

I didn't believe a word of it, so I tried calling Rolf and finally tracked him down to a hotel in Cape Town. 'I've heard that Queen are about to be invited to China.'

'Who are Queen?'

'Rolf!! How can you be so out of touch? They're one of the biggest rock groups in the world.'

'Why do they call themselves Queen. It's not a very good name.'

'They're outrageous, that's why. Haven't you heard of Freddie Mercury. He's a flamboyant genius – he flaunts his bi-sexuality. To be honest, he's the best thing in British pop.'

'Would you be happy if they went to China?'

'Don't be crazy. It's exactly what I *don't* want. I'm calling to see if you've any ideas how to stop it happening. I thought perhaps your Mr Wu could help.'

'I'm sure he could, but first we'd have to give him the right information. Why don't you make up a little report on Queen – outline what they're about, what the word means in slang terms – tell him about this Freddie guy. Can you get hold of any pictures of him? You know the Chinese authorities hate that sort of thing.'

I got the idea. I spent the next couple of days making two presentations – the sort of thing people searching for investors prepare about their product. I put together a brochure about Wham! and another about Queen – twenty-five copies each, and they looked very good indeed.

The Wham! brochure had pictures, biographies and reviews, all slanted to show how family-orientated the boys were – how middle-class, how morally correct and clean-cut. They dressed in simple clean clothes, did their hair nicely and always invited their parents to concerts.

The brochure on Queen was quite different. There were pictures of Freddie Mercury and of each individual musician. In all the pictures, the clothes were outrageous and the make-up as thick as pictures could be found to show it. And there were other things too.

The first page was a blow-up from the dictionary showing one of the definitions of 'queen' – 'A male homosexual, especially if adopting the female role'. Sprinkled liberally throughout the brochure were pictures of drag queens in Brazil, muscle maniacs on Santa Monica beach, naked men cavorting onstage in gay clubs, and two men kissing at the Sydney Mardi Gras, one rather butch, the other lipsticked to the upper limits. Pasted all over the place, in letters decorated with sparkles and spangles, were the words 'homosexual', 'gay' and 'drag-queen'. Yet the brochure wasn't at all offensive. It was the sort of thing that might have been put together by a gay fan in praise of his favourite group – glitzy and camp.

Without telling him about the brochures, I asked Kaz to fix me a meeting with the people making the movie in China.

'Porodyusa is the person to talk to,' he told me. 'He's the one who has been talking with Queen.'

The next day I was in Tokyo talking to him, a pleasant man and very dapper, neatly dressed in a suit and tie and strictly in the business of talking a deal. 'I think we can help your group get into China,' Mr Porodyusa told me, 'but they will have to agree to write and perform a title theme for the movie we're making. It's a Japanese–Chinese co-produced war film. So far Queen have not agreed to write a title theme.'

'*We'll* agree,' I said at once. 'Help me get Wham! into China and you'll get your theme.'

Then I showed him the folder on Queen and told him, whether he helped me or not with Wham!, I would be sending it to key people in different ministries in China.

Mr Porodyusa was shocked. 'This is not something you should show to too many people.'

'On the contrary, I intend to show it to everyone.'

'But that would make it very difficult for us to get Queen into China.'

'Good! You can help Wham! instead.'

I could see he was taken aback by my aggression, but he agreed anyway.

The next morning we flew to Beijing where he took me to meet someone at the All-China Youth Federation, Zhou Renkai – a bulky man with a greasy pockmarked face and a dingy tweed suit, the seat of which hung six inches lower than his bottom. It was a brief meeting and seemingly not productive.

'Mr Napier-Bell manages a pop group and is interested in them coming to play in China,' explained Mr Porodyusa, then watched in embarrassment as I handed Mr Zhou copies of my two folders, one on Queen, one on Wham!.

As we left the office Mr Porodyusa said, 'Be careful of Mr Zhou. He's mad about money. He will ask payment for everything he can think of. On the other hand, if you want him to help, it would be best to give him all he asks for.'

*

To start with Zhou asked for lunch, which I provided at the Great Wall Hotel.

He said he'd been a cocktail pianist in Shanghai before the revolution but there wasn't much of the cocktail bar about him these days. Two decades of communism had hardened him up; he was manipulative, scheming and greedy, and spent a great deal of time exploring the more malodorous parts of his body with his fingers before sniffing them.

'We would need money for everything,' he explained through his translator. 'If a pop group comes to play in Beijing, it will have to pay for the hire of the hall, the printing of the tickets, the printing of the posters, even the salary of the people who sell the tickets. But the money from ticket sales will go to the All-China Youth Federation.'

Although he spoke as if it was within his powers to say yes to a visit by Wham!, I still wasn't going to get drawn into asking that fatal yes-or-no question, 'Can Wham! come or not?' I had to avoid giving him the chance of saying no.

Despite some misgivings, something told me Zhou was the right person. He may not have been in the upper reaches of the Chinese power structure but he held an important position in the Chinese Youth Federation, and the Chinese saw young people as their future.

At the end of the meal, to make sure things didn't head in the wrong direction, I gave him several more copies of my folder on Queen. As we went down in the lift he looked through it again, shaking his head in disbelief. 'So lucky you tell me about this.'

I called my university friends and arranged another clandestine meeting.

'Do you like sex?' May Ling asked as soon as I arrived.

'Well ... of course.'

What a strange question to jump in with – and usually these students were so reticent about such things.

Pang Yu said, 'We're going to take you somewhere you will enjoy!'

Off we went on a train of bicycles – quite a long way too – and eventually arrived at an unlit alleyway. I found it difficult to believe these socially correct students were taking me to a brothel but I had to admit this was just the sort of street where we might find one.

Instead we arrived at a bustling cafe, packed with young people and raucous jazz.

'Sex!' May Ling said, pointing happily towards the bandstand. 'We all love it.'

And of course what she meant was 'sax', for on the bandstand were four saxophonists – soprano, alto, tenor and baritone – belting out modern jazz 1950s style, sort of Charlie Parker-ish, backed with drums, bass and piano.

To be honest, it was better than sex and I had a thoroughly good time. I asked them what they thought about Zhou and the Youth Federation. Not much, it seemed.

'We are all members,' said Chuen, the pipe-smoker, 'and the organisation does many good things. But it's very political – full of secret police – students spying on students.'

At the end of the evening as we were leaving, sex came up again. Chuen told me, 'People think in Beijing we have no sex worker, but it's not true. I'll show you.'

The others giggled, the girls using delicate hands to cover their mouths. Pang Yu explained, 'Chuen says the two girls serving coffee at the bar are prostitutes. We don't believe him. He says he'll prove it by offering them money.'

May Ling said, 'Chuen's just back from business school in Shanghai, learning the art of the deal, he wants to try out his skills on the bar girls.'

We watched as Chuen approached the girls and spoke to them.

'Se lang,' May Ling hissed out to him, and the others burst out giggling again. 'It means, Sex Wolf,' she told me. 'But Chuen's not really like that. If the prostitutes agreed to go with him he'd be too frightened to do it.'

The girls behind the bar *didn't* agree. In fact they got very angry and berated Chuen who came back with his tail between his legs.

I asked, 'What happened? Aren't they prostitutes after all?'

'Oh they *are*,' Zhang Jin explained. 'But they thought Chuen was trying to buy them for *you*! They were afraid they'd be arrested if they slept with a foreigner so they got angry with Chuen for trying to get them into trouble.'

Zhou's interpreter called and asked for another lunch. It meant staying a night longer than I'd intended and I wasn't sure what to do with myself. The weather was freezing.

I was hanging around the hotel lobby, bored and reading the paper when the girl on reception asked if I'd ever taken the cable car up the Fragrant Hills in the north-west of the city? Or had I visited the park and pedalled a boat on the lake?

Outside it was cold enough that people had their collars turned up, their breath coming out in clouds. I noticed a man sitting on a step in the cold with a little boy in his arms, looking like he had nowhere to go.

'Surely,' I said, 'people don't go on cable cars or paddle boats on the lake in this weather, do they?'

'Oh yes. People in Beijing like the cool air. It cleans the sinuses.'

I decided the best way to pass the time would be a long lunch with a book. Four hours later, having finished lunch and taken a nap, I came back to the lobby to send a telex and saw the man with the boy in his arms still outside in the cold, the boy now asleep. Certain he must be penniless I walked outside and handed him some money – about five dollars in rimimbi. He looked terrified and refused it, shaking his head from side to side. Yet I was sure I'd read the situation correctly – with the weather so cold, why would anyone sit around in the cold all day with a child in their arms if they had enough money to pay for a place to stay?

As I walked back inside, the doorman told me, 'No begging in China.'

It wasn't much of an explanation though it was certainly true that Chinese people didn't like to ask for things directly.

At lunch the following day Zhou said it would be nice to have lobster. He didn't ask for it, he just said it would be nice. I mentioned yet again that it would be nice if one day Wham! could come to play in China. Then I went ahead and ordered his lobster.

Zhou truly loved food. At his previous lunch he'd insisted on ordering drunken prawns. They'd arrived at the table still sober – about thirty of them in a glass bowl. The lid was removed and half a bottle of rice wine was poured over them. Within seconds they were visibly happy.

'Hey guys, somebody's given us a free drink – let's party.'

For a while we watched them live it up inside the glass bowl but once they were suitably inebriated the waiter lifted the lid and threw in a match.

Now they were screaming. 'Jesus Christ! We're on fire. Get out of here quick, we're gonna die.'

Before the lid could be replaced, one single prawn managed to leap to safety on the floor but the others were burnt to death in front of our eyes. They were then served up, soft and succulent, oozing delicious alcoholic juices.

Today there was worse to come. The lobster Zhou wanted was served live. It was brought on a large flat dish that was placed on the revolving centre of the table. The waiter gave us each a bowl of dipping sauce then slit the animal down its back. As we dug our chopsticks inside the shell and pulled out its raw flesh, the still living lobster revolved slowly in front of us waving its claws helplessly and trying to catch our eyes.

'Why are you eating me alive – how can you do this to me?'

I couldn't find the right answer. Perhaps I should have said, 'For the experience,' or, 'That's the way life is,' or simply, 'Because you're delicious.'

Which it certainly was.

Later that day Rolf phoned. 'That little brochure you did on Queen – I've heard it caused a real furore with the powers-that-be. Just what we wanted.'

'I could see they were shocked when I gave it to them.'

'Excellent! And how are things going with your Mr Lew? Is he proving any use?'

Rolf was definitely miffed about my using Lew.

'I can't really tell yet. I gave him the Queen brochure so I guess he passed it on to Zhao's son. And I gave it to Zhou Renkai, the man from the All-China Youth Federation. Apparently it's the Youth Federation who will have to invite any visiting pop group. Do you know him? He likes to eat a lot.'

'I know *of* him.'

I wasn't sure I believed him. I think Rolf was just unhappy about me working with someone he hadn't introduced me to himself.

'In the end he's just a clerk, he'll do as he's told by others,' Rolf said sniffily, and then repeated what Mr Porodyusa had told me. 'But watch out – he'll bleed you dry for money.'

21 SO GRAND, SO BITCHY, SO BROKE

John Maclaren was mid-twenties – bright, pleasant-looking and rather on the scrounge.

I'd known him for some time. Not exactly a friend, but he was always turning up at dinners and parties. He never really settled down to do anything but was always coming up with business ideas that needed financing. Sometimes he found the finance, sometimes he didn't, and though none of his schemes had yet made money he was amusing to be around – Australian, but with a posh accent – snobbish, but with a biting wit – rather proud of having had an affair with a black world champion boxer.

He came to see me with a business idea he'd hit on. 'I've found a backer, someone with money, but I don't have a project for him. I thought you might know of one. It needs to be something in show-business.'

'I hear ideas all the time,' I told him. 'But most of them are rubbish. Finding a good project is much more difficult than finding cash.'

Still, I agreed to meet his backer.

Ron O'Reilly was bulgy in the middle and wore a light grey silk suit. His chubby face was plastered across with a pair of Cartier sunglasses and he spoke with a soft Irish accent. I knew at once he was a Grade A con-man.

'We've bought an old oil refinery,' he explained. 'We're having it refurbished and we're selling it to the government in Azerbaijan. It's a pretty good deal – we bought it for six million and we're selling it for seventy-two. It means I'll have a bit of money over to invest in something fun.'

I'd met many people like Ron O'Reilly and was sure he had no real money. Nevertheless, he was the sort of man through whose hands a great deal of other people's money sometimes passes.

'Who's "*we*"?' I asked.

'My two partners – they're both African chiefs.'

On his second visit he turned up with his wife, a mousy woman bedecked with lavish jewels and designer clothing.

'A cheap piece of trash,' John said behind her back.

I pointed out, however bad her dress sense, Dolce & Gabbana wasn't cheap; so John changed his mind and she became expensive trash instead.

Ron took us to Le Souffle at the Inter-Continental. 'We'll start with caviar,' he insisted. 'Waiter! Beluga please! Four double portions.'

Then he called the wine waiter and ordered Dom Perignon.

'I want to get into show-business,' he told us as he shovelled in the caviar. 'When my oil-refinery deal is completed I'll have the odd million or two lying around and I want to have fun with it.'

When the bill came he produced a wallet thick with credit cards, several of which were returned by the cashier before one was found in good working order. Then, when we got into his Rolls Royce to be given a lift home, I noticed the tyres were bald.

The next day I told John, 'The man's a fraud.'

'Does it matter,' he asked, 'so long as he comes up with the dosh?'

It set me thinking again about the project Graham Chapman and I were working on. Perhaps we were about to find a backer for our ridiculous Jeremy Thorpe musical.

Connie had been getting publicity for it even though Graham hadn't yet finished fleshing out his treatment, and just because I was the manager of Wham! people presumed George and Andrew would do the music. But shortly after my meal with Ron O'Reilly, the project ran into trouble.

The powers-that-be at the Liberal Party had read some of the publicity and didn't much like the idea. Someone from their head office called and threatened me – first with legal action and then blackmail – some sort of public dissemination of unfortunate facts about me (though I couldn't for the life of me think of any unfortunate facts which I wouldn't be perfectly happy to disseminate for myself).

Oddly, someone important from the Conservative Party joined them in these threats while no-one at the Labour Party (whom Graham's piece would make look stupidest of all) said a thing.

Finally I got a call from a very pompous person who claimed to be high up in the Liberal Party but whose name I didn't catch. 'You ought to be shot,' he told me.

Since that was pretty much the thrust of the story in the first place I suggested he should be written into the plot. But when I told my lawyer he warned me, 'When those sort of people make those sort of threats it's usually worth taking heed.'

He was pretty sure, whether we found the finance or not, they would be able to stop our show from appearing in the West End.

To be honest, I wasn't that obsessed with the show, it was my lunches with Graham that mattered. So we went on having them anyway, which when I came to think about it seemed to be the principal point of knowing each other.

* * *

George and Andrew had moved for the summer to Chateau Minerval in the village of Val, the home and recording studio of French jazz musician Jacques Loussier. George would be in charge of making sure the album turned out as it should do; it wasn't necessary for me or Jazz to be there. Nevertheless, I decided a brief visit to the studio would be a good idea.

There couldn't be a nicer place to record an album, especially in the summer. The Chateau had manicured gardens and a swimming pool, and the village of Val was set in perfect Provence countryside, home to Chateau Minerval, one of the region's best wines. I sat around the studio while George played me some tracks and they sounded wonderful.

He told me, 'Since the day we arrived here it's been totally down to me to get this album together. Andrew's just been ligging around, getting drunk, falling in the pool, that sort of thing.'

But he wasn't complaining – rather, he appeared pleased to have the responsibility fall on his shoulders. He even seemed to be enjoying Andrew's bad behaviour. The point was, George had found his true métier – to write and produce himself, the most difficult thing any singer can do.

As I was leaving, a helicopter arrived but I didn't give it much attention. Later I heard it was Elton John, popping into the studio to record a radio advertisement. George must have been overwhelmed; since early childhood Elton had been his hero. But there was more than that to come from this unexpected visit. It was the start of substantial mutual admiration and from then on it was Elton who took over the role in George's life previously played by Andrew.

Andrew had given George the courage to stand up and be a pop star – to be onstage, to be in the public eye – but, with that accomplished, his usefulness had become limited. George was working night and day to make an album while Andrew was getting drunk and having a good time. Elton on the other hand provided the perfect model for George to follow in his new career as a solo artist – in charge of his own business and his own life – able to make every decision for himself, good or bad. He was self-managed, self-sufficient and self-confident. Once George had seen it close up, it had to be what he aspired to from there on.

Which left Andrew precisely nowhere. As soon as the second album had been recorded, released, promoted and sold to its maximum potential, it already seemed obvious – Wham! were due for deletion.

* * *

Allan had taken up with a stylish middle-aged Englishman and they were having a short holiday together in St Tropez, staying at the Byblos Hotel just forty minutes from where George and Andrew were recording. I thought it would be nice, having visited George and Andrew, to drop in on Allan and his friend. Then I decided it would be even nicer to invite Donavon as well. I called London and he asked if he could bring one of the blond swishes who sometimes helped him with his dinner parties. 'Why not?' I told him, then suggested he bring a friend of mine too, a young law student from Malaysia.

I met them at Nice airport and we drove round the coast road to St Tropez, stopping for lunch on the beach at Cannes and for a wake-up swim an hour later in Frejus. We arrived in St Tropez at six in the evening relaxed, good-natured and happy.

Donavon was famous for his see-saw personality; he could be outrageously fun or explosively bad-tempered. Challenged, he could turn into Mike Tyson; otherwise he stuck mostly with Diana Ross – swish, pucker, smile and hairstyle – and this evening was no exception. For dinner he dressed to the nines, or perhaps it was *un*-dressed – the flimsiest of T-shirts with a pair of cotton shorts that were little more than a breath of fabric across his buttocks – as expensive an outfit of shorts and T-shirt as could possibly be concocted, the bottom from Versace, the top from Armani – neither, I suspected, from the men's department.

We dined in the square in the old part of town; Sancerre with lobster mayonnaise, Brouilly with a rack of lamb, entertainment courtesy of Allan's Chinese logic – the same sort of strange logic I encountered every time I went to Beijing.

Over dinner he refused a glass of wine.

'Don't you ever drink?' his English friend asked.

'No,' Allan explained. 'I had hepatitis ten years ago and since then I've never touched a drop of alcohol.'

'Yes you have,' I said. 'Last year when we flew to France together you drank wine with your meal, and you did it again coming back.'

'That didn't count,' Allan explained. 'It was free.'

After dinner, straddling the fine line between tipsy and drunk, we wandered down to the port for brandy and coffee. At midnight Allan left with his friend and a little later, full of liquor, the remaining four of us began rolling back to the hotel by way of the harbour.

Donavon suddenly said something that incensed me. I have no idea what it was except that it must surely have been triggered by a combination of three things – alcohol, the two friends we had with us, and whose bed they would each end up in.

Whatever it was he said to me, I came back with something worse and in seconds we were arguing ferociously. Donavon was the most energised person I'd ever met. When provoked, his usual light-hearted good-humour could switch to pure madness. He would become a fireball of anger and scream abuse, sometimes provoking in the person he screamed at a fury as uncontrollable as his own. He'd done it to me once before, at home, shouting ill-chosen words down the stairs until I boiled over and leapt up them five at a time intending to kill.

On that occasion Donavon had rushed to his bedroom, throwing up a breathtakingly speedy construction of furniture to blockade the door. Now, on the harbour-side at St Tropez, he managed again to trigger inside of me that same intense anger.

He was standing at the edge of the harbour, twenty feet away, a silhouette against the moonlit water, his arms raised, vile expletives screaming through the air towards me.

Primed with alcohol my self-control disintegrated and I ran at him as fast and hard as I could, totally livid. I had no idea what was intended of my bull-like charge. I must have been almost twice his weight and we hit full on sending him flying backwards over the edge of the harbour wall.

As he splashed into the water he shrieked with terror but I paid no attention. Task fulfilled I stormed off into the warm night throbbing with adrenalin and fury, barely noticing his distant cries for help, 'I'm drowning.'

I'd forgotten he couldn't swim but fortunately he was pulled out, the only damage being to his clothes and his pride. The next day, with mutual remorse and a promise from me of replacement evening wear, the thing was put behind us. But with it went our relationship as it had been till then. Thereafter my friendship with Donavon followed in the footsteps of my friendship with Allan – platonic but pricey.

For the rest of that week Donavon and I were at peace (as we have been ever since) and dinner each night was followed by good conversation rather than attempted assassination. I guess our emotions had been knotted too tightly together. Adding too much alcohol to them had been like putting a lighted match to petroleum.

Following on our madness, into St Tropez a few evenings later came George and Andrew. Their petroleum was the result of being cooped up for too long in the recording studio; their lighted match was a bottle of wine in each place they visited as they bar-hopped round town. By midnight they were mindless, staggering round the harbour, screaming vile abuse across the water towards Joan Collins's yacht.

Later it made the papers. My fight with Donavon didn't.

While my own domestic soap-opera had managed to stay under wraps, Connie gave me an idea for putting someone else's on TV. It came up when she was telling me how she'd bumped into the Duchess of Argyle at a party. 'So grand, so bitchy, so broke.'

Margaret, Duchess of Argyle, was now 79. In the fifties she'd been involved in one of Britain's most famous divorce cases. Photographs handed to the judge and the jury (though not to the press) were said to be of the Duchess together with a dog and a member of the royal family. It was never revealed who was doing what to whom but within hours of the photos first making an appearance an out-of-court settlement was agreed.

She had a grand suite at Grosvenor House, given to her for the price of a single room because the hotel thought they gained prestige by having a Duchess live there. She took advantage of this favour quite outrageously, living on free room service brought to her by accommodating room waiters.

An amusing dinner guest, she told stories and anecdotes dating back to the beginning of the century, particularly about the twenties when she was considered Britain's greatest beauty, wined, dined and bedded by every eligible bachelor and many an *in*eligible adulterer.

She had a devoted dog that had never been housetrained. This she took with her everywhere as a deliberate ploy to counter the fact she'd become incontinent. Standing, chatting at the bar with her at the Caprice or Cecconis, you might suddenly realise that a large puddle was forming around her shoes. She would save herself by plucking the poor dog from the floor and giving it a hefty smack, then striding off to the ladies with it under her arm. 'Naughty Fido!'

She wasn't the only woman left behind by time to live out her days in Grosvenor House. One day we were going down in the lift when another woman joined us, about Margaret's age but even more dilapidated.

'How's Jeffrey?' Margaret asked her.

'Dreadful,' her friend replied. 'It's got so bad it takes two of us to help him up in the morning and put him back to bed again at night. We have to wash him and dress him from head to foot – everything – trousers, shirts, shoes, there's nothing he can put on by himself. At meal times, we not only have to cut up all his food, we have to feed it to him mouthful by mouthful, and you can't imagine what a dreadful task it is to get him to the toilet and clean him up afterwards. If he gets any worse I'm afraid he won't be able to drive.'

'Bonkers!' Margaret remarked as we left the lift. 'Jeffrey's not her husband, you know – he's the chauffeur.'

She had a wonderful deadpan humour. Sometimes it was difficult to know if you were being sent up or not. My first lunch with her was at Boulestin in Covent Garden, a grand old French restaurant left over from the thirties, a little faded since its days of greatest glory but with a wonderful wine list.

Because Margaret had known only the best in life, I thought I couldn't get away with cheap wine, so to go with the starters, after a lot of consideration, I settled on a bottle of Puligny Montrachet which was £180. I hoped she would recognise its quality and appreciate my generosity.

During hors d'oeuvre she amused me with a story of great indelicacy about her youth and then, to indicate she'd had enough of the first course, threw what was left on her plate to her dog lying under the table. As the main course arrived the first bottle of Puligny Montrachet ran out and I asked her, 'Margaret, would you like to move onto red?'

She smiled kindly. 'Oh I don't think so, darling. Just stick with this nice house white, don't you think?'

*

Connie had an idea for a docudrama – a real-life soap opera showing the day-to-day life of a 79-year-old Duchess as she tottered around London in the eighties living on her past. It needed further thinking and investment before we took it to the BBC or ITV so I asked John Maclaren, 'D'you think Ron O'Reilly would like to fund its development?'

John thought he would, so Ron was duly told about it and immediately wanted to meet the Duchess. Margaret, a con-woman with a sharp eye for a con-man, managed to get a quick ten thousand pounds out of him in exchange for a letter agreeing to become the narrator-cum-presenter of a TV series following the lives of London swingers of the eighties.

'You must meet Edith, too,' she told him. 'Perhaps we could do it together.'

'Edith' was Lady Foxwell, another woman of much the same class and age. There was something twin-like about them, emphasised by their erratic make-up, presumably applied under the influence. But whereas the Duchess had little connection with the swinging London of the eighties, Lady Foxwell had somehow got herself a job as PR for the Embassy Club in Dover Street, one of London's trendiest young hang-outs.

'How on earth did she get a job like that?' I asked Margaret.

'My dear – the Embassy Club started in the twenties. She probably went on opening night with someone who ran out on the bill and has been working it off ever since.'

Margaret frequently got sniffy about Edith, especially over her penchant for good-looking black guys, but for John Maclaren and me it offered an opportunity to take our docudrama into another area of contemporary society. Starting with Margaret, the Duchess of Argyle, in her supercilious lookout position at Grosvenor House, our programme could move easily on to Lady Edith Foxwell and her trendy pop celebrities at the Embassy Club, and then to the lesser known machinations of black London.

To develop the idea further John and I set up a company that Ron O'Reilly agreed to fund and we started looking for scriptwriters. The big decision seemed to be whether it would be a real-life affair – an extension of tabloid gossip-columns, filmed each week in documentary fashion round London clubs and restaurants – or a more normal sort of programme, scripted and rehearsed.

We called in some experts.

Film director Bryan Forbes came to Bryanston Square and gave us a splendid afternoon of anecdotes, mostly bitchy, concerning his time as a young soldier in the war, as a struggling actor afterwards and of Richard Attenborough's determined efforts to get himself a knighthood. About the slight downturn in his own career, Bryan reminded us, 'Nothing recedes like success.'

But he couldn't see a clear direction of where the series should go.

Graham Chapman thought we should make it fiction but use celebrities to play themselves – pop stars, actors, politicians and sportsmen. We would film it impromptu in the trendiest places in town and he would make up the scripts on the spot. It sounded hilarious but too improvised to be a reliable twice-weekly programme.

Then Lynda La Plante came round. At that time Lynda hadn't yet written her first novel but she was the hottest TV playwright in town.

'We'll get John Gielgud as the Duke of Argyle, Margaret's divorced husband.'

'How can you do that? Surely it has to be all fact or all fiction.'

'Half and half – I'll write characters and blend them with real-life London society – half scripted, half real-life spontaneity.'

It sounded marvellous, though neither John nor I understood quite how it would work.

'Give me three weeks,' Lynda said. 'And you'll see. I'll bring you something to look at. We'll call it *The Legacy.*'

22 RED TELEPHONE

George wanted to do something for charity

'How about a concert for the miners,' Jazz suggested.

It seemed so wrong for Wham!'s image it was laughable, but George liked the idea.

Currently, the miners were on strike and several of the more political pop stars – Paul Weller, Billy Bragg, Tom Robinson, people like that – were about to play a charity concert for them at the Festival Hall. The strike wasn't simply about pay and conditions; it was a strike about the future of trade unions in British society, a flat-out confrontation with the government. Margaret Thatcher had called the miners 'the enemy within'.

Arthur Scargill, their leader, had pushed the miners into putting more than just their livelihoods at stake; he'd got them caught up in picketing and fighting with the police. 'Hooves, truncheon and baton against bone and flesh,' was how poet Barbara Bookes put it in her poem 'Orgreave'.

For a leader to ask you to fight in that way he should at least be a visionary, a philosopher, or a charismatic character, but Arthur Scargill was none of those – he couldn't even do his hair properly. Whenever he appeared on TV he combed the final few strands from the left side up and over his bald head and down the other side. It was such a laughably dishonest attempt to deceive the world – how could you trust such a man? Certainly George didn't. He felt sorry for the miners and their families, not for the union or its leader.

The other artists on the bill at the charity concert were there because they agreed with Arthur Scargill's political objectives, as were the audience. They didn't take kindly to Wham!'s suntans. This was meant to be serious politics and when Wham! performed they were booed.

Afterwards George said of Arthur Scargill, 'I think he's the worst thing the miners could have.'

It caused a stir, but at least George had told the truth as he saw it.

A little later, on another TV interview, he produced more awkward truths. Asked about Wham!'s fans and what he thought of the way they screamed at concerts, he said, 'I think it's ridiculous. I don't have much respect for them.'

That was the side of George which worked against him – he was unable to compromise with what he wanted to say.

* * *

Lynda La Plante came back to us with her first draft script for our TV show, *The Legacy*.

It was tremendous stuff but nothing like what we'd discussed with her – it wasn't a mix of real life celebrity and written story – it was just a great rollicking bit of fiction – a cockney family which went back three generations and were now the centre of London society. And as we sat talking about it she broadened it further and further. 'I'm going to have all the main characters flying round the world, linking up with long-lost relatives in every country they go to. That way the TV show can move all over the globe.'

Meanwhile Connie had fallen in love with the original concept of a reality docudrama of eighties London and was charging round the tabloids drumming up publicity even though the show hadn't yet been proposed or presented to any TV channel or production company. Every day she was on the phone, cajoling journalists to do new stories in the gossip columns.

'Dahlink, haven't you heard? Prince Charles has agreed to do a "bit" part.'

Over the course of a few weeks, she'd not only had the Duchess as narrator and George and Andrew in leading roles, she'd put Princess Margaret in a motor cycle gang and Margaret Thatcher on a trapeze. If it would get a mention in a gossip column, Connie could think it up. Any time the press coverage showed signs of flagging she would throw another famous person into the cast – Princess Diana, boxer Frank Bruno, every pop band in town, even President Reagan in London on a flying visit.

She was plugging John Maclaren and me as 'people about to change the face of British television'. Lord Snowdon took our photographs for the *Sunday Times* and they ran five pages on us. All complete rubbish of course, but the media always liked something strong and specific to say about people, which is why they were so easily led into helping pop managers hype their groups.

At the end of September, I went with Allan to the South of France for a hairdressing convention. It was in a small village near Montpelier, the central square laid with tables and benches for a lunch hosted by the mayor.

It was pleasant sitting in warm autumn sunshine, eating simple food and drinking good local wine together with three hundred hairdressers. And the conversation was refreshingly different.

'How do you get your thickness?'

'Cut on an angle?'

'What gel do you use?'

'Tony & Guy for customers but for shows we use Bostic pottery adhesive. You can make the hair do just anything.'

So different from the world of pop where the lunch would have been at Grosvenor House or the Hilton. Most of these people had their own small businesses and making even meagre amounts of money was essential to them. The man next to Allan was trying to persuade him to buy a gadget for piercing ears.

'You can earn an extra hundred pounds a week. Especially if you have lots of male clients.'

'Why men?'

'Because they're cowards, so they'll pay five pounds extra for it to be painless.'

'How do you make it painless.'

'The girl holds a pink ice cube against their earlobe.'

'What's a pink ice cube?'

'A regular one with a little Ribena added. Pink makes it look more medical.'

The next morning Allan had to do a seminar. As usual we stayed with our Far Eastern theme but it was getting tough. We'd already been through the full gamut of chopstick perms and chopstick weaves but this time I came up with the idea of using a single thick piece of bamboo to create a strange perm. (It had to be strange because, as Allan explained to me, it was impossible to make any sort of attractive style by winding all the hair round one single piece of stick.)

Allan fooled the watching stylists marvellously. 'We call it "bamboo beauty",' he told them. 'The Chinese have a saying – "One stick – many curl".'

He managed to finish it off so well that all the hairdressers went rushing round the beach looking for bits of driftwood to try it out on. When they didn't get good results, Allan told them, 'It only works with bamboo.'

All the way home he was laughing. 'The style was such rubbish. It would have been better using ordinary perm rods.'

'That's the art of selling,' I told him. 'Perhaps, after Wham! have been to China, you should go there too? Show them how to do perms with chopsticks. All those Western hair companies trying to sell their products there will hate us.'

It was strange moving from hairdressing conventions in the South of France to pop management in London, to political diplomacy in China. By October of 1984 I'd already been there eleven times and was just about to go again.

In the studio George was working on a Christmas song. On and on he went with it and just couldn't get the mix right. When he finally did, we realised he'd created another classic, as sentimental as 'Careless Whisper', as hooky as 'Go-Go'.

'Last Christmas' was a wonderful mix of all things familiar – the chugging rhythm of Kool And The Gang's 'Joanna', the chord sequence of the old rock classic 'Mr Postman' and a melody somewhat reminiscent of the opening lines of 'Reunited' by Peaches & Herb. Another perfect example of what a great pop song should be – instantly captivating and full of nostalgic hints. A little over-sugared, but so haunting it couldn't be condemned for being so.

When I left for Beijing I took a copy with me and played it to Zhou Renkai. He'd just demolished a particularly pricey midday meal and asked me back to his office. When he'd finished listening he told me, 'I like it. And lunch was good too. Now you see, I help you.' And he picked up the red telephone that sat dustily behind a heap of files on his desk.

Reputedly these phones went through to Deng himself, though I thought it more likely they would only reach a secretary, or even a secretary of a secretary. Anyway, to thank me for lunch, Zhou spoke to someone in Chinese down the phone and dropped the magic word 'Wham!' into his conversation.

In return for this he wanted more than just another lunch. 'Mr Zhou speak to the top,' his interpreter told me. 'Now you must take him to see Wham! perform. And he must take people with him.'

It turned out Zhou wanted me to pay for eleven people – heads of various departments – to go and see Wham! perform at their next concert, wherever and whenever that might be.

'Mr Porodyusa says Tokyo will be the best place,' Zhou told me through the interpreter.

Had he indeed? I wasn't sure I liked Mr Porodyusa making such expensive suggestions. But since he seemed to be turning into a key player in this whole thing, and since I'd at last seen Zhou pick up his red telephone, I agreed that eleven people could fly to Tokyo to see Wham! play at the Budokan.

The next morning Lew Mon Hung again turned up in the hotel coffee-shop. 'How is our project go?' he asked.

I told him point blank, Wham!'s concert was not 'our' project, it was 'my' project. I also told him the Beijing concert was being fixed by a Japanese film company.

'In that case,' he asked, 'why you talk again with Mr Wu?'

I hadn't done, but at Rolf Neuber's suggestion I'd typed up the sales pitch I'd delivered verbally to Mr Wu the first time I'd met him (about the benefits to the Government of a concert by a foreign pop group, emphasising that while it had to be televised to the world it need not be publicised in China) and I'd sent a few copies to his office. Now, just twenty-four hours later, Lew had got hold of a copy of this and waved it at me stapled to a Chinese translation. It floored me, the speed that this stuff got around town, but I had to give Rolf a few extra points for suggesting it.

'You must meet again with son of Zhao Ziyang,' Lew told me. 'He has deal for you.'

I invested in another lunch and was offered the chance to become the sole agent for the export of Oolong tea, the most popular Chinese tea in Japan. But remembering the Boston Tea Party and the fate of the East India Company I decided tea might be a risky business.

'Well then,' Lew suggested. 'How about open a disco in Canton?'

That was an exciting thought – the first proper Western disco in communist China. There must be leisure companies all over the world who would want to get that sort of prestige.

'Yes,' I said. 'I think I could find backers for that.'

That evening, back at the Hilton in Hong Kong, Professor Rolf called. 'I hear you might get involved in a disco in Canton.'

'I might try to find a backer for one. How did you know?'

'I heard from Mr Wu. Surely you know how fast news travels in Beijing. Straight down the microphones to Mr Wu's men at the other end. I also heard that the typed version of your original sales pitch on the reasons for a Wham! concert made quite an impact. It looks like we're making progress.'

He was doing it again! I hated it when he said *'we'*, just like Lew.

'Listen,' he said, 'why don't we have dinner?'

It turned out he was in a room on the next floor.

Over more good food and drink, this time at the restaurant in the Regent Hotel, Rolf told me, 'I wouldn't bother with that disco if I was you – I've checked it out already. For a disco, the rules for overseas investment are killing. The investment itself can be refunded from profits, but *only* the investment, after that profits have to be re-invested in China. Importation of drinks wouldn't be allowed – all drinks would have to be Chinese brands.'

Our table was next to the window, looking out over Hong Kong harbour at night. I'd always connected that view with times when I was free and on my own. Now I seemed to have no privacy left at all.

'Rolf – how do you know all that?'

'Wu told me, so that I could advise you correctly. And another thing, the disco would have to open at 5 p.m. and close at 10 p.m with no hard liquor. The whole thing would be under the control of the local government, it would be little more than a youth club.'

'Why are you able to get so much information? What do you want it for?'

'Other people want it. I just get it for them.'

'But why?'

Rolf put down his knife and fork and answered with care, as if this was meant to be a once-and-for-all explanation. 'Do one silly thing when you're young and you'll be pressured by these people the rest of your life. I accepted a fake degree in teaching and a title to go with it. I became a professor of languages – and let me tell you, a very good one – but in doing so I got myself a lifetime obligation. It's like getting yourself tattooed one drunken night when you're a teenager – it stays with you forever.'

We were interrupted by a bellboy who came to find me with a telex from Mr Porodyusa. He wanted to know how my meeting with Zhou had gone. Had Zhou asked to take people to Japan for a show by Wham!? Had I agreed? Had I confirmed with George yet that he would write the theme song for their movie?

Rolf asked, 'Anything important?'

'Some Japanese people. They're making a movie in China and they've offered to help me get Wham! an invitation.'

'I know about them. It's a big production. They'll probably be able to help you. They know about me too.'

I was certain he was bluffing; just trying to impress me by saying he knew them. There were too many people getting involved in Wham!'s trip to China and I had no idea who was doing what.

'It's a big war film, isn't it?' the professor added. 'About the Sino-Japanese problems in the nineteenth century.'

I had no idea about that either.

* * *

Bit by bit Jazz and I were giving Wham! everything they'd asked for. Once China had happened we would get them to the heights we'd promised – the biggest group in the world. But if they then broke up and didn't tour, there would be no profit for us in having done so. It was becoming more obvious each day that George could hardly wait to leave Wham! and become himself yet we were only at the stage of launching their second album. We did it in October with a 'World Premiere' for celebrities and journalists at Xenon, a night club in Piccadilly.

During the evening, Bob Geldof came over and spoke to me. 'Did you see that TV programme last night about Ethopia?'

I hadn't, but I'd read about it in the morning paper. It was the first time the world had been informed about the plight of these people.

'I want to do a charity record,' Bob said. 'Give the proceeds to Ethiopia. I want every famous singer to come and sing on it. D'you think George would do it?'

I couldn't imagine he wouldn't. No-one could be more genuine than Bob and no-one more deserving than starving Ethiopians.

I asked, 'Who else have you got?'

He shook his head, 'No-one yet. Just starting out.'

'And who's putting the record out?'

He shook his head again. He was just at the beginning of it so I made a few business suggestions about maximising the income from the record and asking the distributor to handle it for nothing. Bob seemed grateful for the advice but later I felt guilty I hadn't offered to get more involved. Anyway, the next morning I asked George and he jumped at it.

He also came up with another great song. His fourth super classic, 'Everything She Wants' – gritty, funky and meaningful – about a hopelessly cooled-off marriage. At CBS it was decided to put that and his Christmas song on the same record. 'You'll get four weeks at Number

One,' they told us. '"Last Christmas" for two weeks before the 25th and "Everything She Wants" for two weeks afterwards when everyone's clubbing.'

In November we heard that 'Go-Go' had gone to Number One in the USA, Al Teller and CBS America having done as they'd promised and given it maximum promotion. Shortly afterwards the album also topped the American charts, as did 'Freedom', Wham!'s new single in Britain. I put a copy in the post to my student friends in Beijing, though I doubted they would get it.

In the middle of the month Bob Geldof recorded his charity record for Ethiopia, 'Do They Know It's Christmas?'. Andrew had also been invited but on the day in question he overslept. At the time it didn't seem of much importance but four weeks later when the record was huge and the video was being shown worldwide it was clear that everyone who was anyone had been at the recording. Except Andrew.

It was probably another nail in Wham!'s eventual coffin but for the moment things couldn't have been going better. In January they would leave for Japan for ten days, then Australia for a fortnight and America for a ten-day tour of venues with one-thousand capacity – better to be sold out with people queuing than to have a single empty seat in the house.

Before that, though, there was Christmas in the UK. Wham! were booked to play four days at Wembley Arena including Christmas Eve. 'We want it to be the best Christmas show ever,' George announced. 'An end of year outing for all our fans.'

On the first night the atmosphere was amazing. The VIP box was packed with stars and George and Andrew blew a thousand kisses to the audience – 'Happy Christmas!'

Schmaltzty, perhaps, but a wonderful party anyway.

After the show Elton John breezed into the green room and landed a kiss on George's lips. 'Brilliant', he pronounced.

Donavon and Allan were there too, dressed to the nines, trying to outdo each other as usual. They asked Connie, 'Who's got the best outfit?'

'I have,' she told them.

Then Princess Di turned up, so they asked her too.

'Me,' she replied without hesitation.

Really, though, it was between Donavon and Connie.

23

NOT SO FAMOUS

'You know, don't you, I'm quite well-known in Japan?'

'Well-known! How could you be?' Jazz seemed quite upset by the idea.

We were on the flight to Tokyo. I wasn't telling him to be boastful, just to warn him in advance because he often seemed put out that I was seen as the principal power of our two-man team, like George in comparison with Andrew, whereas the truth was nothing like that.

'You see, I often do interviews for Japanese monthlies.'

'But you can't really be well-known. Those are just pop magazines.'

'No they're not! A lot of them are more serious than that. It's because of my success with Japan. The media were always interested in Japan because of their name and somehow I got the credit.'

Jazz hadn't been to Japan before, so on the second night I thought I should show him around a bit, and that meant nightlife. The Japanese have long known the benefit of having special areas in each city set aside for men to drink, let off steam, have sex or do whatever else they wish to do in their free time. The bars in these areas have wonderful names – 'Erotismatic', 'Beauty & Love', 'Coffee & Peeping'. To Europeans, though, most of these alluring bars are out of bounds. The Japanese simply don't want foreigners in them.

Although a Japanese businessman might come to one of these places for whisky, or sex, the most important ingredient is sheer relaxation – the knowledge that once he passes through the door he will be in a uniquely stress-free environment. The last thing he wants is someone not familiar with the required etiquette causing awkwardness and embarrassment, and it's primarily for this reason that foreigners are kept out. But I knew one place we could get into. It was a small club in Shinjuku where the show was performed by transvestites. Personally I've never been too impressed with transvestites. It seems a singularly bad idea, having found out that you're an imperfect man, to change yourself into an imperfect woman. But this wasn't the evening for such philosophy.

'I've never been there before,' I told Jazz, 'but I'm told the show is excellent.'

On the way in the taxi Jazz suddenly produced a gloating smile. 'D'you know, since we've arrived I've not seen one single person who's recognised you in any way. I can't think where you got the idea that you're well-known here. Maybe you were just boasting.'

'Could be,' I conceded.

When we arrived at the club we knocked and waited while we were peered at from a peephole. Scrutinised and presumably accepted, the doorman opened up and told us, 'Please wait for the manager to allocate your seats.'

When he saw me, the Japanese manager – good-looking and youngish – cried out in English, 'Oh! Mr Simon Napier-Bell, the rock manager.' Then he turned to the waiter and instructed him in Japanese to give us the best seats.

Jazz's face showed intense annoyance.

'Told you so,' I said. 'In Tokyo, I'm quite well-known.'

Seated, we ordered drinks and watched the show. It was frivolous and amusing and Jazz fancied the girls too much to believe they could really be boys until I pointed out the tiny scar they had under each breast.

When the show was finished the manager came across and showed us out with a smile.

'I want to know something,' Jazz asked him. 'How come you knew this person was Simon Napier-Bell, the rock manager? Is he really so famous in Japan?'

The manager giggled coyly, covering his mouth with his hand. 'I met him in London when I was a student, but I think he's forgotten. He picked me up in a gay pub and took me home to his flat. But I don't think he's famous.'

Jazz was happy for the rest of the tour.

Japan is always the highlight of any world tour; slick enough to guarantee everything will work perfectly, quirky enough to provide a new perspective.

Our promoter was Mr Udo – portly and polite, rigidly correct with his business procedures, always dressed in a double-breasted suit, treating everyone in the band's touring party to elegant dinners and a visit to the bath-house if required. And behind the formality was an extraordinary giggling laugh ready for any British joke that could cross the cultural barrier and tickle his Japanese sense of humour.

His crew was masterful. It was possible for a visiting band to turn up with no-one but their musicians and still have the tour run perfectly. Mr Udo's crew would take over the whole show – load and unload equipment, set it up onstage, drive the band around and do everything else that was needed.

On the first night of any tour, having got the group's gear set up onstage to everyone's taste, Udo's crew would take a series of Polaroid photos. Thereafter, every night, at every venue they travelled to, the group, their backing band, their dancers and singers would find everything set up identically.

At the first day's rehearsal, Tommy Eyre, Wham!'s keyboard player, sent out for Kentucky Fried Chicken and coke. He wanted to eat while he rehearsed so he borrowed a small table from the dressing-room and put it next to the keyboards. Because the table turned up in the Polaroid photos it was commandeered by Udo's crew and taken round the entire tour, appearing onstage every night in the same place.

With Wham!, the biggest problem Udo's crew had was keeping them safe from teenage girls. To begin with pop stars think the attention paid them by fans is fun, but it can easily turn dangerous. At a radio station on the first afternoon the usual tight-knit plans of Udo's team went wrong. George and Andrew with me and two security guards left by a back door; there should have been a limo waiting outside but there wasn't – instead there were thirty or forty teenage girls.

For a few seconds George and Andrew stood their ground smiling insecurely, presuming the two security guards could deal with it, but for a gang of girls this size two guards and a manager were not enough. Individually these girls looked like harmless dolls – petite and perfectly mannered. Together, in a fit of mania, they could turn into a Mongul horde. And when it dawned on them that George and Andrew were standing just twenty feet in front of them, the horde attacked.

'Sagatte!' yelled the security men. 'Stay back!'

'Fucking hell!' said George.

'Get back inside,' said Andrew.

But we couldn't. The back door to the radio station had shut and locked itself behind us.

'Let's get out of here,' I shouted, and pushed George and Andrew in the direction of where the limo should be coming from. The security guards stayed between us and the girls, one of them yelling furiously down his walkie-talkie, trying to raise our driver. 'Rimo wa doko? Where's the limo?'

Before we'd taken three steps the horde was on us, the girls fighting their way past the guards, screaming manically, grabbing at George and Andrew – pulling their hair, tearing their clothes, shrieking as if they were possessed.

'Shit!'

'Sagatte!'

'Rimo! Rimo!'

Nothing any one of us said could help, nor was it likely to. These girls were star crazed; they didn't really know what they wanted, their obsession with Wham! was based largely on the presumption that real physical contact with their idols was an impossibility. But now, with their idols suddenly in front of them, they'd gone completely berserk. A girl bit into the cheek of one of the guards – another got hold of Andrew's hair and started tugging it – half of George's body was protected by his security man, the other half was open to the grasping hands of ten or twelve girls.

The whole thing lasted just ten or fifteen seconds but for those brief moments it was pure blood lust. Andrew kicked. George shouted. The security men hit out and the girls clawed and shrieked.

Then the limo screeched up beside us. In a flash the boys and the security guards were in the back with me in front with the driver. The strange thing was – this was what these sex-mad girls really wanted. They preferred their idols locked behind glass in a car. That's how things were meant to be. That way they could crawl all over the limousine, screaming, rubbing their bodies against it as if the car itself was the object of their sexual frenzy rather than the passengers inside.

We inched away slowly, the driver anxious not to injure any of the girls clambering around us. One screaming teenager stretched herself across the bonnet and tried to hang on. A pretty little girl with dyed blonde hair, only fourteen or fifteen, she pushed her lips against the windscreen in front of me and started furiously french kissing it. As the car eased away she slowly slid off to one side keeping her tongue pressed against the glass as she went, leaving a snail trail of saliva across the windscreen.

The driver cursed and turned on the washers.

'The girls excite too much,' he grumbled.

The next morning Zhou and his gang of Chinese bureaucrats arrived to see Wham!'s show at the Budokan. I was sure this would be the end of my efforts to get Wham! into China.

At the concert they were given seats at the back of the first tier where they had a panoramic view of the whole auditorium. The show was chaotic – Japanese girls could scream even more loudly than their counterparts in Britain. All round the hall manic teenage girls stood on their seats, screaming, weeping and urinating, while at the back of the first tier twelve stiff-faced Chinese stared inscrutably across the sea of hysteria towards Wham!, midgets on a distant stage.

When I asked Zhou afterwards if they'd enjoyed the show, his translator made a face. 'He's not sure if it's OK for Beijing.'

A few minutes later Mr Porodyusa met us in the lobby and said he'd organised dinner for them. 'And for anyone who wants it,' he added, 'there's the bath-house too.'

I thanked him for his help.

'Not at all,' he said most politely. 'After all, this is our joint project, isn't it?'

He was the third person to think this way. But I had to give him credit – the next morning when I spoke to Zhou again, his translator told me, 'Mr Zhou say he like everything. Perfect! No problem if Wham! play Beijing.'

The visit to the bath-house seemed to have done the trick.

Three days later, on a day off, we were stuck in a hotel in Kyoto in the most miserable weather. It was bucketing with rain.

In the lobby I bumped into Tommy Eyre, our keyboardist, looking lost. 'The bastards went without me,' he said, referring to his normal drinking partners from the band.

'So let's go somewhere for a beer or two,' I suggested.

We borrowed a couple of big umbrellas from the front desk and found a bar in a small road behind the hotel. When we opened the door the barman tried to stop us coming in, waving his hands and saying 'No open'. But Tommy had a winning way with him. He just sat down and smiled.

'Beer,' he told the man several times. 'Japanese beer – very good.'

And since the only reason that Japanese try to keep foreigners out of their bars is to avoid embarrassment and trouble, and since it was quite obvious to the barman that to make us leave was going to cause more embarrassment and trouble than allowing us to stay, he gave us the beers.

'Not much of a town for a day off,' Tommy commented as he got stuck into the first bottle. 'Reminds me of a tour of the States I did with Joe Cocker. Thirty days in a row we played and everyone was begging for a day off. Then when it came it was in Billings, Montana. Have you ever been to Billings? There's just a broken-down Holiday Inn and a bar in the middle of town where they still have a place to leave horses.'

The barman came across and pointed at his watch. 'Closing in ten minute,' he told us, which seemed a strange thing to do at twenty-to-one in the afternoon. He just wanted to get rid of us, but unfortunately for him a group of Japanese businessmen arrived, obviously regulars, and settled down in a corner, overriding his decision.

Once he'd delivered their drinks to them he approached us and again pointed his finger at his watch. 'We are now close.'

'He doesn't really think we're going to leave, does he?' Tommy asked.

'At school they learn everything by rote,' I explained. 'They're taught that repetition is good because its consequences are predictable. Accordingly, this barman thinks that if he repeats himself often enough we'll finally leave.'

The barman was still standing next to us waiting for our response so Tommy pointed across the room, guiding his eyes to where the five Japanese businessmen were drinking happily in the corner. 'Yes – closing – very good, we like it,' Tommy said. 'Two more beers please, Yoshi.'

The barman simply went and got them.

In the corner a TV was showing scenes from some vicious student riots that had taken place in Tokyo the day before – an unusual sight in Japan. Youths ran around breaking shop windows and setting cars on fire and there were thousands of police with batons knocking them off their feet and spinning them into the air with water cannons. One picture showed a student walloping a policeman on his riot shield, knocking him to the ground.

'Whooeeee,' Tommy said in a satisfied way, for he was a typical Scot and not a great lover of authority.

One of the Japanese businessmen from the corner was passing by us on his way to the toilet, a serious-looking man in his mid-thirties with horn-rimmed glasses. 'Yes, it is very good,' he agreed in rather good English.

'Really?' I asked in surprise.

'Yes,' he nodded. 'People should protest while they're still young. That way, when they leave university and get jobs, the protest will all be gone out of them and they will become better citizens, better Japanese.'

He continued on his way to the toilet.

'Funny lot, these nips, aren't they?' Tommy said, finishing off his second bottle. 'But they make good beer. Ready for another, are we?'

The Japanese businessman passed us on his way back from the toilet. 'What are you people do in Kyoto?'

'We're on tour with a rock group,' I told him.

He drew a deep, excited breath, 'Aaaah, loku-gloop.' And he called out to his friends on the other side of the room.

Suddenly we found ourselves in the middle of a party. The stuffy besuited businessmen bought us beers and began asking questions.

'You ever meet the Beatle?' one of them wanted to know.

'You know Lolling Stone?' another one asked. 'When I at university I ruving Keith Lichard.'

Having recorded with almost every British rock act there ever was, Tommy had met them all. When he told the Japanese, they went mad. One of them played some frantic air guitar and explained, 'We all big loku fans since university. Today is my birthday so we come cerebrate. What the name of your gloop?'

'Wham!'

'This is not good name for loku-gloop.'

'You're wrong,' I corrected him. 'It's a very good name indeed.'

'When are you play?'

'Tonight.'

I had a bunch of tickets in my pocket so I gave them one each. Then it was party time till 2 p.m. when our new friends announced they had to get back to work.

'What do you do?' I asked.

'Banking,' one of them replied. 'But all at different bank. Today we come early to lunch to cerebrate Ishi's birthday. Now we must go back.'

'What are your names?' Tommy asked.

They replied like a school roll-call. 'Ishi', 'Yoshi', 'Kazu', 'Tats', 'Dennis'.

'Dennis?' Tommy and I echoed simultaneously. 'How can you be called Dennis if you're Japanese?'

'My father live in England for ten years. He fall in love with clicket. He call me after his favourite clicketer – Dennis Compton.'

Outside it was still bucketing but the five of them tottered off umbrella-less through the downpour, blind drunk, ready to run the city's banks for another afternoon.

24 SOMERSAULTS

For a tubby forty-five year old I was getting surprisingly good at somersaults.

I'd learnt them at Jomtien beach on the Gulf of Thailand where my coach was Ade, a young man with a tendency to high-pitched squeals when things got exciting. The trick was to run fast down the beach towards an incoming wave and throw yourself forward and round in a loop as you reached it, landing flat on your back in the shallow surf as it rolled out again. I had a few false starts including one time when I misjudged the wave's movements and landed bang on the top of my head on dry sand amid shrieks of laughter from my chaperones. But I soon got the knack of it; then became rather good.

Ade persuaded me to push the boundaries of human endeavour even further. We tried a twin somersault, running at the water hand in hand and spinning into the air at precisely the same moment, landing on our backs in the surf still holding hands. This raised so much applause from people on the beach that we set about training others, then started experimenting with a line of three.

Soon, under a clear blue sky, on the golden sands of Jomtien bay, we were doing line somersaults – nine at a time – one plump Englishman flanked on each side by four slender Thais, running, hands clasped, to the water's edge risking communal hara-kiri if a wave were to recede at the wrong moment, but to tumultuous applause from our audience on the beach if we succeeded.

All this, of course, was an integral part of getting Wham! into China.

'You know,' Ade told me, 'you are half naughty school boy, half big man.'

After their visit to Japan, Wham! had gone to Australia for ten days. Jazz had been happy to go with them, always pleased to be the man in charge.

As usual, I was equally happy not to be; always pleased to be the man behaving badly on the beach.

At the beginning of February Wham! would move from Australia to the States, the first date being at the Palladium in LA. With George making increasingly frequent references to his impending solo career, Jazz and I knew, to keep Wham! together we needed to make them as big as we could as quickly as possible. The gig in China would be an essential ingredient in shooting them to the top in America, so after a week on the beach perfecting my somersaults I planned to go back to Beijing.

As I was about to leave I had a problem. For more than a week I'd had a slight pain in my right ear but in the last couple of days it had grown from an itch to a throb. On my last evening in Thailand it turned into a continual drumbeat and I went to bed dosed with whisky and aspirins. By the morning it had become an all-out nightmare. It felt like something deep inside my ear was growing, like some sort of hatching science-fiction monster. I could feel the egg, already six inches across, ripping my whole head apart; shortly a full-size space-dragon would be born through my aural cavity.

I went to see an ear specialist at Thailand's best hospital, Bumrungrad. He was a charming man who'd practised for twenty years in the USA. He shoved an inspection gadget into my ear and peered down it studiously. 'You have a tiny little fungus growing at the bottom.'

'*Tiny*?!' I exploded. 'It must be the size of an egg at least.'

'Maybe,' he said. 'But only a fly's egg. However, these things are serious and must be treated. It's looking very sore and I need to dress it for a few days. Then when it cools down I can take another look and decide what we'll do next.'

I told him I was going to Beijing and he asked me when I was coming back. 'I've no plans to do so. After Beijing, I'm going to Los Angeles, in about four days' time.'

'That will be perfect. I'll write you a note for Dr Benjamin at the Beverly Hills clinic. He'll sort it out for you; he's an old colleague of mine.'

Having first dripped some sort of medication into my ear, he sent me next door where his nurse dressed it for me. It was a peculiar dressing – it came in a cardboard tube like a Tampax. The nurse held it close to my ear and pushed it in with tweezers. I couldn't see what she was doing but she told me, 'This dressing is a long thin thread, very fine, nearly twelve feet long and we push it in slowly, packing the ear from bottom to top. But be careful when you're in the shower, don't let your ear get wet or it will swell. And if you do accidentally get it wet, take it out at once.'

The next day I was back in Beijing; it was Zhou's feeding time. At the Great Wall restaurant there was a new specialty he wanted to try. A large pan came to the table in which there was nothing but a squirming wriggling mess of tiny black fish, slippery, ugly and just two or three inches long. They had orange-red eyes, so that looking into the pan what one saw was a throbbing black mush and hundreds of gleaming red dots. I couldn't think of anything more sickening or inedible and I really couldn't believe Mr Zhou was going to eat these things, or worse still, expect me to eat them too. If I was going to, I had at least to be sure that some progress was made after my months of heroic lunching.

I told Zhou, 'I've been thinking, *if* one day a British pop group were to come here, as we've talked about so often, and *if* it were to be Wham!, the ideal place for them to play would be the People's Gymnasium.'

His translator struggled to reproduce the subtlety of my grammatical construction in Mandarin.

Zhou was silent a long time, watching our fish being prepared. It was one of those cook-at-the-table dishes and a chef of some sort had arrived with a trolley on which was a wok and a primus stove.

The chef picked up the pan of fish and poured them into boiling fat. At first, to watch it almost made me retch, but after just thirty seconds the black mush had turned into a mass of crunchy crispy things, like whitebait. And when they were placed on a big serving dish, sprinkled with coriander and edged with a ring of sweet plum sauce, they looked so delicious I could hardly wait to be offered some.

Nor could Zhou. And once his mouth was full of the crispy red-eyed minifish with plum sauce dribbling down his chin to form a brown dew drop, he waved his chopsticks in my face and finally responded to my devious statement.

'He agrees', his translator explained. 'He thinks he will be able to invite Wham! to play at the People's Gymnasium a little later this year. But he wants to take you to meet the minister. If the minister agrees there will be just one more person to give approval.'

'Who?'

The translator raised his eyebrows, surprised I didn't know. I presumed he meant Chairman Deng – but for all I knew it could have been Zhou's wife.

After lunch we went to meet the minister.

Zhou's driver managed to arrive at the ministry on the wrong side of the road – a dual carriageway – and although it was pouring with rain Zhou decided we should get out there rather than continue another few hundred yards and do a U-turn.

'Cannot be late for the Minister,' his translator explained. 'We all run across the road. I give you umbrella.'

Zhou and I dodged across the wide avenue with the interpreter holding an umbrella over the two of us, the largest part being reserved for Zhou so that a stream of rainwater ran down my neck.

A few minutes later we were waiting in a conference room with a highly polished wood floor and lace-covered armchairs. The minister turned out to be rather nice. Dapper and well-suited, with no hint of a Mao outfit or a dreadful tweed jacket like Zhou's, he was the epitome of sophistication. Through the interpreter he explained he'd once been a film director in Shanghai, which tallied – he was probably the same minister who was in charge of Mr Porodyusa's Sino–Japanese co-production which had led me to Zhou in the first place. This was as productive a meeting as I'd ever had and I felt I was finally getting somewhere.

Then, just as we were getting along famously, I suddenly had a pain to end all pains in my ear, so acute I yelped. It was right where it had been the day before when the Thai nurse had inserted her 'please-don't get-it-wet' bandage. I realised, while we'd been crossing the road, the interpreter had skilfully engineered about twelve gallons of rainwater into my right ear. I grabbed at it, trying to pull out the bandage as the nurse had said I should do if it got wet, but it was hard to find a loose end to get hold of.

The pain was enormous – my ear was about to give birth – a thousand little animals were heaving and shoving, struggling to get out. I grabbed again at the bandage trying to find a loose end while still attempting polite conversation with Zhou and the minister, both of them now far more interested in my efforts to grab a thread of bandage than in what I was saying. And then I managed to get hold of it.

The nurse was right about it swelling – what had gone in as silken thread came out as a damp, half-centimetre wide bandage. My first tug got about three feet of it out, the second tug another three feet. I remembered her saying it was nearly twelve feet long. There was nothing I could do now but keep pulling, and inside my ear still felt like a bursting balloon.

The conversation dried up. They were transfixed with what I was doing. It appeared to be some sort of conjuring trick – pulling a half mile of bandage out of my ear. I'd once seen a naked girl onstage in a Bangkok nightclub do something similar, producing a string of Christmas bunting from her pussy. Now it was my turn. More and more and more, until in the end there seemed to be twenty feet of it, not twelve, strewn around the floor. And it still wasn't all out. I stood up, tethered by the bandage still hanging from my ear to the pile of it already heaped around my feet.

'Excuse me, minister,' I asked. 'You don't happen to have a pair of scissors, do you?'

The minister pressed a buzzer. A maid came in but just as she did so I managed to remove the last bit of bandage from my ear.

I picked up the heap on the floor and put it in her arms. 'Maybe you could throw this in the bin.'

Zhou looked distinctly shaken, as if his world was falling apart. But the minister was laughing.

'Excuse me,' I told him, 'I got an ear infection when I was in Thailand.' He didn't hear me; he just laughed and laughed.

Later, when it came time to leave, I felt I'd made rather a good friend.

25

NO PHOTOS

At Los Angeles airport the immigration officer carefully studied the 'me' standing in front of him (a sun-tanned pop manager, freshly arrived from triumphant somersaulting on the beaches of Thailand) and compared it with the 'me' in my passport (bad-tempered and unshaven, photographed in a photo-booth at Victoria station in a rush to get to the passport office before it closed).

'You don't look like your picture,' he complained, and wasted time looking from the photo to me and back again. 'It looks like a different person.'

I was impatient. I wanted to see the opening gig of Wham!'s first tour of America which was due to start one hour from now at the LA Palladium.

'What d'you do?' he asked.

'I manage pop stars. In fact, the group I manage is Number One in the States at this very moment – Wham!, with a song called "Careless Whisper". I'm trying to get to the opening night of their tour.'

The mention of their name made no impact on him whatsoever. 'Never heard of them,' he drawled, still turning the pages of my passport.

That was typical of America. A couple of hit songs were never enough to get a group's name across. People would get to know the songs from the radio but still wouldn't know the name of the artist. It was for exactly that reason that Jazz and I wanted to get Wham! into China, so their name would be splashed across TV news broadcasts and national magazines.

'It isn't a very good picture,' the immigration man said, staring at my passport photo with obvious disapproval.

This guy was getting just *too* annoying. 'It was taken in a hurry,' I snapped.

I looked at my watch and sighed loudly. It annoyed him and he glared at me suspiciously. 'I'd have thought a manager of pop stars would have made sure his passport had a really good shot.'

'For God's sake,' I grumbled. 'It's a travel document not a bloody record sleeve.'

A silly remark. With Wham!'s show due to start in sixty minutes, I'd just earned myself a body search.

I saw the show the next night, in San Francisco – a biggish venue and well-filled. Jazz told me, 'In LA the tickets sold out in ten minutes. And it's happened again in New York.'

Despite this good reaction from American fans, George still seemed intent on Wham! coming to an end. Andrew was aware of this now, and appeared to accept it, though George was still talking about doing one more album – 'to give Andrew something extra before it all finishes.'

When we reached Dallas he called a meeting in Jazz's suite. 'I want to make a schedule for finishing Wham! and going solo,' he told us.

'But I've almost pulled off China,' I pleaded. 'In another week it might be confirmed.'

George looked pleased; but it didn't change his mind. He'd decided Wham! would break up and that was that. He wanted them to go out while they were at the top. 'But to thank the fans we'll play one last gig – a really big one.'

I shrugged; Jazz argued. He was always more persistent than me. 'Where would you play it?'

'Wembley,' George said without hesitation.

'That would be so unfair on your American fans,' Jazz pointed out. 'You can't think only of Britain.'

Andrew nodded and George reconsidered. 'OK. You're right. We'll play one in Britain and one in the USA.'

'West Coast or East Coast?' Jazz asked. And two minutes later the number of gigs was up to three.

Andrew had a comment, and a helpful one too. 'To be honest – we should probably play somewhere in the middle as well.'

'Nope!' George was not going to be dragged any further away from his original plan. 'Three will be enough.'

'What sort of show do you want?' Jazz asked. 'Just a bare stage and play all the hits, so that it doesn't cost too much and we can make some money?'

'No!' Andrew insisted. 'When we play our last show it has to be the best one in history.' And George agreed.

Over the next week Jazz and I drew up a budget for putting together a stadium-size show for the US. There would be the best sound and lights we could get and the full band Wham! were using for their current tour of America. George and Andrew also wanted new merchandise to be designed by Katherine Hammet, so that too had to be added to the cost.

Bit by bit the plan for the two big American gigs came together, and so did the costs – the whole thing would lose around five million dollars.

Jazz persuaded George, 'Why not play a few more gigs – not a lot, but just enough to amortise the cost? And we'll be careful to spread the gigs evenly around the USA so that everyone gets a chance to see one of them.'

For Jazz and me, the most important thing was that we didn't call it a 'goodbye' tour; Americans wouldn't understand. For America, Wham! was just beginning. For them, this was a 'Hello' tour. And we still hoped – once Wham! started packing stadiums, receiving accolades and earning millions – George might change his mind and wait another year before starting his solo career.

In the end we got George to agree to eight dates and nothing would be said about it being a goodbye tour. It would be called Whamerica!.

* * *

'There'll be no pictures, I'm afraid. Not if it wasn't agreed with Connie.'

'But it was,' the lady journalist snapped back at me.

In London, George and Andrew were doing an interview for an American magazine. Connie was busy elsewhere and Jazz was still in America. I'd gone along to make sure everything was alright, but it wasn't. The journalist had brought a photographer with her and I knew for sure George hadn't been warned.

Andrew arrived first, not in the hire-car that had been sent for him, but walking in off the street wearing a big smile and a shiny tracksuit.

'What happened to your limo?' I asked.

He shrugged as if he had no idea what I was talking about. 'I took a cab.'

The limo would be waiting outside his flat, and since this was in the days before mobile phones it would probably stay there at thirty pounds an hour until the driver got hungry or realised it was bedtime.

Andrew drifted off into his own world. He sat down, drank from the journalist's half-empty glass of mineral water, then picked his nose. The journalist, about to introduce herself, put out her hand to shake Andrew's then quickly withdrew it when she realised what it was he was inspecting on the end of his finger.

George arrived wearing old jeans with his hair in a mess and a runny nose. He smiled broadly and seemed to be in a good mood but I knew he would never agree to be photographed looking as he did. He wandered across to the stereo and put on a tape of 'Everything She Wants' – not yet released in America.

'It's a bit different, isn't it?' George said about the single. 'It's more of a club record than the last few. Hopefully it should get us back some of our older fans. It's more *us*. More about sex.'

The journalist looked blank. 'How d'you mean?'

George was in a talkative mood. 'Well, "Wake Me Up" was sexual on a kind of soap opera level. I mean, it was very kind of kiss and cuddle whereas this is ... like ... more about sex ... closer to the way we are now. When we started, it was alright to say "18 year olds – they haven't had much sex", but at 22! People fall in love ... the rest of the time they have sex.'

He was giving the journalist plenty to quote from, though whether it had any substance I wasn't sure. I didn't usually sit in on these interviews, I only read the results after they'd been edited and polished. It certainly wasn't easy listening.

George started talking about their first American tour. It appeared to have given him a new viewpoint on a whole lot of things. 'I always thought I was incredibly ambitious. I thought nothing could stop us becoming the biggest stars in the world. But you get to the stage where you realise you're chasing your own tail. On that tour, we had to do things, stupid things, like meeting record company people and their families and doing the autograph bit. It was just horrible.'

There was no doubt about it, he was no longer enamoured of the idea of being the biggest group in the world. The fame he'd so longed for was becoming a burden. The falseness of Wham!'s image was telling on him. It was meant to be two young guys being themselves, but the more successful Wham! became, the more difficult George found it to keep on playing the role of a second Andrew. His impatience was understandable. It wasn't simply a matter of ego; he felt he was wasting his creativity on something false. He was still unsure of his real nature, but to go solo and write for himself was the best way to find out. I could see that breaking up Wham! and becoming George Michael wasn't a petulant whim, it was necessary to his mental well-being.

The photographer wandered into the room, his equipment round his neck. George looked up angrily. 'No not today. I'm sorry I just can't. I've got a cold. My nose is red and my hair is dreadful.'

The photographer looked to the journalist for an answer. She looked to me. 'Can't we just do one?'

I shook my head and the photographer wandered off again, sulking.

Andrew, still laid out on the sofa, yawned loudly and the journalist looked across at him. 'So you don't like America?'

I wanted to interrupt and remind them both that this interview was for an American magazine, but it wouldn't have made much difference. George was in full flow so I left him to it.

'It's a completely different ball game being a star over in the States. It's just full of completely sycophantic bullshit – at least in the UK there's some attachment to reality. There's no danger of turning into a Michael Jackson figure – locking yourself away and going a bit barmy.'

He pulled out a grubby-looking handkerchief and blew his nose – a real ear-blaster – then took a peep into the hanky to make sure it was all there. 'Ugh! That was huge ... Now, what were we talking about?'

Andrew suddenly spoke. 'Pop stars like to attach a mystique – a cosmic importance – to what they do. Onstage that's fine – it's all part of being a performer – but offstage it's stupid.'

I was uncertain what he meant but George understood. 'Yeah – we've always approached things in terms of show-business and entertainment, without attaching it to our personalities.'

The photographer came back into the room, still hopeful of a shot.

'No-o-o-o!!!' George yelled, like shouting at a wet dog about to shake over the guests. 'I've got a cold for God's sake. Look ...' He pulled out his hanky and blew another monster blast. 'Phllab-phlutter-gerspaaaschterblughhhhhh!'

The cameraman gave up and put the lens cap on his camera.

Andrew yawned.

26 INVITATION

I'd always presumed, if I finally got an invitation for Wham! to play in Beijing it would be something formal – a letter on headed paper from a government department, something with a seal on it, something delivered by messenger from the embassy in London, perhaps with a military band marching up to our offices blowing bugles and banging drums. But the Chinese played me at my own game.

At the beginning of March, having spent eighteen months going backwards and forwards to Beijing, avoiding questions that could result in a negative reply and proposing instead scenarios that started with the word 'if', I came out with my final one over yet another lunch at the Great Wall Hotel.

'*If* you were to invite Wham! to play a concert at the People's Gymnasium, it would be really nice if it were to be on April 7th.'

Without even referring to Zhou, the interpreter told me, 'There will be one important condition; you must do nothing to publicise the event within China.'

As I nodded my acceptance, Zhou smiled.

'It's agreed then,' the interpreter told me.

That afternoon I flew to Singapore. Before the Chinese could change their minds I wanted the news announced all over the world. I called Jazz in London and told him, 'It's fixed. Get all the press you can.'

He wasted no time; when I woke up next morning it was on the front page of the newspaper hung on the door knob of my hotel room.

I'd gambled that the Chinese really *had* meant to invite us. But in just the same way as I'd avoided a formal question, the Chinese had avoided a formal invitation – it had been delivered with nothing more than Zhou's smile. Since it was now headline news all over the world I presumed they wouldn't dare backtrack, but I still wasn't totally sure.

To make certain, I played one last game of 'never ask yes or no'. When I got back to London I telexed Beijing asking for a plan of the Workers' Stadium with the seating laid out as it would be on April 7th. Two days later the plan was couriered to me. It showed the stadium set up for a concert rather than a basketball game and on the stage area was written the word Wham!.

The concert was confirmed but we'd forgotten about the cost.

To do this concert we had to pay for everything – from the hire of the concert hall to the cost of printing the tickets – yet we had to donate the income from ticket sales to a Chinese charity. There would be diplomatic banquets to welcome the group and facilities would be provided for the world's press. The Chinese would decide how much to spend on all these things but it was Wham! who would foot the bill. On top of this there would be the normal cost of taking a major rock group and its equipment to a country on the other side of the world where nothing could be hired locally. The entire trip had to be financed by Wham! themselves.

Jazz and I were faced with an immediate bill of half a million dollars – for the band, the crew, the wages, the transport, the hire of lighting and sound equipment. So we called Paul Russell, the new managing director at CBS, 'Can we borrow five hundred thousand dollars, please? We need it by tomorrow morning.'

Amazingly, Paul agreed to consider it, but only if we agreed to make a full-length film of the event which CBS could sell as a video.

Jazz and I went away and worked out the cost. It would be another half million. With three weeks to go, we were trying to borrow a million dollars from a company which normally required a month's notice for a fifty pound loan. Yet the next morning Paul Russell called us at ten. 'The cheque's in reception. Come and pick it up.'

We now had the money, the crew and the musicians – the tour manager could start arranging things. But with only three weeks to go we had to find a suitable film director. On the chance of coming up with a movie good enough for cinema release, Jazz wanted to use a feature film director. My father having been a documentary film director, I knew a little about the subject. I said I doubted someone from features could cope unless they also had experience of documentaries.

'In that case,' Jazz said, 'why not use Lindsay Anderson?'

I couldn't think of anyone in the world more likely to add to our difficulties in hurriedly putting together this complicated trip. Nor could I think of anyone more likely to dislike Wham!'s happy-go-lucky view of the world. Lindsay Anderson had a reputation for being difficult and complex; permanently dissatisfied with both himself and most of the people around him.

For someone like Jazz who was both a movie buff and instinctively left-wing, I could see Lindsay's appeal. For me it was different: I'd known him since I was ten. He'd been one of a group of documentary film directors working together out of a building in Soho Square in London. My father had been another.

Later, after he'd made *This Sporting Life* and *If*, Lindsay had become the most famous of the directors to emerge from this group, something of a cinematic superstar, but to me he was simply the person I'd always known; amusing, cantankerous, sometimes brilliant, sometimes boorish, with an Oxbridge background yet a devout left-wing activist; always angry with life. And in all these things he was almost a twin for my own father, which is probably why they found themselves in the same film company doing the same job.

Lindsay would hate it when he realised Wham!'s reason for playing in China was no more than publicity; he would want to make his movie political and provocative. But Jazz called him anyway.

Lindsay agreed at once. He wanted to cover the tour in a massive way, with four separate film crews each capable of working on their own without him, each with a top cameraman. It was the reverse of the technique he'd used to make his successful documentaries – the concept of the tight-knit crew. On this project he wasn't going to be a documentary director; he was going to be a Hollywood mogul – Francis Ford Coppola making *Apocalypse Now*.

The film would double the cost of Wham!'s trip to China but CBS wouldn't fund us without it. Having gone chasing after Lindsay there was now no time left to look for someone else. We had no option but to go ahead.

In the middle of March, three weeks before the show was due to take place, I was back in Beijing and bumped into Lew Mon Hung.

'Zhao's son says you should get publicity for your concert inside China,' he told me. 'Some people in government agree, others say keep it quiet. Do you want me to help you get press?'

To begin with I'd believed what I'd told the Chinese authorities, namely, I didn't care if China stayed as tightly shut as ever, this concert was simply for promotional purposes in the West. It was this that had sold them on the idea, but as the date got nearer I began to get interested in what effect the event might have on young Chinese people if only they knew about it.

Professor Rolf too had been trying to persuade me I should publicise the event within China, so I contacted Chuen, the pipe-smoking student at Beijing University, and asked if he could help spread news of the event in the university paper and on notice-boards.

Soon, rumours about it began to spread from Beijing to other cities. Articles about the concert appeared in independent newspapers in Canton and Shanghai and I was told that one of them had been closed by the authorities. To begin with I was worried the publicity might cause the event to be cancelled, but when I thought about the amount of international press we'd received I realised it would be almost impossible for the Chinese to pull out at this stage. From the first day it was announced, the story of Wham! going to China had been non-stop front page news throughout the world, and every day Connie milked the media for more. When it finally took place there were going to be journalists and photographers from every major newspaper in the world.

Nevertheless, to protect the event even further I went to see the British ambassador in Beijing, Richard Evans, and persuaded him to attend. This gave me enough pressure to persuade the Chinese that they should reciprocate with a member of the Central Committee. With this parity of people attending, the Chinese government announced they would recognise the concert as an official cultural exchange, the first since Margaret Thatcher's historic meeting with the Chinese leadership at which it was decided to return Hong Kong to China in 1997.

Obviously the Chinese authorities were still hoping to 'contain' the event in one concert hall of fifteen thousand 'safe' young communists and keep news of it out of the Chinese newspapers. It was for outside eyes only. And the awful truth was – no-one in China had ever heard of Wham!.

This was something I wanted to conceal from the hundreds of Western journalists who would attend the concert so I hatched a plan to make the Chinese attending the concert familiar with the music.

Mostly they would be well-behaved young people given permission to attend by their local cadre. They would be there because they were inquisitive, not because they knew the music. I decided to take a well-known Beijing pop singer to Hong Kong and make a cassette of her singing Wham'!s songs in Chinese.

Lew Mon Hung organised it for me. On one side of the cassette were the Chinese versions of Wham!'s songs and on the other side the original versions. We would give two free copies of this with every ticket sold so that before they came to the show the audience could learn the songs and also have a spare cassette. By this method, tickets wouldn't only go to the privileged few with spare cash. Tickets were being sold at the same price as the cost of a cassette in a record shop. If someone couldn't afford a ticket, they could borrow some money, buy a ticket, collect two free cassettes and sell one in the market to recoup their outlay. This too would help spread the word about Wham!.

Lew asked for an exorbitant sum to cover the costs of recording and copying the cassettes, much more than it could actually cost. 'This whole thing only happen because of me. You think is because of Japanese film-producer, or your friend the professor, but not so. Only because I speak to the Prime Minister son.'

It was more likely to have been a combination of all three of them – Rolf had introduced me to Wu; Lew was friendly with the Prime Minister's son; the Japanese had introduced me to Zhou Renkai.

Since I had no way of telling who had been the most important, I decided to give him what he asked for.

'It's a good price,' he insisted.

And for him, it certainly was.

27 TEARS

Two weeks before Wham! set off to make history in China, George made some for himself. It was at the Ivor Novello Awards, at the Grosvenor House ballroom in London.

Unlike other industry award events the Ivors are aimed squarely at songs and songwriters, not record producers or video makers, nor even artists. Having eaten, drunk and gossiped for two hours, it was time for the cream of the music industry to watch the opening of envelopes. Best International Hit went to Duran Duran; Best Film Theme to Paul McCartney, and then came the one we'd been waiting for – Best Song of the Year.

Elton John, who was opening the envelope, deliberately made an awkward job of it, fumbling it, taking more time than was necessary, reading the result to himself before finally coming out with it ...

'George Michael!'

George went onstage to take the award, the youngest person ever to receive an Ivor. Elton stepped back to the mike and said, 'George Michael is the greatest song-writer of his generation – in the league of Paul McCartney.'

And then George cried.

Some people said he faked his tears, but I'm sure he didn't. George could fake a laugh (he faked one nearly every time he was photographed, always producing the same, forced, toothy smile), but I'm certain he didn't fake his crying. He always kept his emotions under tight control, and tears, once they start, can so easily get out of hand. If anything, I felt he'd been trying to keep them bottled up but hadn't quite managed it.

Anyway, I was quite touched.

A couple of weeks later George showed more unexpected emotion. In Hong Kong, Wham! were set to play two shows before they went to

Beijing. These two performances had been arranged to subsidise the cost of the concerts in China and also acted as good warm-up gigs.

We were in the Meriden, not the hotel of my choice, but because our tour manager had found the best deal there I'd forsaken my usual suite at the Hilton. The venue was just down the road – the Coliseum – Hong Kong's best indoor stadium. Apart from the twenty or so journalists who were travelling with us, dozens of other news crews and journalists were turning up from all over the world, pestering me and Jazz for interviews in lieu of George and Andrew who would do none.

On the first morning, the hotel manager complained to me that George had been rude to a woman in the coffee shop, a hotel guest. I guessed she'd come pestering him with dumb questions or requests for an autograph when he was sitting over his morning coffee. I was sympathetic to his having been abrupt to her, yet I was surprised; he was usually patient and calm with people like that. But perhaps he was tired from the previous day's flight, or hungover, or had something else on his mind.

In the end it seemed to be the latter for he got more and more touchy throughout the day. Ten minutes before the evening performance was due to begin he called Jazz and me into the dressing room and told us, 'No photographs. I want you to ban all photographers.'

George has often said he sees his managers as 'there to do his bidding'. Jazz and I accepted that, among the thousand other things a manager had to do every day, a bit of 'doing George's bidding' was necessary to keep things running smoothly. So we told George, 'OK – no photographers.'

George usually came out with these requests when he was feeling his most insecure. He appeared to have a deep psychological fear of photographs. He never admitted it, but I think he felt a fraud about his pop star good looks – afraid, perhaps, that one day an off-the-cuff photograph might reveal the podgy bespectacled schoolboy he'd once been.

Jazz and I went off to the bar for a drink. The show was due to start in ten minutes and the photographers had all been given photo-passes. Since there was no pit for them to work in we'd told them to sit wherever they liked and with twenty thousand people now in their seats it would be pretty impractical to start walking around throwing them out. Moreover, there had been no ban on fans taking in their own cameras so there were probably another two or three thousand amateur photographers inside. When pictures appeared in the next day's paper and George complained, we would tell him the newspapers must have bought them from a fan. And if the pictures were no good, and he complained about that too, it would excuse us even further – 'Should have let the professionals stay.'

After ten minutes in the bar, the show was still not under way. We had another drink and waited another ten minutes then Jazz drifted off to the dressing room to see what was holding things up. He didn't come back, so after another ten minutes, with the crowd getting restless, I wandered off in search of information.

I found one of the band in the dressing-room corridor. 'Seems George is having a bit of a nervous breakdown,' he told me. 'He's crying and says he can't possibly perform.'

Good artists need to have the odd unexpected emotional breakdown; it's part and parcel of being creative. George was simply confirming my confidence in his artistic nature, and since he had many able persuaders around him – Andrew, Connie, Jazz, the band – all capable of getting him onstage, I left them to it and went to the bar for another drink.

Despite my confidence it was quite a long time before I heard the first few screams, the ones that signalled the band's arrival onstage. Then I heard the deafening ones for George and Andrew.

I left the bar and went into the auditorium. Wham! were playing as well as ever, so with the gig under way I wandered off to have dinner at Dateline, a little club I knew on the Hong Kong side, then back to Kowloon and the Canton disco to drink myself into a happy state of retirement.

The next day I got up at eight, strolled along the seafront and took the Star Ferry across to the Hong Kong side where I visited my favourite bookshop; I had the feeling a week in China would require some good reading. Having made my choice, I started a new Anthony Burgess over coffee in the Mandarin lobby, then read it through lunch at Le Pierrot.

When I got back to the hotel Jazz and Connie were running round looking for me. 'Have you seen the *Daily Mirror*?'

It was hardly likely I would have done; it was only three in the afternoon and in London just eight in the morning, but already someone in London had telexed Jazz with the news that the *Mirror* had run a story about George having a breakdown – which, they said, put Wham!'s Beijing concert in doubt.

John Blake, the show-business editor for the *Daily Mirror*, one of twenty journalists travelling with us, had got himself an exclusive. The night before, Connie had insisted to the journalists that the late start was caused by the keyboard player. Whether or not they believed her, I didn't know, but either way John Blake was the only one to break ranks and file the story, which seemed not at all beneficial to the event in China.

Luckily we had a lawyer with us – Tony Russell was making the trip with his wife. So Jazz, Tony and I got ourselves into a conference room at the hotel and called Robert Maxwell, the owner of the *Daily Mirror*.

Tony told him straight out, 'First, the story is untrue and we'll be suing for libel. Secondly, it's harmful to political relations between the two countries. Wham!'s concert is an official cultural exchange and our Ambassador will be attending it. If your paper harms the event in any way, I'm sure he'll report back to London.'

What he intimated, though didn't actually say, was that it could jeopardise the knighthood Robert Maxwell so longed for. It was a clever mix of legal threat and personal intimidation and a little later Maxwell called John Blake and yelled loudly.

The next morning we flew up to Beijing, Wham! and their management in first class, the crew and the journalists in economy. The journalists – friends and competitors alike – were together in their usual heavy-drinking block of seats. Only John Blake sat alone, ostracised, with two empty seats next to him in the front row of economy.

We arrived in Beijing in a jovial mood – over a hundred of us – George and Andrew, their parents and friends, the road crew and the journalists. Out of all of them, I was the only one who'd been to China before and as we stood in line to go through immigration it occurred to me that this was the first time I'd ever been there with an officially issued visa from the Chinese embassy in London.

It did me little good. As everyone else was waved easily through I was confronted by a sour-faced officer who studied my passport with great deliberation. Finally he handed it to a woman officer standing next to him who led me to a small room.

After leaving me alone for a few minutes the woman reappeared with a dozen or so passports which she scattered across a table some six feet in front of me. 'Which one is yours?' she asked, in clear but pleasantly accented English.

I picked mine out easily, though instead of telling me I'd done so she left it where it was and picked up a file. 'Now then, Mr Bell ... This file contains everything about you and your group. For instance, let's start with *you* ...'

She searched in the file for a moment and pulled out a typewritten sheet. 'You share a house in London with two friends – Allan Soh and Donavon Nelson. Your bank is Barclay Bank in Soho Square, London. Your house is on lease, you don't own it outright ... Right?' She paused. 'And you spend a lot of money on travel and eating in restaurants. Why do you spend so much?'

Whatever this was about I decided to resign myself to it. 'It's the music business,' I explained. 'It just seems to push me into extravagance.'

She returned my sheet to the file. 'Well, it's not really our business. We're just letting you know we have a very good file on you and your group – political viewpoint, credit rating, tax return, newspaper report, that sort of thing. And I notice you always get your visa at same travel shop in Kowloon?' She waved the file in my face. 'Just letting you know, that's all.'

Two minutes later I was back with the others collecting the luggage. There didn't appear to have been much point to my interview; perhaps the authorities thought it served some sort of psychological purpose, and maybe it did. I was strangely nervous for the rest of the time I was in Beijing and I never again went to the travel shop in Kowloon.

28 THIS SPORTING LIFE

'**B**loody Chinese – bloody English – bloody road crew – bloody everybody!'

It was Lindsay versus the world.

'It's people really,' he grumbled. 'That's the real problem. Bloody people!'

From the moment he'd arrived in China, Lindsay had turned into a tyrant, stalking round in a hugely bad mood until he fell over on the Great Wall and twisted his ankle. After that he was confined to a wheelchair where he grew ever more malignant, ordering his film crews around with bestial shouts of foul-temper bizarrely interspersed with hearty laughter. Even on his best days he was always grumbling.

The embassy were to give us a party – it was something I'd arranged based on the fact that the ambassador, Richard Evans, was going to attend the concert. Lindsay latched onto it with glee. He was determined to get shots inside the embassy grounds of members of the dying British Empire which he could intermix with scenes of Red China.

Lindsay had trouble getting his film crew into the embassy grounds so by the time he was ready to start tracking his camera around the party-goers his mood was worse than ever. He was eager to dig up people who spoke with accents last heard in the days of the Raj. And he actually managed to find some.

'A pop star's manager, are you?' said a middle-aged gent in a decaying white suit. 'How a-a-a-a-wfully interesting. And what exactly does one have to do for them? Change their nappies?'

Annoying as he was, this relic from the British Empire had hit it on the head. It was strange – he was so unmodern, so unworldly, yet so instinctively right. 'And what does one call the person one manages?' he asked. 'One's client? One's protégé? One's bank balance? Haw, haw, haw.'

Lindsay was having a field day.

'I've heard about groupies,' a braying woman told me. 'Will there be any here in China?'

'I doubt it. To be honest Wham! aren't really known here. It was a bit of a coup getting them in.'

Her husband butted in. 'Well, Sybil, maybe you could be a groupie for the afternoon. Oh haw, haw, haw.'

Again, he was pretty near the mark, for Sybil was undoubtedly undressing Andrew in her mind if not already sniffing round his genitals.

A man approached me holding a packet of cheese crisps, a good few of which he crammed into his mouth before he spoke. He looked somewhere between Greek and Filipino but spoke American. 'You're the manager, aren't you? Listen – we really approve of this Wham! thing, like we really approved of the Hong Kong agreement. We see Hong Kong as a Trojan Horse being taken within the walls of China.'

'That's the second time I've heard that,' I told him. 'Some students at Beijing University said it. Who do you mean by "we"?'

He filled his mouth with more crisps (they appeared to be the essential fuel of his conversation). 'Government policy-makers.'

'Which government?' I asked. 'America's? China's? What nationality are you?'

'Can't tell you that,' he said, screwing up his empty crisp packet and dropping it on the lawn. 'I just wanted to tell you, there are a lot of people in government who don't believe for a moment that Hong Kong will be subjugated to the will of the old guard of the Central Committee. They think it will be a source of new thinking that will slowly permeate China. And we'd also like to see more publicity within China for your Wham! concert. It may seem a small thing to you, but cumulatively, events like this can revolutionise the way young people in China perceive things.'

He was lecturing me and I didn't like it. 'Wham! just want to play a concert,' I told him brusquely. 'They aren't interested in changing the world.'

I moved away and found myself next to one of the embassy's junior attachés. 'Who's that man I just escaped from?' I asked. 'What does he do?'

The junior attaché looked disapproving. 'CIA, I think. He imports trouble! Such a pain, those people.'

In the following days Andrew became engaged in a running battle with the British tabloid photographers – dozens of them. They followed

Wham! wherever they went – Tiananmen Square, the Great Wall, the Forbidden City, the toilet. They were *really* intrusive.

Andrew's answer was to do his best to make sure they didn't get a decent picture. He wore dark glasses, turned up his collar, frowned ferociously and turned away when he saw them about to snap. The trouble was, he often turned right into the lens of another photographer, waiting on the off-chance. The resulting shot would look angry, ugly and blurred – certainly not flattering.

George, on the other hand, resigned himself to the inevitable. However many photographers there were, he posed patiently, stretching a plastic smile across his feelings and giving them something they could use.

'Andrew's his own worst enemy,' he told me. 'When he gets home and sees the pictures of himself he'll understand why he should have been more co-operative.'

This was George the career pop star, for when it came to meeting boring dignitaries he showed no such patience. He realised at once there was no benefit in meeting them, nor any downside in refusing. Andrew, on the other hand, found time for all of them, shaking hands endlessly, making friends wherever he could.

As did Connie. Wherever she went she was photographed, mostly by other tourists – flouncing across Tiananmen Square, posing in front of Chairman Mao's portrait, organising photos of Wham! on top of the Great Wall, parading round the Forbidden City followed by Tony Russell and his wife and other members of the Wham! party. For the Chinese who'd been delegated to look after us – the interpreters, the drivers, the guides – it wasn't George and Andrew who were of interest, it was Connie and her super flamboyance. Allan once nicknamed her Miss Fluorescence, and in Beijing's drabness that's just what she became.

'What do you think of China?' she was asked by an officially sanctioned government journalist.

'Dahlink,' she throbbed back. 'It's a country of sex gods.'

I doubt the quote made the papers. 'Sex and God' were the country's two most forbidden subjects.

The night before the concert the government gave an official state banquet at which Wham! had to meet five hundred dull dignitaries. The food was mostly inedible – fish lips, chicken's feet, duck's knees, that sort of thing.

I tried sucking on a chicken's foot but it was like chewing rubber. Another dish was slightly better. 'What is it?' I asked a waiter.

'Steamed pancreas of pig.'

Like most of the people in our party I was already planning my real dinner of the evening – something later in the hotel coffee shop.

When he'd organised the guest list Zhou hadn't consulted me, yet I spotted not only the Japanese film people but Lew Mon Hung too. Lew came over. 'It was me fix all this. It's OK – yes?'

Mr Porodyusa and Mr Zhou had both told me much the same but I'd given up caring who'd done what in relation to Wham!'s visit. I was in an excellent mood, glowing with pleasure from something I'd seen that afternoon.

In a market place I'd watched as money changed hands for Wham! cassettes (the ones we'd given away with the tickets), and earlier in the evening when I was being pedalled back to my hotel in a trishaw I'd heard Wham! music drifting out of a bar. It was very satisfying to see Western-style hype working so well in this bastion of censorship.

'To honourable guests from United Kingdom, the Chinese people would like to propose a toast ...'

Another dull dignitary – poor man. Around him swirled a messy banquet of several hundred people, most of them already unsteadily drunk, many of them wandering round the hall chatting to friends. He was the eleventh or twelfth person to propose a similarly dull toast, and as the number of toasts increased, people's interest in them diminished and the chatter grew louder.

From the Wham! benches there was an ever-growing level of raucous laughter, the sheer volume of rice wine making everyone feel good despite the awfulness of the event. Actually, the rice wine was pretty awful too but I'd discovered a trick. On the buffet table were dishes of plum sauce to eat with various crispy fried things. A teaspoon of that with a tumbler of rice wine made quite a tasty cocktail and I'd soon put away five or six of them.

Someone tapped me on my shoulder and when I turned round ...

'Rolf ...!' (I almost didn't recognise him, his wonderful sweep of silver hair had been reduced to a dark-coloured crew-cut) '... I thought you couldn't come here?'

'I never said that! I simply said, Professor Rolf Heinrich *Neuber* might encounter some difficulties. Henry *Nueber*, the English journalist, has no such problems.'

With short hair he looked extraordinarily Chinese.

'Don't worry,' I told him. 'No-one's going to recognise you with that ghastly haircut. Are you going to join us at the top table?'

'No – I'm happy where I am – with a table of journalists, mostly Chinese, some of them on the dissident side. Have you had anything much in the Chinese press?'

'I'm not really meant to, but I've got a friend at a local university who's been helping.'

'I know.'

He pointed to his table of friends and among them was Chuen, my pipe-smoking friend from the university. Rolf took me across and introduced me to the others, who included the strange American I'd met at the embassy party, the one who 'imported trouble'.

'This is Leon,' Rolf told me. 'He's an attaché at the Greek embassy.'

'I thought you were American,' I told him.

'Like Rolf, I'm lots of things. Will Wham! sing "Freedom"?'

'I think so. But it probably doesn't mean the same to them as it means to you.'

'Never mind. It's a good title.'

We were interrupted by Zhou, without his translator, telling us about problems at the venue. 'Your crew too slow at gymnasium. Too many come to party. You must pay Chinese worker to help.'

I didn't believe him; he was just after money. I checked with our tour manager who was at the banquet and he called our stage manager who was at the venue. 'No problem,' he assured us. 'Everything's going fine.'

Zhou didn't agree and there was little I could do but pay up. If I didn't he would simply bring work at the venue to a halt. I doled out five hundred dollars for his mythical extra workers and went back to feasting.

Rolf said, 'I want to meet Lindsay Anderson.'

'I didn't know you'd even heard of him.'

'Of course I have. He made one of my favourite films – *This Sporting Life*. I was living in Bournemouth at the time. That film showed better than anything I've ever seen the way man's physical force can be organised and coordinated – the way those rugby teams played – so ruthless, so perfect.'

'You're sounding like a Nazi again.'

'But I'm not. Surely you know that.'

This wasn't the time for such portentous debate, the room was too raucous. I searched through the hubbub for Lindsay and found him hobbling around on crutches.

'I don't have time to run around meeting your business contacts,' he grumbled. 'We're in the middle of filming the minister and he's so drunk that if he stands up to make another toast he might fall flat on his face. I don't want to miss it.'

I dragged him over to Rolf and made him shake hands. Rolf said nothing, just smiled and stared into his face. Then Lindsay was off, back to the inebriated minister and his imminent topple into Wham!'s movie.

Rolf left me after that, but during the rest of the banquet, with hundreds of drunken people perambulating around the great hall, I saw him speak with both Lew Mon Hung and Mr Porodyusa. He was such a mystery.

When I next passed Lindsay he said, 'Interesting man.'

'But you didn't even speak to him.'

Lindsay shrugged. 'He had an interesting face.'

29

STAY IN YOUR SEATS

In the VIP box, I sat sandwiched between the British Ambassador and General Xiao Hua, a senior member of the Central Committee.

Below us the auditorium was packed with cameramen. In a roped-off area in front of the stage were more than seventy TV crews; behind them, two hundred stills photographers and hordes of international reporters.

This was normally a sports stadium. Now, the downstairs arena contained the stage, an area in front of it for TV crews and photographers, and then seats for four thousand. The next tier was seating for six thousand and above that were two more tiers of two thousand each. Behind the stage there was cheap seating for a thousand. Our VIP box was high up between the first and second tiers.

Every one of the fifteen thousand seats was filled with chattering young Chinese. In case their excitement should boil over, a thousand members of the People's Police stood round the walls downstairs, ready to stop trouble before it could start.

The lights went down, the audience cheered, the band came onstage, the first chord was struck and George and Andrew bounced out smiling and waving.

So this was it. The moment I'd spent eighteen months travelling backwards and forwards to China to witness. With seventy TV crews and two hundred photographers in front of them, Wham! were just twenty-four hours from being front page news in every paper in America. But instead of bursting into song as he was meant to, George hesitated. With all those cameramen and TV crews training their sights on him, he opened his mouth and not a sound came out.

Just a couple of days ago, he'd asked me, 'There won't be too many photographers will there?'

'Of course not,' I told him sarcastically. 'It'll just be you and fifteen thousand Chinese teenagers. Who'd be interested in taking a picture of that?'

He really hated photographers, and the sight of two hundred of them plus seventy video crews had caused something to happen he'd never experienced before. George – always overconfident, always cocky, never nervous – was experiencing his first attack of stage-fright.

With cameras flashing madly and TV crews following his every move he ran to the far side of the stage, clapping with the beat, trying to loosen himself up.

By now I was as nervous as George – when things went wrong he could be unpredictable – but he recovered quickly and somehow pushed out the first line, croaky but audible. Then the second line, stronger and more confident, and suddenly the stage-fright was gone. The show was on the road.

The next song was 'Club Tropicana'. George bounced round to the back of the stage, clapping his hands on the beat, encouraging the spectators seated behind the band to do the same. They hadn't a clue; they thought he wanted applause and politely gave it.

If the audience seemed interested rather than ecstatic, it was probably because of an announcement during the interval. An authoritarian Chinese voice had blared through the speakers, 'Stay in your seats. Don't dance!', and for the moment that's what they were doing, especially downstairs, intimidated by the sight of so many police and soldiers. But they were enthusiastic nonetheless and cheered hugely, letting out strange bursts of clapping which had no relevance to either the beat or the start and finish of songs. In the context of a normal pop concert, this show was never going to work, but as a bizarre event it was red hot.

By the end of four songs, I realised something strange was happening. The TV lights and camera flashes, which at a normal concert would be directed at the stage, were being directed at the audience. The world's media hadn't come to see Wham! play in Beijing, they'd come to see the Chinese *watching* Wham! play in Beijing.

'And now,' George announced, '"Bad Boys"!'

'Ba-ba-ba doo-wah,' chanted the backing girls, Pepsi and Shirley.

From our seat in the circle we could see the upper terraces. Away from the police and the prying cameras of journalists the upstairs audience was more boisterous. One big block, perhaps a thousand people, were foreigners with tickets from their embassies. By the end of 'Bad Boys' they were standing up and dancing. The Chinese near them took confidence in their numbers and copied them. Then scattered groups around the other upper tiers started to do the same. Some of them even got the hang of clapping on the beat, even learnt to scream when George or Andrew waved their butts.

Downstairs, though, the audience remained more careful of what they did. The film crew had turned hugely bright lights onto them. These Chinese kids probably didn't realise this was a documentary for CBS Records, they thought it was the secret police taking a filmed record of anyone who misbehaved.

'This song has been Number One in our country,' Andrew shouted. 'Let's hope one day it will be Number One in China too. "F-R-E-E-D-O-M"!'

Upstairs the groove was growing. With no in-built sense of self-control some of the Chinese kids were getting dangerously over-excited. People danced around the terraces, not with style and rhythm, but with manic swinging arms, pouring out energy like punk rockers on speed. It wasn't just the music that was driving them, it was a new-found sense of self-expression. Of freedom.

Below, the world's journalists were unable to see what was going on above them, but from the VIP box we had a perfect view. Thirty minutes had passed. Next to me the general from the Central Committee sat stony-faced and silent. The audience downstairs still behaved meekly, but upstairs, fuelled by the contingent from abroad, the audience was becoming more and more excited. On the other side of me our ambassador appeared equally unresponsive to what was going on. He knew all too well, if there were any complaints from the Chinese government it would be him on the receiving end.

'Careless Whisper' calmed the crowd for a moment but then Wham! crashed into 'Young Guns' with its sexy dance routine and catchy vocal riff, 'Da-doo-wah doo-wah.'

Some of the TV crews had escaped from their special area downstairs and were starting to climb up the terraces, roaming up and down steeply raked balconies, their handheld lights sucking up small groups of demented dancers like garden lights attracting whizzing night insects.

Downstairs, the impassive guards of the People's Police still prevented people from moving around or attempting to dance but upstairs there was no-one stopping what was going on. The few guards that were there watched bemused, enthused even, sometimes smiling as people jammed themselves into the pools of light that came from the handheld cameras.

"'Wake Me Up Before You – *GO! GO!*'" The upper tiers took George's yell on the last two words of his announcement as further encouragement to throw off their inhibitions. They began to throb magnificently – almost as well as the crowd at the Glasgow Apollo had done fifteen months earlier.

We were now forty-five minutes into the show. Downstairs the audience were still subdued, sitting politely, nervous of the filming and the lights. The stills cameramen, still held captive by security guards, were pivoting from side to side, looking up into the terraces, trying to see the bizarre goings-on, shielding their eyes from the lights of the downstairs film crew, searching for stories.

And all the time Wham! poured out the music.

As they reached the end of 'Wham! Rap', with just two numbers to go, a teenager downstairs started dancing in a distant corner, smoking a cigarette, drinking from a bottle of rice wine. He was grabbed by half a dozen of the People's Police and it caused a miniscule rumpus.

Just what the world's media had been looking for! They rushed to film it, leaping from their restricted area, the guards unable to contain them, competing with each other to shine lights on what was happening. Some of the stills photographers, finding themselves pushed back by the police, struggled with them so that the single drunken fan became the cause of a skirmish between photographers, TV crews and police, which of course was filmed by others.

"'I'm Your Man.'"

The band pounded into its last number, the last three minutes of the show. Downstairs, filmed by the TV crews, the police took away the lone dancer. Upstairs the kids jived on. Then the band hit the last chord and the houselights came up.

From all round the hall there was cheering but next to me General Xiao Hua looked shaken. The passionate reaction of the young Chinese in the upstairs terraces was new to him, as was the rumpus downstairs, and he didn't like it.

I wanted to have the entire audience on its feet for the encore, so being in the emperor's seat I stood up and applauded furiously. The general was forced to follow suit and so was our ambassador. Then everyone in the auditorium.

I'd decided to stand and clap till the band came back, then stay standing throughout the encore to keep the audience on its feet with me. But it didn't work.

George and Andrew had had enough. Playing a one-hour concert in such a bizarre atmosphere had taken its toll. They were back in the dressing-room recovering.

The next day we received international newspaper reports by telex. It was intriguing. On the front page of all the British tabloids was the story of the police beating up a boy for dancing.

It was a distortion of the truth. The incident had been right at the end of the concert and the boy had been drunk and probably abusive. Moreover, the guards had done no more to him than British police would do to a rowdy football fan.

Interestingly, the American papers had chosen not to write about that. Instead they concentrated on the audience's desire to learn what rock 'n' roll was about – 'Rock and roll history made in a riot of enthusiasm' – and particularly noted the subdued audience in the downstairs seats.

A lot of what they'd observed had been caused by that announcement before the show, 'Stay in your seats.'

It had been all my fault. Wham!'s warm-up act was Trevor, a break-dancer who had to perform for twenty minutes. I thought he wouldn't be able to hold the audience for that long so I'd told him, 'After the first couple of numbers, jump off the front of the stage and move among the audience dancing.'

It had caused a near riot. He was dressed in a flowing jump suit made of white parachute silk and he'd flowed right into the audience. They were all on their feet trying to copy his movements, swirling around him, kissing him, shaking his hand, terrifying the authorities who had never seen such subversive stuff. The order to stay seated had been the result.

I thought about the quiet man from the Central Committee who'd sat next to me – General Xiao Hua. (In English his name meant 'Little Flower' and I couldn't help wondering whether American troops would have been equally prepared to storm the beaches of Iwo Jima if their commanding officer had been called 'Little Flower' rather than McArthur.)

He was pleasant enough, in an impeccably cut Western suit. Before the show he'd told me his daughter had just come back from university in America and had brought a Michael Jackson record with her. She'd been teaching him how to dance and he'd enjoyed it.

After the show his face was filled with concern and he didn't talk to me again. He'd been closely watching what had gone on upstairs and he hadn't liked it, especially the way the foreign contingent had influenced the normally well-behaved Chinese youth around them.

He'd just had a lesson in how subversive Western pop culture could be. The dangers of introducing it to China's young people must have been all too clear to him.

30 THE LAST POST

'**O**ne of the trumpet-players is giving me trouble.'

Jake, our tour manager, woke me earlier than I wanted. It was only eight and I'd been hoping to sleep till midday.

'What d'you mean – "trouble"?'

'It's Raoul. He says he can't travel. He says he's possessed.'

I managed to blink myself awake and remembered that today the crew and most of the touring party were travelling to Canton to prepare for the second gig.

'He probably took the wrong drugs,' I said. 'Tell him this is work, not a holiday. Fill him up with coffee and give him to one of the security men to deal with.'

After that I went back to sleep till early afternoon. We'd celebrated heavily after the show and there'd been many previous days without sleep to be made up for.

Late afternoon, Jazz and I went with George and Andrew to a TV studio to make a satellite broadcast to New York for *Good Morning America*. Afterwards we went back to the hotel looking forward to a quiet, unpressured dinner but there at the reception desk was Zhou. He rushed at me jabbering while our interpreter tried to keep up with him. She was Leng Leng, a Chinese–American student, the first interpreter we'd been able to trust, but what she now told us we could hardly believe. One of our musicians had hijacked the plane to Canton.

Zhou's story was that Raoul, the moody trumpet player, had gone mad on the plane and rushed the cockpit with a knife. The plane had gone into an emergency dive and landed at the nearest military airport. Raoul had been subdued and driven to hospital accompanied by Dave Moulder, one of our security men. Then the plane had flown on to Canton.

It sounded serious and unexplainable, but it was over. Whatever had happened had been dealt with; we could play the gig in Canton with one less trumpeter. But as Jazz and I were about to go to the restaurant Dave Moulder appeared. He was our best security man – six foot two and sixteen stone – a mercenary in Africa, a member of the Saudi royal bodyguard and cool in the toughest emergency. Dave had never been known to be ruffled by anything but now he was distraught.

'I need a drink,' he told us. 'I've had one of the worst days of my life.'

That morning, when he'd been told to pick up Raoul and get him to the airport, Dave had found him in a strangely vacant state. 'I'm possessed by the devil,' Raoul had told him.

Half carrying him, half pushing, Dave had got him to the airport and onto the plane but as soon as the plane was off the ground Raoul had pulled out a penknife and shoved it into his own stomach.

'I jumped forward to stop him damaging himself,' Dave told us, 'but he started struggling violently. Two other people rushed forward to help but he was more than we could handle. He was demented.'

A stewardess, thinking it was a hijack, rushed to tell the flight crew. The pilot put the plane into a steep dive dropping twenty thousand feet in seconds which threw Raoul and the people struggling with him crashing to the back of the plane. Then the plane headed back to Beijing and made an emergency landing at a military airport.

As the plane came to a halt, police and medics rushed on board to subdue Raoul with tranquillisers, but he kept on struggling. Eventually Dave and the medics got him enough under control to carry him to a waiting ambulance. 'I've killed myself,' he told Dave. 'I'm dead. The body you're holding is an exorcised shell.'

Not yet completely subdued, Raoul refused to get into the ambulance until someone fetched his trumpet from the plane. Then, still insisting he was dead, he allowed himself to be lain on the floor of the ambulance with his head sticking out the back door.

'As it moved away,' Dave told us, 'he played The Last Post.'

At the hospital, even though there was a penknife sticking out of his stomach, Raoul refused to register as a patient. Afraid the tranquilliser would wear off, Dave decided to bring him back to the hotel.

'It was the only thing I could do. He's upstairs now. Asleep.'

*

I called an after-hours emergency number at the British Embassy.

'We need help,' I told them.

Fifteen minutes later it arrived – three people from the British consulate with a doctor from the Australian Embassy, the only one they could get hold of at that time of night.

The doctor went to inspect Raoul in his room. 'He's *just* conscious,' he told us when he came back. 'His wound is superficial but his mental state isn't. He's in extreme psychosis. I've given him more tranquilliser but when he wakes up properly he'll be intensely dangerous.'

'How long will that be?' I asked.

'About four hours. Before then you'll need to get him into a top-security mental hospital.'

'How are we meant to do that?' Jazz wanted to know. 'In Beijing, in the middle of the night?'

The doctor shrugged. 'I've no idea – it normally takes four weeks but you've got four hours. The Chinese don't commit people to mental institutions lightly. Regulations are strict, and for foreigners they're even stricter. They don't want to create a diplomatic incident by institutionalising a foreigner.'

He wrote out a note outlining his qualifications and saying Raoul must be committed immediately. Then he left.

One of the three men from the consulate asked, 'By the way, he *is* British, isn't he?'

And then we remembered – Raoul was the only non-British person in the band. 'No. He's Portuguese.'

And they too disappeared into the night.

Jazz and I were left standing in the lobby of the hotel at 1.30 in the morning with three hours to go until a potential lunatic woke up and started terrorising the hotel.

Then we were faced with another lunatic – money-crazy Zhou was back in the lobby, shouting.

'I need money. When plane does nose-dive, old lady have heart attack. Now in hospital – two hundred dollars a day. China Airlines need twenty thousand dollars for cost of come back to Beijing. Ambulance for your musician was one hundred dollars...'

He was having a field day but I'd had enough. 'Shut up, you greasy goat,' I snapped. 'We've got no more money for you. Moreover, you're in big trouble. You're directly responsible for inviting a maniac to China. He's nearly killed a plane load of innocent people and now he's back in this hotel.'

Zhou went red with anger. He didn't understand what I was saying, he was just furious at the way I was saying it. But when his translator explained what I'd said Zhou's face changed from red to white.

Encouraged, Jazz joined in. 'The doctor says if he's not in a mental hospital in three hours' time he might kill someone, and if he does *you* will be directly responsible. You'll probably end up in jail.'

Zhou's interpreter (almost certainly an officer in the secret service) appeared to confirm to him that what we'd said might be true – Zhou could well end up bearing the responsibility. And five minutes later he was helping Jazz and me, phoning round the city's mental hospitals.

At first it seemed an impossible task but after an hour Zhou said he'd cracked it. At 4 a.m. an ambulance arrived with a doctor dressed like a baker come to deliver the morning bread – white overalls with a French beret. Ten minutes later Raoul was in a straitjacket in a wheelchair being trundled through the lobby.

But now there was another problem. The mental hospital wouldn't accept patients prior to official committal proceedings unless the patient was accompanied by a family member, though for foreigners a person of the same nationality could be substituted. We knew no-one who was Portuguese but decided any European face would do. So, because Jazz and I had to leave for Canton with George and Andrew first thing in the morning, we went and woke Dave.

'No!' he protested. 'I can't be with Raoul any more. I'll go mad.'

'That won't matter,' I told him. 'You'll be in the madhouse anyway.'

After they'd left, Jazz and I started worrying about Dave. He was over-tired and distraught. Under strain, it wasn't inconceivable he might take a fit and start smashing up the hospital.

'We could all end up in China for years,' said Jazz, so around 9 a.m., while I took George and Andrew to the airport, he decided to go to the hospital with Leng Leng and try to retrieve him.

Zhou insisted his secret service interpreter go too, so the three of them took a taxi to the mental hospital an hour away on the far side of Beijing where they found Raoul sound asleep at the far end of the ward. Dave, though, was anything *but* asleep. He was highly agitated – pacing up and down and hitting the wall with his fist as shuffling mental patients mumbled at him and fingered his clothing.

Jazz grabbed hold of him. 'Come on, we're getting you out of here.' But as they headed out of the building a doctor chased after them with Zhou's interpreter.

'You can't leave,' he insisted. 'One of you must stay with your patient. It's the law.'

Jazz, Dave and Leng Leng strode on and got into the taxi but the doctor rushed up and stood in front of the car. 'You're Chinese', he told the driver, 'you must not obey these foreigners. I am a doctor and I order you not to leave.'

The taxi driver turned off his engine and the doctor wrenched open the door. Jazz, Dave and Leng Leng leapt out the other side of the car and marched off down the road.

They were in the middle of nowhere, an hour's drive from the airport and God knows how long on foot, but then the taxi driver turned up. The fare on his clock was more than a week's wages – doctor or no doctor he couldn't afford to lose that much.

Sixty minutes later they were at the airport with me and Wham!, just in time to catch the flight. But there was one more obstacle – Zhou was there too, alone and hysterical.

'The hospital take my man,' he told us. 'They make him stay till trumpet player get better.' He pointed a finger at Dave. '*You* should be there, not him.'

Dave moved forwards threateningly but we held him back.

Then we headed for the gate, Zhou running behind us hurling Chinese abuse. But without his lackeys he was unable to do much and we had Leng Leng, our pretty interpreter, to charm us past all obstacles and out through the departure gate. China was over.

There was still Canton to come, but it was a breeze. The Canton concert was like something in London or Manchester – the kids knew the songs, knew the routines, had been receiving albums from Hong Kong. The truth was, as soon as that plane took off from Beijing we were free. The concert we'd worked so hard for was over. Zhou and his secret police were behind us.

Two days later, at Hong Kong airport, Jazz and I said goodbye to each other, both heading for a week's holiday – Jazz in the Far East, me in

Mexico. Earlier, over breakfast at the hotel, we'd sat poring over endless reports from around the world about the Beijing concert. Wham! were everywhere – newspapers, magazines, TV news, TV interviews.

Fifteen hours later I went through immigration in LA. It was the same terminal I'd been through two months earlier when 'Careless Whisper' was at Number One yet no-one knew the group's name.

I passed easily through immigration but when I reached customs I was confronted by the same officer who'd given me a fifty-minute body search on my previous visit. 'Hey man,' he said, cheerfully, 'you're the guy who manages Wham!, aren't you? We've been watching them non-stop on the news all week – ABC, NBC, CBS – whatever channel you turn on, there they are. Have you got any records on you? My daughter's crazy about them.'

By the time I'd stopped and pulled out a couple of autographed singles there were other people asking too.

'Wham! is it? Hey, they're huge.'

'Congratulations, buddy. We love them.'

'How the hell did you pull off that thing in China?'

It was just as we'd planned. A week of non-stop TV newscasts had given us everything we'd hoped for.

Wham! were the best known and most talked about group in the world.

PART III
APRIL 1985

31

HAPPY BIRTHDAY

'So far we haven't made a penny.'

Rolf looked surprised. 'Why on earth not? I thought managing pop groups made millions.'

'I only wish it did. Unfortunately management doesn't work like that. Unless the group does a major tour, the money just dribbles in slowly. But Wham! don't want to do long tours. In fact, George wants to finish the whole thing and go solo.'

From the look on his face Rolf was more upset by the news than I was. 'That's terrible. After all the work you've done. There must be a way of capitalising on it before it finishes?'

It was April in Southern Mexico. To wind down after the excitements of Beijing, Rolf had invited me to his house for the weekend. Mid-afternoon he'd met me at Villahermosa airport in tropical heat but we were now in the air-conditioned coolness of his limo.

'Anyway,' he said, changing the subject, 'happy birthday! Forty-six, isn't it?'

I pouted, not too thrilled about reaching such a great age. 'Where's your house? Is that where we're going?'

He nodded. 'About sixty miles north, in the hills behind the coast, quite near the town of La Venta – green and tropical with a perfect view across the Gulf of Mexico.'

On either side we were passing communities which could also have been called green and tropical, though hardly perfect – people living in shacks made from cardboard boxes covered with sheets of plastic, jammed among trees and thick foliage.

'If a pop group doesn't tour, how do its managers make money?' Rolf asked, drawing my attention away from the scenery outside.

I sighed. 'They don't really. George and Andrew probably have half a million or so each in their bank accounts but because we agreed to manage them for a smaller than usual management commission Jazz and I have only earned around a hundred and fifty thousand pounds in the two years we've been doing it. Just enough to run our offices and pay our staff.'

'Why don't you try and sell your management company?' Rolf suggested. 'Or float it – go public?'

I said nothing. It felt obscene to be driving through the middle of these poor people's lives enclosed in a bubble of luxury discussing something quite unrelated to them. Rolf seemed to sense it too for he suddenly changed the subject and launched into tour guide mode. 'These people are living in what once was the Mayan empire, so different from the Aztec one, but where we're going was the seat of an even older empire, that of the Olmec ...'

When we arrived at the coast it was easy to spot his house; it was another Bavarian castle, hardly different from the one in Chiang Mai.

'One thing about you Rolf – you're consistent.'

He tilted his head to one side, accepting what I'd said as a compliment. 'Come and look at the terrace.' He took me through the house to an enormous marble-floored balcony that overlooked a vista of wooded hillside stretching down to the sea. 'It's wonderful, isn't it? I like to sit out here and listen to music – relax and forget the world.'

'What d'you listen to?'

'Jazz, mostly.'

A few minutes later we were seated on thickly cushioned chairs listening to Miles Davis as Rolf rolled a couple of joints. 'You know,' he said, 'I've got a friend who would probably buy your management company if you wanted to sell it. He's crazy about show-business and he has far too much money. I used to go to school with him in Shanghai.'

The last thing I wanted was to get involved in business with Rolf or his associates; I just wanted to keep him as a friend. 'Maybe later,' I said. 'First, Jazz is going to fix a stadium tour of America. You never know, if it goes well George might change his mind and let the group go on for a while. That would be better than selling the company.'

Rolf lit a joint and handed it to me. 'Just trying to help.'

'Of course! Thanks!'

He looked at me strangely. 'You know, you wouldn't find it as bad as you think being involved with me in business.'

It was as if he'd read my mind. Moreover, I felt strangely threatened by his having done so, though I couldn't think why. But when I lay back against the cushions and inhaled the soft Mexican grass any worries I had about it drifted away. As the light faded to dusk we relaxed in adjacent chairs, drawing silently on our joints as Miles Davis meandered through *Sketches of Spain*, music and smoke mixing lazily together in the warm evening air.

The next morning his boyfriend arrived.

'This is Manolo,' Rolf explained. 'He got married yesterday. The ceremony was at his village, on the border with Guatemala. I was meant to go, but with you arriving I couldn't make it.'

Manolo was twenty-three or four and wore a thin voile shirt with simply cut black trousers. Fine limbs, a firm torso, sparkling eyes and a topping of spiky black hair – he just oozed sex.

'Are you tired of your wife already?' I asked him.

Manolo grinned broadly, his eyes flirting furiously.

'It's only a marriage of convenience,' Rolf explained. 'The bride's father is the village headman. Manolo prefers to be away from the village; that way he can live as he pleases.'

Mid-morning the three of us set off in Manolo's car to drive round the coast looking at Olmec carvings and Mayan ruins. It was hideously hot but Rolf and Manolo didn't seem to care and made me walk up a mile of steps to look at an ancient temple. At the top, as we gazed out over acres of tropical forest Rolf suddenly asked me, 'Have you got any money? I mean – *real* money?'

Dripping with sweat and itching from insect bites, his question made me suddenly sharp-tempered. 'For Christ's sake, Rolf! Don't tell me you made me climb up this bloody hill just to ask for some money?'

'Simon needs air-conditioning,' Manolo said. 'Let's go back to the car.'

As we started back down, Rolf said, 'You didn't need to shout at me. I was just thinking – if you can't make money out of Wham! maybe I could help you make money from something else.'

I was embarrassed I'd snapped so I tried to explain. 'To be honest, I don't have much. What with all the travelling I did to fix Wham! in China and the lack of any real income from the group, it's been getting pretty tight. But I've never cared too much about money, so don't worry about that. As far as work's concerned I prefer not have too much long-term commitment. I like my home life to be settled and my business life to be an adventure. Right now I feel like Wham! is beginning to tie me down.'

Rolf shook his head as if I was plain foolish. 'How can success tie you down?'

'It's not the success, it's the feeling of being tied to George's angst – his moodiness, his determination to finish Wham! just when we've achieved what we set out to achieve.'

'So why not let him break the group up and manage him as a solo artist?'

'It wouldn't change anything. I think he has angst in his soul.'

When we reached the car, Rolf asked, 'D'you want to look at another temple? There's one down the coast made entirely of oyster shells.'

'Absolutely not,' I insisted.

We decided on lunch and Manolo drove us into the hills to a restaurant with a fabulous view and a peppery dish-of-the-day made from rabbit. Afterwards we snapped pictures of each other before going back to the house for an afternoon swim.

Manolo wanted to play tennis.

'I'm terrible at it,' I told him. 'I've always been a squash player, not a tennis player.'

'He'll teach you,' Rolf said. 'He's an excellent coach. Everyone who plays with him goes away the better for it.'

Manolo and I went and found the necessary equipment from the games room then climbed down the terraces past the swimming pool to where the court was. I played terribly, as I always did, and Manolo tried to show me how to hold the racket.

'You mustn't flick your wrist like that. That's only for squash. Look ...'

He stood right in front of me, the tips of our tennis shoes almost touching, his left hand on my right hand, which was holding the racket, and told me to take my arm back as if I was going to play a stroke. My arm went back with his left hand resting on my wrist, his body stretching across me.

'Now forwards – don't bend it – and follow through.'

As my arm played an imaginary stroke Manolo kept his left hand on my wrist but held his body where it was so that my forward movement pressed me tightly against him as our arms rose in the air in an intimate waltz.

'Smile please!'

Manolo jumped away.

We turned to see Rolf on the terrace, lowering his camera having just captured the moment. He acted as if nothing unusual had happened and proceeded to mix cocktails from bottles he'd brought on a tray from the house.

Throughout dinner Manolo seemed unsettled. Afterwards he suggested I play Mastermind, a board game in which you had to put rows of pegs into rows of holes, remembering which ones had been tried before and which ones hadn't. With a good understanding of how the game worked, and a perfect memory, it was possible always to get it right in just four turns. Sometimes playing well, providing you had luck, you could do it in three, but Manolo won in three time after time. Over thirty games, I won four times in four while he won twenty-six times in three. I thought again about the construction of the game – without doubt, to win in three turns required luck or an ability to know something unknowable.

'Amazing, isn't it?'

Rolf was standing looking down at the board as Manolo considered his next move.

'Any idea how he does it?'

'No – but I talked to some research scientists in Tokyo and they think in certain people it's a natural phenomenon. They want Manolo to go there for a week of tests. I'm wondering whether it could have some sort of business application? Perhaps he could use it to tell if shares would go up or down.'

'How d'you do it, Manolo?' I asked.

He shook his head. 'I've no idea. Sometimes I'm as surprised as you are.'

I went to bed puzzling over it. My room was on the lower floor of the house, off the open-plan kitchen and dining area. The bed was king-size and the room spacious, decorated all in white, with sliding windows that opened onto a small balcony overlooking cliffs that fell into the Gulf of Mexico. Rolf told me to use the air conditioning but Manolo told me differently.

'Don't!' he said. 'Open the door to the breakfast-room and the breeze will blow in from the terrace and out the door the other side. You'll be cooler and you'll sleep wonderfully. The sea air is much better than air-conditioning.'

I followed his advice and ten minutes later was lying comfortably in the dark enjoying a half-dream and the sea breeze.

I was almost asleep when I heard a noise from the kitchen area beyond the open door. In the dim light I saw Manolo walk across to the refrigerator and open it. As he did so a shaft of light fell across his torso and thighs, naked except for hipster briefs. He stood there for ages, fiddling around, choosing a drink, drinking it, not moving from the small area lit by the refrigerator, white cotton against dark skin, directly in my eyeline.

I pretended to be asleep until he left then got up and closed the bedroom door, locked it and turned on the air-conditioning.

32 TALENT NIGHT AT THE APOLLO

In May 1985, George Michael was invited to sing at the Harlem Apollo. The theatre was having a grand reopening after being renovated. Motown Records were turning the event into a mammoth TV show at which every living 'great' of black music would perform. And with their eye on the biggest possible worldwide audience they were including a few white performers too, among them George. They were surprisingly generous in their hospitality. Although they only wanted George on the show, they'd also invited Andrew as a guest, plus Jazz and me and publisher Dick Leahy. And they flew everyone by Concorde.

I was probably looking forward to going to the Apollo even more than George was himself. I had a special memory of it; I'd first been there when I was 18, en route to Canada, to which I was emigrating.

I'd flown by way of New York because I was crazy about jazz and wanted to tour the city's jazz clubs. To pay for my emigration I'd sold my collection of jazz records which had given me enough for my airfare and a balance of one hundred and fifteen dollars, a hundred of which I'd paid into a bank account in Toronto before I left England. So for twenty-four hours in New York I would have just fifteen dollars.

The flight arrived in the early morning and I took a bus to 42nd Street from Idlewild airport, and for just $1.99 found a hotel in Times Square with fluorescent-lit corridors, steel doors and a treble-locked room that looked like a cell. But it was only for storing my bags; I was off on the town. In the evening I would go to jazz clubs; in the afternoon I wanted to visit the Apollo Theater in Harlem.

All the black jazz greats had played at the Apollo and I was determined to see one of them. Afraid of how much it might cost to get in and not wanting to waste any money, I set off at ten in the morning to walk there and asked someone the way.

'All the way up,' they replied. 'Just keep walking up Seventh.'

I did – for eighty blocks.

I got there in the early afternoon hoping to see Lionel Hampton's Band or Earl Bostic, but topping the bill that day was Louis Belson. I was disappointed. Belson was white and it felt wrong to have come all this way to see an act that wasn't even black. But the show was magnificent.

What disappointed me most, though, was that I was unable to see the Apollo's famous Wednesday night talent show. Many greats from Billie Holiday to Louis Armstrong had started at the Apollo talent shows, some of them not going down too well with the famously tough crowd. Luther Vandross was among those who got booed off several times before finally making it big. Bad audience reactions were famous.

In the late fifties, around the time I went there, some young people queuing for the Wednesday night show were interviewed on TV.

'Why d'you come here on talent night?'

'To see amateurs.'

'What's the big draw?'

'Booing people.'

Rehearsals for the Motown show started at 9 a.m. George was near the beginning of the show so we went there early, which turned out to be the best thing we could have done. What was so special about the rehearsals was the intimate chatter and bitchery that went on between the artists, an A–Z of American black music. Among them was a smattering of white faces, including Boy George, who refused to say hello to George Michael but hopped around the famous black faces, not at all shy to introduce himself. Boy George had the advantage that his face (or at least the make-up on top of it) was well-known to them while in America George Michael was known only by his songs.

The morning rehearsals produced an extraordinary duet between Joe Cocker and Patti LaBelle. Joe, tense and jerky, interjected odd staccato phrases into Patti's swooping gospel lines like nut chips in smooth ice-cream. Their disparate voices and odd body movements rose to a musical orgasm that left them both visibly shocked by its intensity. It had the stars who were watching applauding furiously.

Later there was something even better. With most artists finished with their rehearsals and gone back to their hotels, Billy Preston sat down at the piano to sing 'Try A Little Tenderness', a tribute to Otis Redding. It started out quietly with the band playing in the classic style of great soul recordings, tight and understated. But as the song progressed from verse to chorus and back to verse again, a ripple of tension could be sensed from the watching technicians and the band began to play even tighter. As he hit the second chorus, Billy's voice snapped into another tier of emotion and a shiver could be felt from everyone listening.

When Billy flowed into the last middle eight, the usually blasé technicians were turned to stone – he wasn't just singing a song, he was pouring out his life – and when the drums doubled into a tattoo of eights going into the last chorus there were tears running down Billy's face.

Yet when it finished there was no cheering, just silence; most of the artists had left the theatre and the technicians were far too embarrassed to show they'd been moved. It was the cold silence of a rehearsal in an empty theatre. The production manager's voice came over the PA. 'OK Billy, you're cleared, that'll be fine. See you back at 9.15.'

I went back to the hotel. If in forty years I'd never heard anything that good I was unlikely to hear something else that could match it that afternoon.

There was another reason why I left. I'd been thinking about Rolf's suggestion that we might float or sell our management company and had suggested it to Jazz.

'Great!' he'd told me. '*My* project can be fixing Wham!'s stadium tour of the States. *Yours* can be finding a way to sell the company.'

Shortly afterwards a friend recommended me to someone in New York. 'Rupert Clarke. A real whiz-kid finance person. Everything he touches turns to gold.'

I found Rupert's offices in one of the smaller buildings at the World Trade Center, buzzing smoothly, with rows of people sitting at computers in an open-plan office. His own private office overlooked the ferries that ran across the water to the Statue of Liberty and Staten Island. Rupert was early thirties, thin, impeccably suited and English.

· 'Easy-peasy,' he said, when I explained what it was Jazz and I would like to do with our company. 'We'll back you into an inactive public company. The general public will love the idea of buying into Wham!'s management.'

I wasn't sure what 'backing into' an inactive company meant. 'Why can't we go in forwards?'

'It's not the way it's done.'

He studied his computer screen, fiddled around on the keyboard, then nodded with satisfaction. 'Here's one. An inactive company – quoted on the Nasdaq and based in Atlantic City. It made its money distributing jukeboxes in the 1930s and now owns small seaside hotels on the East Coast. Leave this all to me. I'll get things prepared and we'll put the issue on the market at a peak moment. When will Wham! be here touring? That would be the moment to do it.'

'We're planning a stadium tour for later in the year. How much d'you think we could raise?'

'My guess is you'll be able to raise around ten million in cash and retain thirty per cent of the new combined company. You'll be paid with shares in the new joint company and half of those shares will be sold on the Nasdaq. I'll give you a list of our charges.'

He handed me a booklet and it worked out that he and his company would take around two million dollars for organising our flotation. But what the heck, that left Jazz and me with four million each and we would still own thirty per cent of the company.

'Is that it then?' I asked Rupert. 'Nothing more you want from me at the moment?'

'We'll want your company's financial records. Put me in touch with your accountants in London and we'll sort it all out for you. We do deals like this all the time. Just keep me informed about when the tour will happen.'

It seemed all too easy. At last we were going to make money from managing Wham!.

I passed the rest of the afternoon by dropping in on Walter Yetnikoff, the president of CBS Records.

Walter was a strange guy: intelligent, sensitive, much loved by all CBS's artists, but obsessed with swapping rough talk and foul language with friends like Alan Grubman, New York's top music lawyer. On their office walls, Walter and Alan kept framed faxes of insults they'd traded, full of words like *ball-buster*, *motherfucker*, *cocksucker* and the like.

I talked to Walter enthusiastically about the publicity we'd created from Wham!'s concert in Beijing. 'It's made them big enough to do a stadium tour, which is just what we intended.'

'So it was all just a gimmick was it?' he asked. 'Just for publicity.

There must have been an easier way of making all those newscasts. You could have got George caught with his pants down in some sort of big way. You know – screwing a film star's wife – causing a divorce, something like that.'

'That's such bad taste,' I told him.

'Don't be such a fag. Good taste never got anyone anywhere.'

'What about Corbusier? Or Frank Lloyd Wright?'

'Who the fuck are they? More of your fag friends?'

Walter wasn't homophobic but gay society seemed to annoy him – like a party he couldn't get into – I don't think that he particularly wanted to go, just that he hated not being invited. In fact, we got on really well and he was always helpful.

'We're thinking of selling our management company,' I told him.

'If you want someone to come in with you, you should talk to Alan Grubman, he's always got his finger on the pulse. Or maybe Irving Azoff.'

Alan, the lawyer with whom Walter traded his macho faxes, just didn't seem the right partner for Jazz and me, nor did Irving Azoff who was famous for sending his enemies such presents as gift-wrapped live snakes. 'I don't think it will be necessary,' I explained. 'I've just seen someone about floating the company on the Nasdaq. It's being taken care of – which leaves me without a project. I'm bored with management, it ties me down too much. Think of something fun for me to do.'

'Why not get CBS into China?'

'Are you sure?'

'Sure I am. But the deal would be – *I* get the credit, not you! I'd love it. It would annoy the hell out of Tisch.'

Currently, Walter was having a battle with the overall owner of the CBS corporation, Laurence Tisch. They simply couldn't get on and fought on every occasion.

Walter had an extraordinarily detailed employment contract. It outlined every last thing to which he was entitled including his right to travel first class, to stay in a suite in a five-star hotel, to eat in the best restaurants and to have full American breakfast.

Recently Tisch and Walter had travelled together to Los Angeles. At the Beverly Hills Hotel they'd had a breakfast meeting with some other people from CBS. Walter didn't want a full breakfast, he just wanted a bagel but there wasn't one included on the American set breakfast. He ordered one specially and Tisch pointed out that this was not something his contract authorised him to charge to expenses. So he made Walter pay for it personally.

After that Walter never travelled without a bagel in his brief case. Any time, anywhere, whether it was a CBS board meeting, a music business charity dinner or the next seat on an airplane, if he was with Tisch, Walter would put his briefcase on the table in front of him, take out the bagel and leave it on top. It annoyed Tisch unbelievably, but not enough to satisfy Walter. He was always on the look-out for more and better ways to annoy him. Getting himself publicity by arranging for CBS to set up in China struck him as the perfect method.

'I'll charge you through the nose for my costs,' I told him.

Walter laughed. 'No problem. You can even have bagels for breakfast.'

'And a handsome fee for pulling it off. Perhaps one per cent of all CBS's turnover in China for ten years.'

Walter raised the palms of his hands in a gesture of compromise. 'Let's talk about that when it happens.'

At the Apollo that night the audience was the executive elite of the music business. To the general public it wouldn't have looked star-studded; to people in the industry it was breathtaking. Big industry events could sometimes draw a third of these people; to pull them all in one evening was a testament to Motown.

Smokey Robinson was compere and pushed the show smoothly through its first half hour. Then it was George's turn; he was going to sing 'Careless Whisper' and he strode out with his usual cool confidence.

'Are you nervous?' I asked just beforehand.

'Not a bit,' he replied, nor did he look it. But sometimes it worried me. George wasn't natural. Artists about to walk out onstage are *meant* to be nervous, as he'd found out in Beijing.

He flowed easily into the first verse and hit the chorus in good voice, but there was something amiss. Some of the musicians had read their parts incorrectly and played a wrong chord as he hit the chorus. By the third bar most of them were back in step. It was a bad glitch, but most artists would have struggled on and ignored it. Not George. He stopped singing and the band tailed off behind him. The cameras kept turning and the dinner-jacketed audience shuffled uncomfortably. George told them, 'I'm sorry. The band were in the wrong place as we hit the chorus. I'll have to start again.' He leant over the front of the stage and talked to the conductor.

There was really no end to his self-confidence. He walked back to his camera start mark and turned again to face the audience. Amazingly, before he could start singing they burst into applause. This was a show-business audience and they knew cocksure class when they saw it.

George acknowledged it with a slight bow of his head and started the song again. He sang as well as I'd ever heard him sing and when he hit the passionate ad lib-style third verse the audience burst into more applause, almost drowning out his singing.

When he came offstage I asked him, 'Weren't you nervous when you had to start a second time?'

'Not at all,' he told me. 'I would have just gone on till we got it right.'

In the finale someone else tried to do just that and nearly got booed off the stage. Sammy Davis Junior had stretched the show out with an hour of tap-dancing and the audience was tired and hungry. By one o'clock in the morning, having been there for six hours, people were shuffling in their seats. Diana Ross was supposed to be joining the cast for the finale, arriving by helicopter from Atlantic City where she was working in cabaret, but despite the show running an hour late she still hadn't turned up.

In the end the finale was done without her. Bon Jovi sang 'I Want to Know What Love Is', then the rest of the cast came on to join them.

The show was finished but the posh celebrity audience was kept a few more moments while the stage manager waited for the producer to give him the all-clear on taping. Then Smokey Robinson came on and announced, 'Ladies and Gentlemen, I'm thrilled to tell you, Miss Diana Ross has just arrived. Please stay in your seats and we'll reshoot the finale.'

I'd gone up to a seat in the circle to watch the end of the show and from all around me I could hear mutters of disapproval at being kept longer – people were just too tired and hungry. Behind me a man jeered. Encouraged by him other people booed too, not loudly, sort of under their breath.

The guy behind me told his wife, 'That bitch always comes late. I could murder a burger. I could murder her too.'

The finale restarted, Bon Jovi began singing their hit and Smokey Robinson announced, 'And now, Miss Diana Ross.'

Out she came in dazzling white, her arms swinging above her head, her smile wider than her face. For a few seconds things moved along smoothly, but then she did a George Michael and stopped singing.

There was some talk between her and the stage manager and his reply came over the PA. 'Diana – don't worry if you do a little something wrong – we've got this thing covered with twenty cameras. There'll be plenty of cutaways we can use. Just keep on going.'

Smokey Robinson came out and told the audience, 'Please, when I announce Miss Ross, I want you all to applaud.'

Next to me, a man said, 'When we were kids we used to stand down the front and throw bad fruit.'

It started again, but the audience (now even hungrier and tireder) didn't do well with their applause. And dammit, she stopped the show again.

Smokey Robinson came out and begged the audience, 'We're going to do it one more time, but please, when Miss Ross comes out this time I want you to give some real big applause.'

The audience had had enough. Instead of applauding they booed. Not just a little. Loudly. And the guy who'd said he used to throw fruit stood up and booed loudest of all. I was shocked. How could a show-business audience boo a star of such stature? But remembering the traditions of Apollo talent night, I shouldn't have been surprised. Many members of this audience had once been poor kids growing up in Harlem. Sitting there in their dinner-jackets with their bejewelled wives, they must have longed for the good old days when they went to the Apollo on a Wednesday night for a good evening's booing. Now Diana Ross had given them their chance.

She didn't stop the show again and twenty minutes later we were all out of there, heading into a gargantuan marquee on a parking lot, hung inside with crystal chandeliers, the Count Basie Band playing for us while we banqueted till dawn.

George, in an excellent mood, was much congratulated. Miss Ross was nowhere to be seen.

33 SIX THOUSAND BICYCLES

'**B**efore *me*,' Frank Barsalona liked to tell people, 'rock promotion was the asshole of show business. Lower than the rodeo.'

Frank had been my booking agent for The Yardbirds some twenty years earlier and was now considered the biggest independent agent in America. Frank claimed to have virtually invented the rock concert business.

He'd had a vision – acts and promoters and record companies working in coordination, and it worked – all his artists ended up with long-time careers; The Who, Led Zeppelin, Earth Wind and Fire, Bruce Springsteen, U2. He also had an Italian name, which gave him extra leverage. It was just a name and nothing more, but his Italian heritage made people nervous of crossing him. It allowed him to push for better deals.

I introduced him to Jazz and they got on well. With just a handshake they agreed that Frank should become Wham!'s American booking agent, which was the way Frank liked to start things off. No-one ever went back on a handshake deal with Frank Barsalona.

That done I flew to Beijing, looking for permission to get CBS into China. I'd asked Lew Mon Hung to help me with it and we met in Beijing.

Even though Rolf had been pressing me to bring him in on anything I did in China, I didn't want him involved. It wasn't because I didn't like him, the very opposite in fact, I'd rarely met anyone whose company I enjoyed so much. It was simply that I didn't understand what he wanted out of my business dealings whereas with Lew Mon Hung it was all too clear – quick cash. Since Rolf would inevitably find out what I was doing, I called and told him anyway. All he did was sniff down the phone – a bit put out but nothing worse than that.

With Lew's help I found my way to the right person for setting up with CBS. He was in charge of the State dance university in Beijing, where promising young dancers were sent at ten years old, staying until they were good enough to join the National Ballet. In talks, I made fast progress on the project. It was likely the government would agree and we fixed another meeting for two days' time. That meant forty-eight hours of boredom in Beijing, so for the first time since long before Wham!'s show I contacted my student friends again.

Actually I'd called several times since I'd last seen them but my calls hadn't been returned. This time one of them called back – Pang Yu – and surprisingly she agreed to come to the hotel for lunch with a friend.

I took them to the rooftop restaurant where they appeared not at all overawed by the hotel's posh surroundings. Pang Yu told me both May Ling and Chuen had now completed their studies and left university; my other friend, Zhang Jin, the first one I'd met, had moved to another department and Pang Yu saw less of him. Her new friend, the one she brought to lunch, was a solid-looking girl and rather plain, called Lua. Conversation was stiffer than it had ever been before but Pang Yu had always been the least talkative of the group.

Lua spoke English the best of all the students I'd met. She asked if I'd learnt any Chinese during the time I'd been coming to Beijing.

'Not really,' I admitted. 'Just taxi stuff – "left", "right", "straight ahead", and all the numbers.'

She looked at me disparagingly, 'This shows quite a lazy nature on your part.'

'That's right,' I agreed. 'I *have* been very lazy about it, but it just didn't seem necessary. Language is a funny thing – you can speak ten of them then find yourself in an eleventh place where none of them are understood and you'll be as helpless as someone who's never bothered to learn a single one. In the end I decided I wouldn't waste any more time learning languages except where it was vital for what I was doing.'

Pang Yu asked, 'What happens when there are written signs? How do you know what they say? "Toilet" – "Men" – "Women" – things like that.'

'I just watch where other people are going. It's not so unusual. In London I have a Singaporean friend who speaks five Chinese dialects but he can't read a word of Chinese.'

'You know Chinese people in UK?' Pang Yu asked sharply. 'Why you never tell me that before?'

I was shocked. She'd jumped out of her shell with a zing – not like the quiet girl I thought she was. They were odd, these two girls. I felt I was being quizzed.

'He's a business partner,' I told them, skirting the basis of my relationship with Allan yet tempted to drop it right in their faces. 'And I have another business partner who's black. Should I have told you that too?'

I don't know why, but I felt like being rude; something about the way they were speaking drew it out of me.

Lua said, 'We have a student at the university who is black. From Tanzania. He has learnt to speak beautiful Chinese.'

This, I felt sure, was intended as a criticism of my laziness.

'But he smells,' Pang Yu added.

My fair-mindedness in matters of race leapt to the poor man's rescue. 'Most Chinese have no odour glands under their armpits; as a result, in China when you go in a hot crowded place there's never any smell of sweat. In Europe and America, the only reason it isn't smelly in crowded places is because we wear deodorants. Your black student obviously couldn't bring enough deodorant with him to last an entire year in Beijing.'

'And your black friend in England, does he smell?' Pang Yu asked.

'Absolutely not. He wears deodorant like everyone does.'

'And do you?' Lua asked.

'Of course!'

Lua now embarked on a scolding. 'You agree that Westerners all smell and that you cover it up. Why are people in the West always blaming the Chinese government for covering things up when it is so much part of your own character too?'

'What d'you mean?'

'You often accuse our government of covering bad things in society or in history – but what's the difference?'

'You're talking about political things – governmental mistakes – am I right?'

'Yes – and you do the same in your country too – that's what I'm trying to tell you.'

'Sometimes it happens, but in general we have a more open society. We have freedom of the press. We accept investigation more easily. We make ourselves more open to criticism.'

'But you still cover bad smells, so what's the difference? An under-arm stink or a political stink? You see – in the West you're just hypocrites.'

She was so aggressive, and her logic so bizarre. And it was strange – never before had I managed to persuade a student to come to this hotel yet suddenly these two girls were happy to eat lunch there. Then I realised ...

Of course! More secret police! Lua's English was just too good for her not to be. China, I could see, was going to be much less fun the second time round. The intrusion of people like this at every level made being there just too uncomfortable.

'What subjects are you taking at university?' I asked Lua.

'I'm forbidden to give details. What about you? What business are you doing here at the moment?'

Now she was really pissing me off. 'I'm seeking permission to set up a foreign-owned brothel.'

It appeared she hadn't understood. Or perhaps she was just *pretending* she hadn't. Or *hoping* she hadn't.

'When it opens, would you like a job?'

Lua answered with silence. The waiter came to clear the dishes.

'Dessert?' I asked. 'Ice cream, fruit? No?'

Tired of being spied on in Beijing, I went back to Canton. I wanted to visit the record company that had released Wham!'s cassette and check on sales. But when I got to their offices they'd disappeared.

In their place was another record company which was nothing to do with them. Nobody spoke English so I said 'Wham!' a few times and sang a few bars of 'Careless Whisper'. The girl on reception understood perfectly and wrote an address on a piece of paper. 'Car, car,' she said, and I understood equally perfectly.

Thirty minutes later I was dropped off by a taxi at what looked like a series of aircraft hangars on the outskirts of town. It had once been an airport but was now a film studio and I found the record company's office next door to a suite of rooms occupied by Bernardo Bertolucci who was there filming *The Last Emperor*.

When I pushed open the door the managing director was sitting at his desk eating duck noodles. He recognised me at once but with his mouth full of food greeted me only with a wave of his chopsticks.

'How many cassettes did you sell?'

Even as I spoke I realised it was rather impolite not to have first said hello, but then he hadn't either. Anyway, he didn't appear put out.

'Not sure,' he said, slurping up more noodles. 'I don't think we counted.'

'How could you have not counted? You have to pay us a royalty on each cassette sold. Do you think you sold one hundred thousand?'

'Maybe,' he agreed, smacking his lips. 'Yes – one hundred thousand, OK.'

'Or was it more like two hundred and fifty thousand?'

'Could be.' He raised the noodle bowl to his mouth, draining what was left. 'Yes – two hundred and fifty thousand.'

'Or could it be five hundred thousand?'

He put the bowl on the desk and wiped his mouth with a cloth. 'Five hundred thousand too expensive. Better say two hundred and fifty thousand.'

It was a strange way to arrive at a royalty statement but it felt amicable enough and for me this was a game, not a serious piece of business.

Surprisingly, once we'd agreed on the number of cassettes, he seemed quite keen to sort out the payment (presumably getting him off the hook for any cassettes sold over and above that figure) and he told me the money would have to be paid in Rimimbi, which were not convertible.

'So how can the group use it?' I asked.

'Can buy things.'

'What things – silks, carpets, gems?'

'No – must buy things approved by government. Here ...' He reached into the drawer of his desk and pulled out a typed piece of paper. 'I give you list.'

It wasn't much use, it was in Chinese, but he translated. 'Must be things the government finds hard to sell – bulldozers, earth movers, steam locomotives, bicycles ...'

'Bicycles,' I told him. 'They sound OK. How many?'

I expected them to cost about twenty dollars per bike but he surprised me. 'I get you special price – just four dollars each.' (Which probably meant the real cost was two dollars, for surely he would be taking a handsome profit for himself.)

That afternoon he took me to the bike factory to have a look. They were simple and sturdy, no gears, but wouldn't fall apart. 'They're made for the army,' he explained.

'Tell them three dollars each,' I suggested, and he didn't even propose it to the factory manager, just agreed there and then. So I knew I'd been right about him doubling the price.

It still wasn't settled. There were official forms to fill in before he could use the Rimimbi from our record sales to purchase the bikes for us. This was going to take time but at least I'd set it in motion. When Wham!'s royalties finally came in they would be paid with six thousand army-issue bicycles.

'Where you want them sent?' he asked me.

I hadn't a clue. But two days later, back in London, I spoke to a friend who dealt in commodities. He told me about a fifty thousand pound deal he'd recently done in Rumania for which he'd received payment in coal. This had been swapped for one hundred million rubber bands from South Korea which he'd exchanged for two hundred used wine casks from Bulgaria which he'd sold in Chile for twenty thousand pounds.

He said he had a contact in Paraguay, an army man, who would use the bikes for what they were meant for – soldiers. Taking a small commission for the work involved, he agreed to ship the bicycles to Paraguay where we could be credited with twenty-seven thousand kilos of best Paraguayan coffee. 'And coffee,' he explained, 'is as good as cash.'

'Don't rush things', I told him. 'We haven't got the bikes yet.'

34 BIT OF A NUTCASE

Live Aid was destined to be the biggest live music event ever – a transatlantic charity concert to be held simultaneously at Wembley Stadium in London (where George and Andrew had been invited to perform), and at JFK Stadium in Philadelphia. There would be a live audience of two hundred thousand and a television audience of more than a billion. Yet I didn't want to go.

I don't really know why. I guess it was to do with absolutely everyone being there. It was like being asked to join in community singing, like holding hands and singing 'Auld Lang Syne' on New Year's Eve. I just don't join in well at these communal events.

Or was it simply because it wasn't me who organised it?

Anyway, since there was some leftover business to sort out with the Japanese film people, I got on a plane and flew to Tokyo.

At the Shinjuku Hilton I had dinner alone, intending to go straight to my room and sleep. But having undressed and got into bed I found I just wasn't tired enough. Maybe I'd gone too easy on the wine at dinner, or perhaps life just wasn't meant to finish so early that night. Either way, I got up again and went to Mako, one of the few gay discos in Tokyo that allowed Japanese and foreigners to mix. There, life was as it was meant to be at that time of night – noisy, fetid, chaotic and exuberant. I couldn't think what had made me want to go to bed in the first place.

Eight whiskies and three hours later I moved on to a small late-night place next door, the Regent. Sitting there at the small bar, pleasantly soporific, I was spoken to by a young man who plied me with drinks and conversation until around four in the morning. Then he persuaded me we should walk back towards my hotel together. Halfway there he pointed upwards to an apartment building and told me he lived there. 'Why not come in for a drink?'

He wasn't my type, this young man, I couldn't really say why, he just wasn't. But the night had reached that vague alcoholic point where rolling around in bed with someone seemed the right thing to do. Besides, so few Japanese ever invited people to their apartments, it was sort of flattering.

By Japanese standards it was a pretty good apartment for a young single man, right in the centre of town. He must have been doing well.

'I'm an architect,' he explained. 'I've managed to make the flat look bigger than it really is.'

It was true – he had – though in essence he was still living the usual miniaturised life of all Japanese city dwellers.

A few more whiskies and a bit of music and he pointed at the futon on the floor.

'Come on. Now we go to bed.'

I'd changed my mind. I really had no interest in this young man. I wanted my own crisp clean bed at the Hilton and tomorrow I had to meet with the Japanese film company. I got up to go. 'Sorry, I can't. I have a meeting at nine. I need to go back to my hotel. It's five-thirty already.'

He walked across the room to stand right in front of me, almost nose to nose. 'Listen, Simon, I was afraid to say it earlier but from the first second I saw you I knew this was something special. I'm twenty-seven and I never found the right man to love. But I've always had a vision. Tonight when you walked into the disco, you were that vision. I could not believe it.'

This was some big turn off. All I wanted to do was to get out of there.

Tears were welling in his eyes. 'That face I have seen always in my dream,' he said desperately. 'That face is now front of me. It is a miracle from Buddha.'

I had a headache. I was uncomfortable. He was mad. I headed for the door.

'No, Simon, you cannot leave. You must stay. Please. You are my dream come true.'

I wrenched open the door – stepped out – headed for the staircase – this had definitely not been the right thing to do.

He flew after me, grabbing at my arm. 'Simon, you don't understand. Your face has been engraved in my mind since I was a little boy.'

I strode down the stairs, through the lobby, into the street – it was dawn and cool, the fresh air washed pleasantly on my flushed face.

I set off down the street but he followed me, running round me in circles of despair.

'Simon – I need you.'

Above our heads windows opened and people looked out as I searched frantically for a taxi. I saw one, waved it down, climbed in quickly and slammed the door. But the lunatic still followed.

'Heelton,' I told the driver in my best Japanese taxi-language. And we were off.

As the taxi sped away I turned to look through the rear window. The young Japanese man was standing in the centre of the street, dishevelled and miserable.

'Bit of a nutcase,' I thought. 'Must be more careful in future.'

That afternoon I had my meeting with the film company. I'd always worried that George might not like the idea of writing a theme song for their movie and so far had never actually asked him if he would. I was relieved to learn that the film company had changed their minds; they didn't want a theme song after all.

That was that. Tomorrow I would fly to Thailand for a few days and watch Live Aid on cable TV in the comfort of a suite at the Oriental Hotel. For the moment though, I needed to get some sleep. So around five in the afternoon I went back to the Hilton and had an afternoon nap.

It was a bad move. I woke up at nine in the evening feeling great – refreshed and clear-headed, ready for anything except going back to sleep again. Almost inevitably I began to think how nice it would be to plunge back into the jumbled jungle of youth at Mako's, sipping a whisky, having fun, the music washing over me. But because of that ghastly mistake last night, I couldn't. Just suppose I met that mad creature again?

After a dreary half hour in the lobby bar of the Hilton, I decided it would be OK. Most Japanese didn't go out every night of the week and having been there on a Thursday he surely wouldn't be there on a Friday too. Besides, I would be careful to scout around before I went in. If he was there, I could make a quick exit before he spotted me.

I got there at 11 p.m. and it was throbbing. To the left of the entrance was the dance floor, heaving with movement. To the right was the bar, packed with interesting faces. I spun my eyes round the room. No, he wasn't there, I was in luck.

I edged my way through the crowd. Faces turned to say hello, some attractive, some to be avoided. The place was provocative – explosive even – all the fun of the fair. How could I have even thought of not coming? And the music too – just perfect!

I reached the bar, pushed gently through a group of giggling Frenchmen wearing two many rings and bangles, and ordered a whisky. Taking a sip, I relaxed, turned round and leant with my back against the bar surveying the scene. And then I saw him. He was on the far side of the room and hadn't seen me. So I turned swiftly back to face the bar and leant there sipping my whisky, hoping he wouldn't see me.

After a few minutes I turned casually round to survey the room and he was right there, just ten feet away, pushing through the crowd towards where I was standing, though apparently he still hadn't seen me. Then his eyes flicked up and we were looking straight at each other. There was no way of avoiding him now. If I walked away he might start chasing me and screaming.

Unsure of what to do I hesitated, then decided directness was the best approach. 'Hullo,' I said. 'How are you tonight?'

He fixed me with wide-open eyes, oozing with innocence.

'Hullo mister. First time in Japan?'

* * *

While I was still in Tokyo, Rolf called from Singapore. He was with the school-friend he'd mentioned to me when I was in Villahermosa, the one who might like to buy our company. Why didn't I come and see them?

I really didn't want to be involved in business with Rolf or his associates but since I was already in the Far East it was difficult to refuse to fly to Singapore, just a few hours away.

I arrived mid-afternoon and Rolf was waiting at the airport to take me straight to the meeting. 'He's a strange one is Shu,' he told me in the back of the taxi. 'Like me, he's a product of third generation Shanghainese – half Chinese, half Japanese, with a touch of Maori from his grandmother. He has a pan-Asian food business. Very rich. Another member of our murky world.'

It was odd; when I'd first met Rolf he'd insisted he knew nothing about any 'murky world'. Later admitted he knew a little. And then – well – quite a lot. Once he told me, 'You think of me as loving art, architecture, clever talk, good wine and fine food, but there's another side of me you don't know. I love danger, scheming, plotting, back-stabbing, coming from behind, fighting and winning. I enjoy both sides of life equally.'

So, apparently, did this chap Shu.

His offices were in Bukit Tima Road. He was enormous, looking exactly like the composite parts of the nationalities Rolf had described – dark skinned, hugely plump, well-muscled, with thighs like a sumo wrestler and an Asian face with a pert little nose.

'We're both the same age,' Rolf said as he introduced us. 'Sixty-three. We were at school together in Shanghai before I went to Germany as a teenager.'

Shu beamed. Despite being huge and fearsomely bald, even down to his eyebrows, he had the most winsome smile and wonderful teeth. He pressed the intercom and ordered drinks, his voice strangely highish and unsuited to his size.

Rolf whispered, 'He's taken a fancy to you, I can tell at once. You're his type. I'm sure he'd like to sleep with you.'

It was a shock, like having someone suggest you might like to lie down in the path of a Sherman tank.

A waitress arrived with bottles of sake and three crystal tumblers. Shu split the first bottle between the three glasses and handed me one. Alarmed by the news of his sexual predilection I gulped nervously and much too deeply, and I felt instantly tipsy.

'Simon – Rolf tells me you're on the verge of selling Wham!'s management company.'

I lied politely. 'It's too late. We've done the deal. It's being floated on the Nasdaq.'

'I'll increase whatever you're being offered. You know, I'm very interested in getting into entertainment.'

'It's not an offer, it's a deal. We're committed to it. We're getting ten million dollars.'

'Well I'll pay you fifteen.'

Was it the company he was offering the money for, or was it me? It was twenty years since I'd last had an older person say they fancied me. I'd forgotten how uncomfortable it could make me feel.

I sipped more drink. 'Why would you want to pay so much for my company?'

He flashed his winsome smile and topped up my glass from the second bottle of sake. 'How else would someone in my position be able to move instantly into the entertainment world at an internationally successful level?'

'I have a partner,' I said. 'He would have to be consulted, and anyway, as I told you – we've already confirmed the deal.'

'Twenty million?'

I felt under pressure – I wanted to change the subject – I gulped more sake. 'Tell me about you and Rolf. What is it you do exactly? Is your company your own? Who do you work for?'

Shu frowned. 'What do you mean by "Who"?'

Another sip of sake removed another layer of caution. I gestured at Rolf, sitting opposite me. 'I've often wondered,' I told Shu, 'if Rolf might be connected with the Yakuza?'

Shu burst out laughing. 'You must be crazy – you have to be seven generations pure Japanese to get a look in. As far as the Yakuza is concerned, anyone of mixed race is a peasant.'

Rolf was laughing too. There was a noticeable intimacy between the two of them, not surprising if they'd known each other since they were at school.

Shu picked up a remote control from his desk and pointed it at the TV. 'Listen, let's sing some karaoke. I love it – I do it all the time. I've got all the Wham! songs.'

A minute later this mountain of a 63-year-old was dancing across the room clutching a microphone, singing 'Young Guns', reading words from the office TV, imitating George and Andrew's onscreen movements. It gave a new dimension to his offer to buy the company – he was just a big groupie. It was too awful to cope with; I drank more sake.

Shu finished the song and came over to top up my glass, finishing off the second bottle. 'Is there any chance of getting George and Andrew on the phone. I'd love to say hello to them.'

I was beginning to feel ridiculously tipsy; I'd drunk almost a bottle of sake in twenty minutes, but I tried to explain. 'Artists don't like things like that. A manager is expected to keep undesirable people away – not bring them nearer.'

'Undesirable?'

Shu killed the music and stood in front of me. I was drunk. Things were unsteady. He floated before me like a barrage balloon.

'I mean,' I tried to explain, 'artists like their privacy. They don't want to be introduced to everyone who comes along.'

Throughout all this, Rolf had been sitting silent. Now he said, 'Forget it, Shu. Simon didn't mean anything. Give us another song.'

And off he went again, this time on 'Wham! Rap'.

I drank more. And when he started on 'Last Christmas' I drank more still. Why didn't Rolf get me out of this?

I tried closing my eyes and drifting away but Wham! songs kept coming; when I opened them again the mountain was in front of me wiggling his hips the way Andrew did onstage. 'Come on – do it with me!'

Had I heard him right? I'd been half asleep. Did he mean *sing* with him, or was he asking me to *sleep* with him? I didn't know and I started rambling incoherently, trying to avoid triggering his anger. 'Look – you're an interesting person, and you have a certain stature, but ...'

He responded with the leeriest of smiles. I'd not often felt so uncomfortable.

'We should be going,' Rolf told him, deciding at last to help me out.

'Not till you've both done a song.' Shu pressed a switch on his desk. 'There! You're locked in. To make me unlock the door you'll have to sing a song.'

I said nothing, just stared at him blankly. He flicked the remote control and the sound of 'Everything She Wants' burst out of the speakers. Then he handed me the mike. 'Go on! Let's hear you. Surely the manager knows the songs, doesn't he?'

The sake and my distaste for the situation washed away my last bit of caution. I took the mike and spoke loudly. 'Rolf – tell this idiot to open the door and let us out of here.'

As the upset rose in Shu's face, Rolf was out of his seat, standing between us. He spoke in Shu's ear and the music was turned off at once. 'I think you're drunk,' Rolf told me quite sharply. 'I'll take you back to the hotel.' He pushed the button on Shu's desk and the door opened.

Shu dropped into his office chair, breathless from exertion, sipping sake. He told Rolf, 'If he wants to stay it's OK. I wasn't offended.' And to me he said, 'I'm sure you didn't mean anything bad. Why not stay and have dinner with me?'

I was already out of the door.

A few minutes later Rolf and I were heading for the Hyatt in a taxi. 'How could you have got me into something so awful?' I protested. 'Why didn't you stop him earlier?'

'We're old friends – since school days. I didn't want to spoil his fun. He wasn't doing any harm.'

Round midnight, when I'd slept off the sake, we had a late-night supper in the hotel coffee shop and Rolf half apologised.

'I'm sorry. I didn't realise you couldn't deal with that sort of thing. But you know, Shu never really said anything unpleasant to you. He gave you sake, offered a deal for your company and sang karaoke. Then you were rude to him.'

'He behaved like an oaf – asking me to call George and Andrew.'

'You could have dealt with it without being rude.'

'I felt threatened.'

'By what?'

I couldn't really answer. 'It's karaoke, I think. Like "Auld Lang Syne" on New Year's Eve – like going to Live Aid. I just hate having to join in with things.'

35 ROUGH CUTS AND HELICOPTERS

Lindsay Anderson had seventy miles of film. This had to be edited into a ninety-minute movie. He took forever to produce the first rough-cut, then summoned us to a small preview theatre in Wardour Street. Andrew came on time; George didn't.

'Where is he?' Lindsay asked inquisitorially.

'He's probably late,' said Andrew shrewdly.

'I know that, for God's sake,' Lindsay snapped, 'but where the fuck *is* he?'

Andrew yawned and sat down. Lindsay stamped and fumed around the small theatre. 'It's only booked for two hours and the film takes at least that long.'

'You'd better extend the booking,' Jazz suggested.

'How can I do that if I don't know when he'll be here? What do we need – an extra fifteen minutes, an extra half-hour?'

'Make it an hour,' I suggested, which was a mistake for it sent Lindsay's face purple with anger. But he went and did it anyway.

George turned up twenty-five minutes late; breezed in with a quick 'sorry', then sat down and started giggling with Andrew.

Lindsay beckoned me and Jazz outside, blazing with fury. 'Aren't you going to say anything to him? How can you let him come late like that without even an explanation?'

He was angrier than it was possible to explain. He appeared to think a manager's job was to crush the artist into a little box and keep him there, to be taken out only when required to do something suitable for an artist to do – sing, perhaps, or smile for the camera.

'Let's just get on with it,' I told him.

Lindsay scowled ferociously and strode back inside. 'Get on with it then,' he shouted at the projectionist down the intercom. 'Run the bloody thing.'

George coming late would have been forgotten if, at the end of the showing, we could have told Lindsay how good it was. But we simply couldn't. He'd made the film so achingly boring we could scarcely sit through it. He was trying to make political commentary, which wouldn't have mattered if he'd managed to capture Wham!'s spirit and personality. But because their happy-go-lucky attitude was everything Lindsay hated most in life, he'd got nowhere near them.

'What do you think?' he snapped in the harsh silence that followed the end of the last reel.

'Some of it's good,' George told him, 'but some of it's boring.'

'Bloody boring,' Andrew agreed. And they wandered off to have lunch.

I didn't want any conflict with Lindsay so I left the problem with Jazz, who seemed quite keen on becoming the film's producer.

He was also keen on setting up Wham!'s stadium tour in America.

Our American booking agent wasn't. Frank Barsalona simply didn't agree that Wham! were ready for such a big tour. He said they should play in ten-thousand-seaters but Jazz disagreed. There appeared to be no middle ground.

The tour was to be in September–October. Frank argued that the weather wouldn't be right for stadiums. Jazz disagreed again.

Finally Jazz simply went and found another agent. Frank said he couldn't because they'd shaken hands on the deal. Jazz disagreed for a third time.

I called Frank to try and smooth things over. 'No problem,' he said, but he didn't mean it. For the months of September and October he booked every stadium in America on behalf of other acts for whom he was agent. No-one crossed Frank Barsalona.

Jazz found another agent to set up the tour and they agreed on less conventional venues. Chicago and Baltimore both had venues for ten thousand people seated in front of the stage and another forty thousand on surrounding grassy banks. For Los Angeles they decided on the LA racecourse. It had facilities for seventy thousand but was a bit long and unfocused. It was also directly under the last mile of the flight path into LA International Airport.

'Never mind,' said Jazz. 'We'll pump up the volume.'

I called Rupert Clarke to give him the dates of the stadium tour so he could finalise our company flotation. By now he'd received all the financial information he'd asked for and on several occasions had assured me that everything was moving forward smoothly. But today I couldn't get hold of him.

'He's not in,' the operator told me.

'Will he be in tomorrow?'

'I don't think so. Probably not for a while.'

I hesitated, hoping this wouldn't set back our plans for getting on the Nasdaq. 'Is he ill?' I asked. 'Is he in hospital?'

'In prison!' she answered bluntly.

At first I was taken back. Then I thought – maybe it's just a contretemps with the traffic police or some unpaid alimony. 'You mean he won't be back for a week or two?'

'Three years,' she told me. 'Though they say he might get parole in two.' And before I could ask her what for, she told me: 'Corporate fraud.'

I paused – perhaps there was someone else in the company I could talk to. 'Is anyone dealing with his work in his absence?'

'No-one,' the woman told me with finality. 'They *all* went to jail. The office is shut down and the company's in Chapter 7. I work for the bankruptcy trustees. D'you want me to put you through to my boss?'

I didn't take up her offer. Our flotation looked a lost cause.

With the American tour almost set and the triumphs of Live Aid and China behind them, with a Number One album all over the world and yet another single, 'Everything She Wants', at Number One in the USA, Wham! and their managers were asked by CBS to attend their annual conference in Eastbourne.

'Do we really have to go?' George asked when I called to tell him. 'I'm busy in the studio.'

'Yes,' I told him, firmly.

'Well in that case, tell them they'll have to provide a helicopter. I haven't got time to waste going by car.'

I wasn't sure whose influence was to blame – Live Aid or Elton – but the end result was that I found myself at a small heliport by the river at Battersea with heavy clouds blowing up and no sign of George and Andrew. I'd told them to be there no later than 5.30.

I was sitting in the little Nissen hut that was the arrival and departure hall and outside was the small green helicopter which was to fly us down to Eastbourne. The helicopter's pilot, rather grumpy, kept telling me that if we weren't off the ground by six he wouldn't take us. The weather forecast said it was clouding over. I hadn't realised till then that helicopters couldn't fly if there was a covering of low cloud.

At ten past six Wham!'s limo turned up and dropped them off. They walked into the hut, George in a distinctly bad mood, Andrew ignoring him by keeping his Walkman headphones tightly in place.

'Let's get going,' I said brusquely, not thinking it worthwhile to ask why they were late.

'Is that it?' asked George, pointing to the helicopter outside the door. 'There *are* two pilots aren't there?'

'Not as far as I know. Just one.'

George pulled his angriest face, all eyebrows and dark clouds round the forehead. 'I told Jazz specifically, if you want us to fly in a helicopter there's got to be two pilots. I won't go.'

The limo that had brought them had already left. I looked at my watch. 'We're meant to be at the conference by 7.30 p.m. Time's getting tight, even by helicopter.'

I went outside and asked the pilot, 'Have you got another pilot available?'

He shook his head. 'No-one else about. What's the problem, don't you like my face?'

George walked out and joined us. 'I've told Jazz a hundred times – I won't fly in a helicopter without two pilots.'

I'd never heard this. Hadn't they travelled to Live Aid by helicopter? Did that have two pilots? I didn't know but it wasn't worth arguing about.

'Can you help?' I asked the pilot. 'Is there a chance of getting someone else?'

'No way. Even if there was, one of you wouldn't be able to go. This is a four-seater. Me and one person up front, and two in the back. Anyway, the idea of two pilots is absurd. There's only one set of controls and the pilot wraps himself all around them. If something happened to him there'd be no chance of a co-pilot getting him out of his seat and flying the thing. That's just the way it is with helicopters. But listen, if we're going, we've got to leave now.'

George had to make a quick choice. He could blow out the CBS conference and piss off a whole host of people, or he could have something good to grumble about for the next few days. He chose the grumble option.

'Alright, I'll go. But I'm telling you ...' He fixed me with an aggressive stare. 'I'm not putting up with all these things going wrong. It's my life you're playing with.'

I looked at Andrew; shouldn't his life be included too? But he was still buried in his Walkman. We walked to the helicopter, climbed in and seconds later we were whirring up above Battersea and the river.

'Eastbourne, wasn't it?' The pilot shouted above the hugely noisy engine. 'D'you know the way?'

At that particular moment I thought it was the most extraordinary question I'd ever heard. I'd been in helicopters lots of times but never in one where the pilot didn't know the way. In my ignorance I thought helicopters were somehow automatically guided to their destination like 747s.

The pilot fumbled in a compartment on his right-hand side and passed a book across to me sitting on his left. It was *Road Maps of Britain*. 'Have a look in there,' he said. 'I think it's the A22. While you're looking I'll head for Croydon. I think that's the right sort of direction.'

I was astonished, I'd never thought of helicopters using road maps, but I did as I was told and found Eastbourne on the map. The pilot was right, the road that led to it was the A22; the only problem was, from a thousand feet above it we couldn't make out the road signs. He grabbed the map from me and flew with one hand while he held the map, looking at it carefully.

'That looks like it,' he said, pointing below then returning his gaze to the road map to make a comparison. 'Yes that's it. Keep your eye on the map, make sure I don't come off that road.'

He handed it to me and looked at the sky ahead. 'Oh shit!'

'What now?'

'Clouds! Look ahead.'

Sure enough, a little way in front of us some clouds were floating along at a lesser height than we were. 'I'll have to go back,' the pilot said. 'We can't land through clouds, and those ones are too low to fly underneath.'

'What d'you mean you can't land through clouds?' I asked indignantly. 'I thought this was a proper helicopter not some homemade thing.'

In my ignorance I'd thought of helicopters as thoroughly modern machines but this one certainly wasn't – it was just an engine with some big blades and a plastic bubble containing four seats. We couldn't fly inside the clouds and if we flew above them it would be too dangerous to come down through them: we might hit an office building or a church spire.

'We can't go back,' I insisted, 'we have to be there in half an hour.'

According to the map, and what I could see below, we were about halfway there, but we'd almost reached the clouds. Suddenly the pilot said, 'Look there's a hole over there.'

More or less in a straight line in front of us, probably some twenty miles away and seemingly on the route of the A22, there was a hole in the clouds through which the sun shone downwards onto the ground below. The pilot made his mind up. 'We'll head for that and hope it stays there for the next ten minutes.'

And that's what we did. Flying in the sunshine above the clouds we headed for the hole and then went down through it. Below us were a few buildings and a large expanse of green. 'That's a bit of luck,' the pilot said. 'It's some sort of park or something.'

A few seconds later we were on the ground and the pilot mopped his brow with relief. George and Andrew had no idea that there'd been any panic up front; they thought we'd been chatting about the price of groceries.

'This doesn't look like the hotel,' George said. 'Where are we?'

'I'm not quite sure,' I told him.

The pilot climbed out, opened the door on my side and I jumped down onto the grass. As I did so I heard a noise; I couldn't identify it at first, it was strange, the communal sound of padding feet on grass, like cattle stampeding. Before I could look round it exploded into the noise of excited children, a hundred maybe, running towards us, a horde in neat uniforms. A girls' boarding school.

I had no time to think further before they were upon us. And if they'd been excited by the arrival of the helicopter, they grew positively manic when they realised it contained Britain's most desirable duo. The screams were ear-piercing and the girls began to rock the helicopter, pushing on the side of it, trying to get at George and Andrew inside.

I grabbed the pilot's arm. 'We've got to get George and Andrew out of here and up to the house.'

It was a futile task. These hysterical young schoolchildren were not a controllable quantity – at least, not by us – but then came the severest and sternest of all sounds.

'Girls ...!'

The hysteria stopped dead in its tracks.

'Behave yourself!'

It was the headmistress.

Ten minutes later we were packed into the back of a minicab heading for Eastbourne, the headmistress rewarded with an autographed album and a kiss on the cheek from Andrew.

I was waiting for George's tirade ... 'No more helicopters. No more conferences. No more managers.'

But he was strangely subdued.

Throughout the dinner and speeches George acted bored and indifferent. When everyone moved on to the ballroom for musical entertainment he grabbed me and said he wanted to go back to London.

The head of Sony Italy had brought a quadruple gold record with him. He asked me to find a moment when he could present it to Wham! and take a picture with them, but George refused point blank. 'I'm not doing it,' he told me. 'These people make enough money from selling my records without me having to hang around and take pictures with them.'

Among the European heads of CBS, respect for George was melting faster than the ice sculpture in the centre of the buffet table. Rather than have him hanging round the conference upsetting people with his sour mood I decided to get a limo and send him back to London. Then I decided I'd like to go too. Jazz and Andrew could stay behind to meet and greet.

We had to wait a long time for the limousine to arrive and George appeared bottled up, not in a good mood at all. When we got into the back of it he spoke almost at once. 'You've got to get Jazz out of America.'

'What on earth do you mean?'

'He's making a mess of things – I've heard he's upsetting people.'

I didn't know if this was the result of something he'd heard during the course of the evening at Eastbourne, from an American record company executive perhaps, or whether it had been something he'd been waiting to tell me since we'd met at the heliport at Battersea. Either way it had to be quashed.

By standing up to Frank Barsalona, Jazz was on the verge of getting Wham! set up with the American stadium tour they'd always dreamed of doing.

'Jazz is setting up a tour for you – in big venues, like you wanted – a stadium tour. It's true he fell out with Frank Barsalona but that just shows you what a good job he's doing.'

George was quiet for a while. 'When I go solo, I don't want Jazz managing me.'

'Jazz is doing just fine.'

I'd already decided, if Wham! were to break up, I wouldn't go on working with Jazz. Even though we were the best of friends, I preferred the freedom of working alone, but that was *my* decision – I didn't want it imposed on me by George. As for ditching Jazz to manage George on my own, my sense of honour said it wasn't a possibility.

George, of course, didn't want a manager with a sense of honour; he wanted a manager who did his bidding. In a recent interview he'd said, 'the reason I chose Simon as a manager was because he's a real arsehole'.

Well Jazz too was an arsehole – stubborn, pig-headed and determined to get what he thought best for Wham!, which at that particular moment meant a tour of American stadiums.

Jazz was doing well. George had got things wrong.

So had Lindsay Anderson.

Lindsay had continued to sort through his seventy miles of film and finally announced his new edit was ready. When we saw it we found he hadn't taken on board any of the criticisms the four of us had made about his previous version. The new one was even worse. Moreover, he'd done an interview with the press in which he'd said of George, 'he has an inflated ego with no interest in anything except his own reality', and of Jazz and me, that we were 'George's puppets, kow-towing to his every need and whim'. At least it made a change from the usual sort of complaints we got from outsiders – that we treated artists with complete disdain and simply manipulated them.

The people Lindsay liked best were misfits; the more someone fitted in with the world, the more he dismissed them. That made George and Andrew the epitome of everything he hated so it was hardly surprising he was finding it difficult to put the film together in a way they would like.

'It doesn't show us as we really are,' Andrew grumbled.

'It's worse than that,' George complained. 'It looks like Lindsay's being scornful of us.'

Having been brought up in the world of documentary films, I would have persevered longer in trying to get a movie that was good for Wham!

while also being unmistakably Lindsay's. But I was overruled. George and Andrew wanted the film made *their* way. And why not? It was *their* million dollars that CBS had lent them to make it with and since George had always made it clear that people around the group were there to do his bidding, why shouldn't film directors be included?

'I want to get involved in the editing myself,' he told us. 'Like when we're making videos.'

So we asked George's favourite video director, Andy Morahan, to come and do it with him. Which left Lindsay to be fired.

Jazz volunteered for the dirty work and made an appointment to meet him, but since I'd known Lindsay for so long, and because he was an old friend of my father's, I thought it might be as well if I cleared the air with him first. Before Jazz could speak to him, I turned up at the cutting-rooms and took him across the road for a coffee to express my regrets.

'I want you to know you're going to be fired and it has nothing to do with me. Nor was your being hired in the first place. If it had been down to me, I would have never let you near the project. You're a cantankerous old bastard who wants to put political and social meaning into every-thing. Just the sort of person who would hate Wham!'

I think he'd realised what was coming and had already resigned himself to being separated from his movie, as if perhaps he'd begun to see that the material really wasn't coming together in a way that was mean-ingful to him.

'You know me,' he said, 'I like films that stir people up – *Incite*ment, not *Excite*ment. Anyway, how's your Dad?'

I told him about a family lunch the previous weekend. I'd been talk-ing with my father about racial prejudice and said how strange it was that some people who are prejudiced still manage to be good people in other aspects of their life. My father completely disagreed. He banged his fist on the table so hard his wine glass jumped onto the floor. 'Intolerant people,' he yelled, 'should be shot!'

Now Lindsay banged his fist. 'They should, they should!' he shouted animatedly. 'And tolerant people too! I hate tolerance even more than intolerance. I *loathe* tolerant people. Tolerance is what you give to noisy children on a beach; tolerance is what you give the mother who can't control her crying baby although it's annoying you to death. Tolerance is simply a temporary gift, offered by someone superior who might easily change his mind and take it away again. For blacks and gays and Jews and every other minority, what's needed is *not* tolerance – it's *indifference*. Complete bloody *indifference*. Then you'd have *real* equality.'

Like all Lindsay's statements, it belied his own character. He'd never in his life managed to be indifferent to anything, just opinionated and usually bloody rude.

And he certainly wasn't indifferent when Jazz turned up later in the day to say he was fired.

36 FUNERAL RITES

Finally, Whamerica!, the American stadium tour. Despite George's reservations, Jazz had pulled it off.

While I'd been trying to sell our management company, and had come up with absolutely nothing, Jazz had fixed eight dates in stadiums across America, six of them already sold out. The tour was due to start in Chicago but for me it started with a Devonshire cream tea.

I was just finishing off my scones and strawberry jam when the lady next to me had a heart attack. Unfortunately I wasn't in a country garden on Dartmoor, I was in the first-class cabin of a British Caledonian plane with Allan, who was coming with me to see the first two dates. Halfway to Chicago the pilot turned the plane around and headed back to England.

Twelve hours after we'd taken off – at just about the time Wham! were due to take the stage on the first night of their stadium tour of America – Allan and I arrived back at Gatwick.

I managed to get Jazz on the phone and wish him good luck for the tour opener. He said everything was fantastic – not only was the show sold out but with fifteen minutes to go until it started the merchandise looked like hitting fifteen dollars per head – an all-time record for that venue.

What a good partnership I had with Jazz. Why had I ever thought it necessary to go to Chicago in the first place? But since I'd promised to take Allan on a few days of Wham!'s tour, we set off again ninety minutes later, though this time we didn't repeat the cream tea.

Chicago was the one place on the tour where Wham! were playing two shows, so the next night we managed to see them. It was good. Good to see the way George and Andrew rose to the occasion; good to see the way the audience rose to George and Andrew. This was way better than their shows in China or Tokyo or Sydney. Something about

America was firing them into a new orbit of performance. Jazz and I had delivered them a sold-out stadium tour in America; now *they* were delivering too, looking like the superstar group they'd asked us to turn them into.

For a moment I almost felt a bond of brotherhood between the four of us – Jazz, myself, George and Andrew. Then I remembered a few weeks earlier George had told me he didn't want Jazz to continue as manager. Moreover, only a week before the US tour started, and with all the tickets already sold, George had changed his mind completely about doing it and was only there now because Jazz had begged our US agent to fly to London and plead with him to do it.

Pop stars – rock stars – what a pain!!

Two years of effort and all it had led to was these eight stadium dates in America. This tour was nothing more than Wham!'s funeral rites.

From Chicago we moved on to Toronto where we woke up to find it raining. Not the sort of rain that could be shrugged off – this was driving, wind-flung rain that crashed against windows in rivers.

Jake, the tour manager, called from the showground. 'We can't rig in rain like this,' he told us. 'There are too many electrical circuits to be installed and tested.'

The rigging should have started a couple of hours earlier, and this gig was the toughest schedule ever. After the show, the stage would have to be unrigged and trucked to the airport where Jake had rented a 747 cargo plane to get it to LA and set up again for the next evening – virtually impossible. 'This gig simply can't start or finish late,' Jake insisted, sounding uncharacteristically panicky.

'We'll sort something out,' I told him, calming him down but with nothing concrete to suggest.

Jazz and I drove through the sheeting rain to the Toronto showground and as we arrived the sun came out. 'There you are,' we told Jake. 'Problem solved.'

Within seconds the crew was in full swing setting up the stage and rigging it. With a good tour-manager in tow, everyone knows, rock managers have little more to do than organise sunshine.

'I'm going to stay here and keep an eye on things,' Jazz told me. But I thought that might be a waste of a nice day so I drove down to Niagara Falls with Allan.

Later, at the show, Allan took a shine to the supporting act, the Pointer Sisters, and they to him. He gave them free hairdos and posed with them for pictures. He also seemed to be getting on enormously well with Jazz and if I hadn't known better I'd have said they were flirting.

'I guess we were,' Jazz admitted later. 'Strange, isn't it. I don't know what happened to me that day.'

Then Wham!'s show at the Los Angeles racecourse. Sold out and glittering!

The racecourse had restaurants and bars way better than most stadiums, and Los Angeles provided celebrities to match. Connie and her counterpart at CBS's Hollywood offices had done their bit. We were overwhelmed with Hollywood razzle-dazzle; music stars, film stars, TV stars – the VIP enclosure was jam-packed.

On the dot of 9.30, the band crashed into the first number like the downward rush of a vast Hawaiian wave. Out of the splattering surf, sweeping across the stage, swooped the figures of George and Andrew – George in send-up biker stuff, his previous clean-cut image forgotten – tight black pants, a chain link belt, the tiniest of flimsy black vests and fingerless black gloves – Andrew in a musketeer's hat and an ankle-length cape.

'Hullo Los Angeles!'

Screams and more screams.

George ripped off his shirt and pumped his crotch; Andrew danced a fandango and flung aside his cape to reveal a bright red suit.

For the opening few numbers I'd planted myself in the middle of the crowd, halfway back on the grass, surrounded by sweating bodies and marijuana smoke.

'They're so horny,' one girl drooled.

'They're making me trickle,' said her friend.

I got out of there and went to the VIP stand. Personally I'd never been able to see George and Andrew as sexy, though it was great to know that their fans did. I saw the show more in terms of its slickness – our computerised lights were the best, we had great back-up dancers, a brilliant band, a pristine white set.

All in all, Wham!'s show was as polished, sharp and entertaining as any I'd ever seen. George and Andrew could steam through a song like 'Go-Go', slip into street jive for 'Wham! Rap', then get the crowd to hold up seventy thousand cigarette lighters at the first hint of the sax solo in 'Careless Whisper'. And the LA show was their best ever.

Backstage afterwards there were stars by the dozen raving about it – Dionne Warwick loved them, even Burt Bacharach, not usually a fan of pop groups, offered praise. But the definitive moment was when Elton John burst into the dressing-room dressed in a bright-coloured tartan suit and flung his arms around George and Andrew. 'Fuck you,' he shouted. 'It took me five years to play a place like this. It's taken you just two.'

37 SELLING UP

The Los Angeles show had been near perfection. It was impossible for Jazz and me not to be proud of what we'd achieved. Surely, we thought, now things were so successful, George's idea of breaking up the group would drift away a little.

We'd done as we'd promised – made Wham! the biggest new act in the world in just over two years. They now had an earning potential of hundreds of millions. If they were to break up now it would feel like having spent two years building the fastest racing car in the world and then – with it sitting gleaming in the driveway – being told you could never drive it. Moreover, Jazz and I *needed* to drive that car. In the two years we'd been managing Wham! we'd made virtually nothing. We had a dazzlingly successful pop group but no cash to go with it.

I tried – more than once – to talk to George about it.

'Why can't you commit to just one more year?'

'I want to start working on different material. Stuff not suitable for Wham!'

'Couldn't you do both? Lots of singers with groups do solo albums and still continue with the group.'

George sighed. 'But that's just the point – I don't *want* to continue with the group.'

'But you'll do one more album?'

'Not if it leads to another tour, I won't. I want it to finish, don't you understand?'

'And what about Andrew?'

'That's between him and me,' he said sharply. 'Anyway, he understands perfectly. There's no problem with Andrew.'

Because we'd had no takers to buy our company, when I got back to London I spoke with my old friend Stephen Komlosey who'd been Robert

Stigwood's partner in the sixties. I told him about the demise of Rupert, my New York contact, and explained how he'd wanted to back us into a public company. Stephen had a rather different idea, more of a 'going in forwards' concept. Why didn't we take over Chrysalis Records?

I don't know why Stephen had this idea, nor why he thought it might be possible, but one day soon afterwards I found myself in a meeting with the board of Chrysalis – Stephen, me and our financial advisers on one side of the table, the Chrysalis people on the other side.

'Your image is dowdy, you're not having current success, you look like a tired old company and you need an injection of new talent,' Stephen told them with impressive bravado. 'Jazz and Simon are prepared to take you over and inject Wham! and all their management earnings into the company. It's just what you need.'

Amazingly, instead of throwing us out, they listened. In fact, Stephen and his advisers talked up such a convincing case for the amalgamation of the two companies under a management team headed by Jazz and me that I began to worry it might happen. For someone like me, who saw life mainly in terms of being free from responsibility, running a record company sounded a profoundly gloomy prospect. Moreover, I'd always thought of record companies as the enemy.

But I needn't have worried; the plan got nowhere. Chrysalis were totally bemused by our audacity. And so was I.

Then we heard that Harvey Goldsmith had done with his company exactly what we'd been trying to do with ours. He'd sold it to a public company, an entertainment group called Kunnick Leisure which owned bingo halls and other similar things. Jazz fixed a lunch for us at Langans with Harvey and his partner Ed.

'When we sold the company,' Ed explained, 'we picked up a million or so in cash plus a few million in shares. If you like, maybe we could use that money to buy your company.'

'Who would be buying our company?' Jazz asked. 'Your company or Kunnick Leisure?'

'I guess it would be Kunnick,' Harvey said, not that it seemed to matter much. 'Get your accountants to set out everything the company might earn in the next three years and let's take a look at the figures.'

Jazz and I sat down and worked it out for ourselves. At this stage, George hadn't actually refused to do a third album so we added royalties from it into the potential income, and then a tour to promote it. And there was a sizeable TV ad for Pepsi in the offing, which Jazz had been negotiating.

When we gave them the cashflow to show to Kunnick Leisure, we told Ed and Harvey, 'Eventually, George might want to break up the group and go solo but we don't know yet when that would be.'

And at that moment we really didn't. After the Los Angeles gig, for a short while at least, it looked like George's idea of breaking up the group had receded slightly. In one of the interviews George and Andrew did for the American press George was quoted as saying, 'There's no doubt that our ambition is to become the biggest band in the world, and I think it's within our reach.'

Did that mean he was planning to take Wham! a bit further before he went solo? We decided the question was best left alone for a while. So while Harvey and Ed thought about whether or not they wanted to buy our company, Jazz busied himself trying to close a deal we'd set up with Pepsi Cola. It would give Wham! three million dollars from which our management company would take a commission of nearly a quarter of a million pounds, an important part of the cashflow we needed if we were to convince Harvey and Ed to buy the company.

* * *

This was a real bits-and-pieces period – life felt fragmented.

Since the end of the American tour Andrew had been mostly in Monaco, learning to race cars, starting at the beginning with Formula Three. There was something of my own character in Andrew. He had dreams of becoming a Formula One racing driver so the first thing to do was move to Monte Carlo, where for tax reasons most racing drivers lived. His approach was the essence of the pop business – get the image right first, the rest will follow later.

George was around in London but not demanding great attention. He was in a morose mood, unsure of what to do next, which left Jazz and me equally unsure while we waited to hear from Harvey and Ed as to whether they wanted to buy our company. For me, in the interim, there was also *The Legacy*.

Connie's publicity for it had become so overwhelming that all the big American TV channels were chasing us for the rights, yet it still wasn't set up in the UK. Lynda La Plante, going with the flow of this new internationalism, took the story further and further from its original roots of a London-based show-business soap opera.

'The original East End family is now scattered all over the world,' she told us. 'There are modern-day relatives in any country we want to film in. They're everywhere – from Rio to Cape Town to the Philippine jungle – doing everything.'

John Maclaren had a bright idea. 'You should turn it into a novel.'

Lynda agreed, in fact she loved the idea, so John and I drew up an agreement giving us joint ownership of the rights and with a few phone calls found her a publisher. Then we flew off to New York to meet CBS and MCA, both of whom were interested in taking the show.

'What you need,' MCA told us, 'is to team up with one of the top independent production companies in LA. Someone with some hot scriptwriters and a few programmes already in production.'

Foolishly, we agreed. Two days later we were in LA meeting them. It meant more people to deal with, more delays and more changes to the original idea. And these people were weird. 'We can't write scripts sitting in the office,' they told us. 'It's too static. We only write in the back of limos.'

So we had a six-hour script meeting in the back of a black-windowed triple stretch driving up and down Sunset Boulevard and Benedict Canyon.

A week later they called us back – they'd had an inspiration. 'Pig farming. It's the only thing that's never been done in big-time soap. We'll take a great chunk of the action to Wyoming and base it round the pork industry.'

'That isn't quite how we saw it,' we told him. 'It was meant to be about show-business life in London.'

'It still can be, godammit. I mean – they all eat bacon don't they! It'll come together beautifully.'

I got back to London to learn that the chap running Wham!'s fanclub had disappeared, as had all the fanclub money. Fanclub members were receiving nothing for their membership fees and the tabloids were running nasty stories – 'George and Andrew rip off their fans' – 'Ten Thousand Wham! Fans in Club Scam'. Things like that.

Usually when something like this cropped up I managed to be away and left it to Jazz. This time I was around and got dragged into it. George turned up at the meeting looking edgy while Andrew arrived from Monaco looking tanned and relaxed and spread himself coolly across an armchair.

Every month ten thousand fans expected to receive a Wham! newsletter together with all sorts of extras – photos and special offers. Running a fanclub is a specialist job. To have it dumped on us with no information other than a list of members was a big headache.

'Perhaps we could use one of those big organisations that run dozens of clubs,' George suggested.

'I checked with a couple,' Jazz told him. 'Just to take it over and reorganise it they'll want more money than we've ever received. It might cost us ten pounds per fan, and we've got ten thousand of them.'

George was shocked. 'One hundred thousand pounds to rescue the fanclub!! And in six more months Wham! might be over. It's not even worth thinking about.'

Now Andrew look concerned too. 'But the tabloids will slaughter us. Perhaps we should find someone else who would run it for a fiver per fan.'

'The problem is,' George observed, 'if we take on someone else and pay money out of our own pockets, for all we know the new person could do a bunk like the last one?'

In the end we decided the most cost-effective action would be to repay every member the five pounds they'd originally paid to join the club.

'Fifty thousand pounds down the drain, but at least it's dealt with,' George said. 'And from here on we won't have a fanclub. We don't need one anyway.'

I had an idea. 'Why don't you and Andrew sign the cheques. No-one will cash them. I mean, what would a Wham! fan rather have – five pounds or a cheque signed by you two?'

George had to be convinced. He felt it was a trick, as if they were deliberately trying to avoid giving the fans their money back.

Andrew got it right away. 'We *are* giving it back,' he insisted. 'If they want it they can have it. If not, they can keep the cheque.'

George and Andrew's signatures were photographed and put into a machine that banks use for large-volume signing and the resulting cheques were sent out with a suitably apologetic letter announcing the termination of the fanclub.

A month later not one cheque had been cashed. The problem had been resolved for a mere five hundred pounds – the cost of ten thousand second-class stamps.

*

A few days later George made his fateful decision. 'I've had enough,' he told us. 'I want to make a schedule for the end of Wham!.'

We still argued with him. Couldn't we hold off announcing it till the Pepsi deal had gone through?

For the moment he acquiesced but we could see he wished he hadn't. He knew all too well the Pepsi ad was a trap. Once it was on air across America, Pepsi would want Wham! back on tour; and one tour would lead to another. And probably to another album too.

George was in an uncertain mood; he wanted to get started on being his real self. 'I feel trapped,' he told me. 'I'm feeling more and more miserable all the time.'

Yet the public had no idea. As Christmas approached, the Top Ten featured two Wham! records – their new single, 'I'm Your Man' and a re-release of 'Last Christmas'. This should have made tying up a deal with Kunnick Leisure all the easier but it was taking too long. If the group broke up before we could pull it off, that would be the end of it. Jazz and I were getting agitated.

Jazz went to see an A&R man at Universal Records to discuss a deal for a new group we might be interested in managing. But instead of talking deals he found himself exploding with fury.

'The music industry's being taken over by niggers and queers,' the A&R man pronounced.

Jazz crossed the room in two strides, picked the guy up by the shoulders and shook him with rage. 'Well, fuck you! My girlfriend's a nigger and my partner's a queer.'

He was going to throw him out the window but realised they were on the ground floor so he shoved him in a cupboard instead.

Since the end of Whamerica! everything had been like that. Nothing was coming together as it should do. George kept telling people, 'Wham! is like a ball and chain.' And for me it felt much the same. Managing Wham! had become a bore; the group was fizzling out and so was our chance of making any money from the work we'd done. I wished I could shove the whole thing in a cupboard and slam the door like Jazz had done with the man at Universal.

With Christmas just a week away George tried again to persuade Jazz and me to cancel the Pepsi deal and arrange a final concert for Wham! at Wembley in the spring. We were just about to give in and do as he said when we finally heard back from Harvey and Ed. 'Happy Christmas, you two! You've got a deal!'

Kunnick Leisure would buy our company for six million pounds, twenty per cent in cash, eighty per cent in shares. The paperwork would be done in the New Year and the deal would be completed at Kunnick's annual general meeting in February.

Even if the shares turned out to be worthless, we would still get six hundred thousand each for the two years' work we'd done. All we had to do was keep Wham! together for two more months.

Jazz and I were over the moon.

38 AMERICAN MUSIC AWARDS

For Christmas I decided on four weeks in Phuket. After three I was interrupted by Jazz.

'We have to go to the American Music Awards.'

I was standing in the hotel lobby looking across a well-kept lawn towards the sea, sparkling under a blue sky. Next to a couple of lazy fishing boats my smooth-limbed beach companions rested on the sand. A few minutes earlier a bellboy had come from the hotel to tell me there was a phone call.

Jazz explained. '"Careless Whisper" has been nominated for Favourite Single and Favourite Video in the American Music Awards. They want George to attend but he's on holiday in Australia. He says we can pick up the award for him, but you know how these things work – if George doesn't turn up they'll lose some of his votes and won't give him an award. And if *we* don't go, *he* certainly won't.'

'Do you really care if he gets an award?' I asked.

'Of course I do. It's like *us* getting the award. As his managers, our stature grows. It'll help us get the company sold.'

I looked again towards the beach and the sparkling sea. I'd been planning to stay another week, another month, maybe the rest of my life. But it was time to get back to business.

'OK,' I agreed. 'I'll come.'

Today was Saturday. The awards were being held in LA on Tuesday and LA was fifteen hours behind Thai time. To get there in time all I had to do was leave on Tuesday afternoon. I could spend at least three more days here.

Jazz read my thoughts. 'You *will* be leaving today, won't you? George wants to know that we're there, on the spot, rooting for him, lobbying, getting him his award. He'll never come if he thinks you're lounging on the beach in Thailand.'

I resigned myself to it and went to my room. I didn't even say good-bye to my friends. If I had done I'd have been tempted to stay a little longer – a lot longer, perhaps.

Twenty hours later I arrived in Los Angeles. Jazz liked the place, I didn't. He arrived around the same time as me and went out to dinner with friends. I sulked in my suite with a bottle of Latour and half a kilo of *foie gras* I'd bought at Honolulu airport on the way.

George had nominations for two categories – but the only one he cared about was Favourite Single. He refused to come unless he was certain to win it. We asked the organisers to check the votes and they told us he was in the lead. Even so, we had to spend the next three days on the phone to him before he finally agreed to come.

He arrived his usual happy self. 'I'd better bloody win this or you'll have screwed-up my holiday for nothing.'

'Don't worry,' Jazz said confidently. 'You'll get it.'

I wasn't so sure. The American Music Awards weren't like the Grammys; they weren't influenced by behind-the-scenes pressure or lobbying by the management, they were voted for by the public and the voting went down to the line.

Nobody would know who the winner was until the last minute.

By the following afternoon George had cheered up and when we set off in the limo he was almost in a good mood. Andrew was meant to be there too but he'd woken late and missed his flight. His absence at the awards didn't matter much; George was happy enough to receive any awards for himself. Apart from in the USA, 'Careless Whisper' had been released as George Michael, not as Wham!, so it felt like the award should be his anyway.

At the theatre, the cars waiting to drop their star passengers queued round two blocks. It was quicker to get out and walk which is what Jazz and I did while George stayed in the limo to arrive in style for the photo-graphers and TV crews. When he did so he grabbed their attention, but only until Whitney Houston arrived, sliding out of the next car in a silver-lamé top slashed to the waist. She was with Clive Davis, the head of Arista Records, and a few seconds later Jazz bumped into them in the lobby.

'I've got a proposition for you,' Clive told him. 'I want George to record a duet with Whitney. They'd be magic together and I'd guarantee you a Number One. Do you think he'd do it?'

Jazz was certain he would but immediately had a better idea – something more prestigious, more impressive, more classy and less pop – a duet with Aretha Franklin (another of Clive's artists). But with Whitney standing in front of him this was not the time to suggest it. He told Clive, 'I'm sure he'd like to. I'll ask him and get back to you.'

The American Music Awards are more about performances than talking. Mainly, it's live music. Acceptance speeches are limited to forty-five seconds. People sit in regular theatre seats, not at tables, and Jazz and I were packed into the middle of a row.

Because in the USA 'Careless Whisper' had gone out as Wham!, the organisers had wanted both George and Andrew to be there, but really this was George's thing. 'Careless Whisper' was his own personal *pièce de résistance*, his greatest work, and he wanted the award for himself.

George sat at the end of a row where he could easily move to the stage if needed. As the awards were announced he looked a picture of enthusiasm, applauding each winner – Bruce Springsteen, Favourite Male Artist – Tina Turner, Favourite Female Artist – Chicago, Favourite Group.

As the moment for Favourite Pop Single arrived, George's smile faded and he became tense and expectant. His hands were clenched on his lap but I could see the huge smile he was holding inside, ready to burst out when his name was announced. And then it came...

'*Huey Lewis and the News.*'

Oh fuck, I thought, there's going to be grumpies tonight.

But watching George's face I saw only the briefest flicker of pain before the smile he'd been holding inside came out anyway. As Huey Lewis passed him to collect the award George smiled congratulations straight into his face. He'd wanted that award more than anything else. He'd flown from Australia especially for it, yet he was managing to look cool and unhurt as someone else went up on stage to collect it.

Next came Favourite Male Video, Bruce Springsteen, and Favourite Female Video, Pat Benatar. Then it was time for Wham!'s second chance of an award.

'Favourite Pop Video. And the winner is ...'

George looked less on edge than previously. Perhaps despair had already set in. Maybe he was already resigned to winning nothing; preparing to live with humiliation.

'Wham! – for "Careless Whisper".'

They'd got it. Or rather George had (for Andrew wasn't even featured in the video). But the smile which burst on his lips wasn't the full release of emotion he'd been preparing for the Favourite Single. It was a smile of relief – relief that he hadn't completely lost face.

He went up alone, played it cool, beamed broadly, said very little and appeared genuinely overwhelmed. But I knew – when he'd missed out on the Favourite Single it had hurt. And with the show only halfway through, there was still another hour to endure, sitting under the cameras, applauding and smiling.

When it finally finished Jazz and I moved out of the auditorium to stand beside George in the queue of stars waiting for their limos. Jazz saw Clive Davis standing alone and went across.

'How about ...' he suggested, 'not Whitney, but Aretha? It would make it so much more credible.'

Clive loved it. 'Brilliant! I'll call her and fix it.'

A few seconds later Jazz was back with us, bursting to tell.

Our limo came and George walked down the red carpet. The crowds screamed but when he reached the car he didn't pose for the photographers like other artists, but stepped straight inside.

Jazz and I followed and slammed the doors.

As we pulled away, cushioned in soft upholstery, the air-conditioning hissing coolly, I told George, 'Pretty good, wasn't it? Two nominations, one award.'

He didn't answer.

I went on. 'Jazz and I are going back to the after-show party. We'll just come a short way with you.'

George suddenly exploded. 'I was humiliated,' he snapped, his face thundercloud grey.

Jazz asked, 'How could you be humiliated when you won an award?'

George's eyes spat needles. 'Because Huey Lewis got Favourite Single! Don't you understand, Favourite Video means nothing. People think it's down to the director, not the artist. You were meant to get me Favourite Single. You didn't do your job properly, man. You fucked up!'

The news about Aretha seemed best kept for later.

The next day George's mood improved hugely. Early evening he said he'd like to take me to dinner, perhaps to make up for having been so belligerent after the awards ceremony – he'd never bought me dinner before, not once in all the time I'd known him.

We went to Dino's on Sunset Strip and George was really easy to talk to; it was something he and I rarely did, chat amicably like that. He was in a reflective mood and told me about something that had happened when he'd been home recently, the first time in a quite a while.

'I wandered down to the bottom of the garden. The other side of the fence there's a farm and countryside. It looked exactly how I remembered it as a kid and I started thinking about all that's happened in the past few years. How trivial it was in relation to what I was looking at, you know – the insignificance of man compared with nature, that sort of thing. For a moment, standing there, it was as if nothing had changed.'

'But d'you really think it *has* changed?' I asked. 'I mean, the way you feel about your family, or yourself – surely that hasn't changed?'

George shrugged. 'About things like that, I'm not sure, but the point of the story is ... While I was standing there with this feeling that nothing had really changed I heard a noise, and there behind the neighbours' bushes were a load of kids with cameras trying to take my picture.'

'And ...?'

'Well, that's it, isn't it? I have to accept that things have definitely changed, and there's no way to put them back as they were.'

I thought he was wrong. 'You'd be surprised how quickly you could get back to being anonymous if you stopped singing, started to live a normal life, got married, had children, grew a paunch. It would take less than a year and there'd be no more kids behind the bush taking photographs, no more journalists hounding you.'

'That's true, I suppose,' George conceded. 'But it wouldn't put things back as they were. I'm not just talking about being a pop star. I'm talking about personal things. I've grown up. I know myself better. I've begun to understand much more about who and what I am.'

I couldn't have enjoyed dinner more, but when the waiter brought the bill, George spoilt it.

'Don't you know who I am?' he asked the waiter. 'I don't think you should be asking me to pay. You're lucky to have me eating here. It'll bring you in business.'

A few minutes later the waiter came back and said, 'That's alright, sir. The meal's on the house.'

I was embarrassed at the time. Later, I tried to find a justification for it. I'd so often seen George do things that were really generous, I felt there must be a good reason for him doing something which seemed so grossly tacky. I remembered what Eartha Kitt had told me about feeling like two different people when she started out – her old self, Eartha May, and the new self, Eartha Kitt.

Perhaps in George's mind, he was still George Panayiotou. 'George Michael' was an invention, a fake character invented to be a foil to Andrew Ridgeley. It was because George had begun to dislike being this fake character so much that he wanted to end Wham! and find a way of being himself. That night, when he went to have dinner with me at Dino's, he had to be George Michael. He wasn't out relaxing, he was playing the part of the pop star. As such, maybe he thought, 'I'm sitting here in this restaurant, working, playing the part of George Michael. I'm giving the restaurant kudos and gossip-column inches. Why should I pay them too?'

I wasn't condoning his behaviour, just trying to understand it. It was so out of his normal character.

If his Mum and Dad had known they'd have killed him.

39   SUN CITY

'You do know, don't you,' Harvey told us casually one morning in his office, 'that the biggest shareholder in Kunnick is Sol Kerzner, the man who built Sun City?'

It was ominous news. He wouldn't have told us had it not mattered, yet it shouldn't have done. After all, when he'd sold his company to Kunnick it hadn't mattered to Harvey. Why should it matter to us?

Jazz asked, 'Has the company buying our company got anything directly to do with Sun City?'

'Nothing at all,' Harvey told us. 'It's just that Sol Kerzner is the largest shareholder. But there are hundreds of other shareholders. Whatever business interests each of them have should be of no concern to us.'

That afternoon, while Jazz and I were still digesting this news, Tony Russell invited us to his office. 'I've heard through the grapevine, you're planning to sell your company to the same people as Harvey did. I'll give you a piece of advice – tell George about it.'

Jazz and I didn't want to. Why should we? It was our company, our money, our decision – we could do whatever we wanted to with it.

'George will feel he should be involved in the decision,' Tony said. 'Because your money comes from managing him.'

Jazz and I decided against it. Next thing we knew, George would tell us where we could go on holiday, what we should eat for dinner, how to decorate our homes. But I knew we were treading on thin ice. With George, I could tell, whenever there was grumpiness it was because of insecurity – a fear of things going wrong onstage or in the media, of having his music disliked by the critics or worse still by the public. Of being seen in a bad light.

Sun City was in Botswana, not South Africa. Botswana was one of the independent homelands created and subsidised by the South African government as a means of reducing its black population.

Most of the world disapproved of this policy for although it created apartheid-free states they were still under the umbrella of South Africa and were born from a desire to segregate rather than integrate.

However, under a shrewd local government Botswana had prospered more than most of the other similar states. It had legalised gambling and granted a licence to Sol Kerzner to build Sun City.

Sun City was a huge complex – hotel, casino, entertainment, holiday homes, sports facilities. There was no apartheid and white South Africans came at weekends with their black lovers – sometimes real lovers, more often short-time mistresses or prostitutes – for under South African law sexual liaison between blacks and whites was forbidden.

Sun City blossomed; Kerzner got super rich; the Botswana government did pretty well, and even ordinary Botswanans found themselves better off than their counterparts in Cape Town or Johannesburg. Major entertainers were paid huge sums of money to sing there – Elton John, Sting and Diana Ross among them – and because the audience was integrated, they did so with no qualms. It became one of the world's *good* gigs, with none of the moral worries about apartheid that came up when the same artists were offered big money to play in South Africa.

Then the anti-apartheid lobby took an interest and decided it was as bad if not worse than South Africa, for although there was no apartheid in Botswana, it compounded the evil of apartheid having been built specifically to sidestep it by the very people who normally supported it.

The moralists were probably right. Maybe it *was* obscene. But so were many things that passed their rigid moral inspection, like the way American record companies ripped off black artists.

Both Jazz and I had to decide what we thought of this, as had Harvey and Ed when they'd sold their company to Kunnick. Sol Kerzner was simply a minority shareholder in Kunnick Leisure PLC, whose shares were publicly quoted and sold on the British stock market. I could see both sides of the argument but came down in the middle. I looked to the media to give me a lead. Nothing untoward had been said in the press about the sale of Harvey Goldsmith's company to Kunnick Leisure, so the moral climate of the moment appeared to say it was OK. Moreover, if people suspected us of racism – *I* lived with my black ex-boyfriend, *Jazz* with his black girlfriend.

My main objection to the deal was the lack of freedom it might present me with. I would be on the board of a public company, there would be frequent meetings and I would be answerable to others. From that point of view I hated the whole idea of it. On the other hand, the cash payment up front would make me pretty well off and ease the financial strain of my domestic life. So, since the terms of the deal were all agreed, I decided for a year at least I would try to be a good board member. All we had to do was wait three weeks for the Kunnick annual general meeting, on which day the deal would be finalised and we would receive a total of six million pounds in shares and cash.

And amazingly, although Jazz and I had sat through endless meetings with lawyers and accountants, although our company records and cash-flow predictions had been subjected to intimate scrutiny, although we'd had to undergo medical examinations to make sure we wouldn't drop dead on our first day as board members of Kunnick Leisure PLC, no-one had ever thought to ask to see a signed copy of our management agreement with Wham!.

Which was just as well, for we'd never bothered to sign one.

40 KITES AND ANCHORS

'**Y**ou should come at once. Something stupendous is about to happen.'
It was Rolf in the middle of the night, waking me up with one of his surprise phone calls.

'Where are you?' I asked.

'In the Philippines. The government here is about to be taken over by the people – a moment of history is about to be made. I'm at the Manila Hotel – I'll book you a room. You won't be disappointed.'

As usual Rolf was a temptation. He was so well keyed-in to everything. If Rolf said come to the Philippines, I had to believe it was worth doing.

'I hope none of your school-friends will be around.'

Rolf laughed. 'None. I promise.'

On the plane I updated myself on what had been going on there. By suspending the constitution then writing a new one, President Marcos had managed to rule the Philippines for twenty years, running it like his own private club, controlling the military, the parliament, the courts, the press, and of course, the money.

His grip began to unravel when a rival politician, Benigno Aquino, returned from exile and was assassinated at Manila Airport. The public reacted angrily, so to prove he still had widespread support Marcos called a presidential election. Aquino's widow, Cory, ran against him and appeared to have won it, but Marcos arbitrarily declared himself the winner. Cory Aquino then addressed a crowd of one million in Manila and called for non-violent resistance. That was when Rolf had called me.

I arrived the next morning around breakfast time. It was obvious during the drive from the airport that the city was in some sort of major unrest. The driver told me, 'The Defence Minister and Deputy Chief of Staff have just defected from the government and barricaded themselves in Defence Ministry headquarters.'

At the Manila Hotel there was a message for me from Rolf. 'I'm at the Ministry of Defence – so is half of Manila.'

When I'd unpacked and showered I went out in the streets to watch. The atmosphere was electric. As I got near the Ministry I saw trees chopped down and buses blockading the streets, protecting the area where the rebels had consolidated their forces. And within that area thousands of people were milling around, not angrily but waving flags and eating candy floss. Surprisingly, among them, I spotted Rolf – it was his shock of silver hair. He had a camera round his neck and was snapping everything in sight.

'Amazing,' I told him. 'Just like Notting Hill Carnival.'

'Don't get fooled, it could turn nasty any minute. It would take just one tank to fire off one round and this whole thing would turn into a bloody battle.'

We bought satay and two bottles of San Miguel beer from a street trader then sat on the sidewalk among local people watching singers and dancers. It was more like an independence day celebration than a revolution.

Rolf lifted his beer bottle, 'Here's to the people!'

By mid-afternoon we'd grown tired of revolt and went back to the hotel. It was strange – one part of town was like a cross between Woodstock and the Hungarian revolution, another like a normal business day. I slept for a couple of hours before meeting Rolf for cocktails at 6 p.m. The hotel was operating as coolly and calmly as normal.

Rolf was still buzzing from the atmosphere in the streets. 'Wasn't it sensational? I got some great photographs.'

We moved from the cocktail bar to the dining room – an oasis of calm amidst the mad world outside – a beautifully cooked French dinner, a wonderful wine.

'Thanks for suggesting I came,' I told Rolf.

'You're lucky you could come here, just like that, on a whim.'

'It's how *you* live too, isn't it?'

Rolf put his glass down and stared at me in surprise. 'Absolutely not! I thought you realised, wherever I am in the world, it's always business, I'm pretty much trapped by it. That's where you and I are so different. Your anchor in life is your two ex-boyfriends. Even though they tie you down and drain your finances, they keep you stable, give you a base from which you can go off and play at managing pop groups or wander round the world having fun. *They* are the anchor to which you attach your kite string?'

'So you don't think I'm really free?'

'Of course not! A kite can't really fly free, that's just an expression. In order to soar high in the sky the string of a kite needs to be anchored. If the string breaks the kite drops back to the ground. The kite's freedom depends on it not being as free as it thinks it is.'

I laughed, 'Why the kite analogy?'

'It's the Chinese side of me. In Shanghai as a boy we flew kites all the time. But you see, my life is completely different from yours. My two boyfriends, Manolo and Lek, are the part of my life to which the kite flies, not where it's anchored. The anchor is somewhere quite different.'

'You mean your business? Your commitment to your "organisation"?'

Rolf smiled. 'These sort of things are best kept private.'

After dinner, as we were going up to our rooms in the lift, Rolf told me, 'Manolo's coming tomorrow. I hope he gets here before it's all finished. It would be a pity to miss it. You remember how he was always winning that game you played together – Mastermind – always getting it in three moves only. We wanted to see if there were any useful applications for that sort of instinct. He's in Tokyo at the moment, doing some tests with an electronics company.'

That evening Marcos imposed a dusk to dawn curfew, but no one paid any attention. A group of rebel soldiers took over the government-run TV station and cut Marcos off in mid-sentence. The next day the streets were more crowded than ever, ringing with live music and spontaneous dancing.

When word spread that Marcos was sending tanks, the crowd moved towards the avenue from which they were coming and sat down across the road in front of them. Not Rolf and me; we hung back nervously, then watched as soldiers came out of the tanks and sat with the people, accepting drinks and cakes and flowers.

I asked Rolf, 'How long do you think this will go on for before Marcos cracks?'

'A couple more days, I think. When the moment is right the Americans are going to fly the Marcoses off to exile somewhere nice – Hawaii or something like that.'

'You mean it's all planned already?'

'Oh yes, but the US has to wait and let it happen organically, so to speak.'

Having spent the day walking round watching things, Rolf and I went back to the hotel for an early supper. It was like watching a day's cricket at Lords, then discussing it over the evening meal. The Marcos government, we decided, was about to be defeated by an innings and a good many runs.

When we'd eaten, Rolf left me with a brandy while he headed for the airport to pick up Manolo, arriving from Japan. After a while I signed the bill and walked back through the lobby heading for my room. By the lifts there was a telex machine which printed out a continuous day-and-night ticker-tape of world headlines. My eyes flicked open in amazement. 'WHAM! SOLD TO SUN CITY.'

I'd hardly got to my room before Jazz called. 'You've got to get back at once. Our deal's in danger. Our management of Wham!'s in danger. Everything's a mess. George was in LA and saw that headline in the *Hollywood Reporter*. He went ballistic. He's getting a plane back tomorrow and wants to meet us the day after. Lunch at San Lorenzo.'

Because I would have to leave first thing in the morning I packed my bag and went to bed but it was only ten o'clock and after an hour I was still wide awake. I put on my swimming trunks and a bathrobe and went down to the pool. It was deserted and unlit but I jumped in anyway and swam determinedly up and down in the semi-darkness, setting myself a target of thirty lengths to ensure I could get to sleep.

After a dozen I sensed a splash behind me and when I turned my head, even in the dim light, I recognised Manolo with a big grin on his face. Though I would have preferred to be alone, I nodded a friendly greeting and kept swimming. Manolo moved across to the other side of the pool and swam up and down in tandem with me so we were swimming alongside each other but fifteen feet apart.

Bit by bit I became aware that he was swimming in perfect synchronicity with me, his stroke, his timing, his turning, all matching mine exactly. And eventually, what had started out as a slight annoyance turned into some sort of camaraderie, and then sexuality. There was no doubt about it, that's what he was putting out and that's what I was picking up.

When I'd done my thirty lengths I stopped swimming, hoisted myself out of the water and sat on a plastic chair in the darkness a few yards from the pool. For a while Manolo swam on, then he too pulled himself out of the water and walked across to where a six-foot tiled wall hid an area behind which were showers. I heard the shower start then heard something splash into the pool just beside me; it was his wet swimming trunks, sinking slowly under the surface.

I wanted no part of it; I stood up to go back to my room and bumped into a silent silhouette – Rolf – standing behind me, watching from the darkness.

The awkwardness was awful.

'I'm off to bed,' I told him. 'I think Manolo wants you to shower with him.'

41

FREEDOM

San Lorenzo was showbiz Italian – very chic, very straight – where the waiters enjoyed telling customers (once they'd finished their meal and had spent a couple of hundred pounds or so) that credit cards weren't accepted.

Outside, the paparazzi crammed the pavement night after night waiting for Tina Turner or Diana Ross to emerge, preferably after some sort of giant row with a boyfriend, or with each other, or with a waiter who'd tipped blancmange down their cleavage.

Such entertainment was not for today; George arrived with his greyest face. Yet he kept things civilised. Over lunch and white wine he wanted to know just what we'd done with *our* company and *his* money.

'Well, it isn't actually *your* money,' I explained. 'It's *our* money – our management commission.'

I remembered Sting having once had a similar disagreement with his manager Miles Copeland. Sting's political views were far to the left; Miles's far to the right. Once, when Miles supported some right-wing cause or other (the sort of thing Sting would go on a march to protest about), Sting objected.

Miles berated him, pointing out that he did an excellent job of managing Sting, which was all that was required of him.

The truth was simple – Wham!'s management company was about to be sold to Kunnick Leisure, a public company, twenty-five per cent of whose shares were held by Sol Kerzner (the founder of Sun City) and the rest by the general public. George thought it looked bad for him. He saw it as *his* money going to Sun City. After all, the headline in the newspaper had told him so.

He decided he couldn't live with it. 'If only you could have done it more privately,' he told us.

Andrew as usual had a more easy-going point of view; the matter of Sol Kerzner didn't seem to concern him greatly.

Jazz argued our case. For my part, I wasn't so sure we had one.

The next few days was like a 'phoney war'. We didn't hear from George and we didn't know what he intended to do.

It was the BPI awards that next brought us together, held in the ballroom at Grosvenor House. Jazz and I were to receive a joint award with Wham! – a special one for getting them into China, for opening new frontiers for the British Music Industry – and it was to be presented to us by Margaret Thatcher's Minister for Trade, Norman Tebbitt.

George turned up wearing a skimpy jacket with no shirt, the thick hair on his chest having been delegated to take its place. From an aesthetic point of view it wasn't a great success but I suspected it was planned as disrespect for Tebbitt, the most right-wing minister in the cabinet.

George and Andrew sat with Jazz and me at the appointed table but there was no light-hearted chatter, just strained politeness as we waited to be called onstage. And once we'd received our award we went our separate ways.

Ten days later George issued a press statement saying he'd terminated his relationship with Jazz and me, and with our management company, Nomis Mangement. He did it without first telling Andrew who'd gone back to Monaco.

The press tried calling Andrew but couldn't reach him, so they called us for our comments.

We delayed them. 'We need to issue our own press release,' Jazz told me. 'Something to stop it looking like Wham! has fired us.'

We jotted it down and sent it out. 'Nomis Management confirm that George Michael has terminated his agreement with the company. Andrew Ridgeley has not.'

We avoided phone calls for the rest of the morning and went for a quiet lunch. As we'd intended, the journalists took our press release to mean that Wham! had broken up. And when the press finally got hold of Andrew in Monaco, because he knew nothing at all about what was going on, he told them, 'Fuck off!'

The *Evening Standard* came out with the headline we wanted:

'Wham! Split!'. But although there was almost nothing about Jazz and me, it didn't change things – we were no longer Wham!'s managers.

Jazz took it badly. 'It's dreadful,' he told me despondently. Yesterday we were managing the biggest group in the world. Now we're just nothing.'

For me, though, it seemed different. Managing pop stars offered two potential prizes, both equally alluring – if they continued to want me to manage them, I earned more money – if they didn't, I regained my freedom. If George had left it one more day to announce his split from us Jazz and I would have received a million dollars each in cash; but it didn't much bother me that we hadn't. Tied to the cash were long-term responsibilities as part of the board of a public company, something I was only too keen to avoid. In due course George and Andrew would settle with us for future record royalties and that would be cash enough to keep me going.

To be honest, the thing I regretted most was having had to fly back from Manila for lunch with George. If he'd said what he'd wanted to say on the phone I could have stayed to see the finale of the Philippine revolution. Instead I'd watched it on TV the evening after our lunch at San Lorenzo. Ferdinand and Imelda Marcos had sneaked out the back door of their palace and been taken by an American military plane to Guam. Cory Aquino was inaugurated president and jubilant Filipinos celebrated in the streets. Free at last.

Like me.

PART IV
APRIL 1986

42 HAPPY BIRTHDAY

'**I**'m coming to take you to lunch.'

'Who's that?'

'It's Rolf, for goodness sake. Don't you recognise my voice?'

I should have done – it was distinctive enough – the Hollywood Nazi.

I was at the Bel Age hotel in West Hollywood. More than ever I was surprised that Rolf should have found out where I was staying; even more surprised that he too should be in LA.

'I'll be there in half an hour,' he told me. 'You didn't think I'd forget your birthday, did you?'

It was just two months since Jazz and I had split with Wham! and each other. I was in LA on some new business. The night before, when the people I'd been meeting had found out it was my birthday, they'd kept me up till three in the morning with drinks to match.

I looked at my watch; it was 11.30 a.m. I pulled myself out of bed and put myself under a hot shower. After five minutes I began to feel better, after ten I was nearly revived. By the time Rolf knocked on my door I was dressed and ready.

'I've got Manolo downstairs – we're going to take you to the best Italian restaurant in California,' he announced. 'About forty minutes out of town – Johnny Milano's.'

Rolf in good form was the most pleasant company anyone could want so I decided to make the best of the lunch he was imposing on me. 'I hope it's going to be good,' I told him. 'I'd been looking forward to a quiet day of solitude.'

He put his arm round my shoulders. 'Never mind, Simon, we can have solitude together – you, me and Manolo over lasagne at Johnny Milano's.'

In the back of the limo with Manolo was another young man, around twenty-something, distinctly chunky with muscles bulging from under his jacket. 'This is Ernst,' Rolf said, nodding at him. 'He's been looking after me lately, if you know what I mean.'

It could mean they'd been sleeping together, or that the young man was his bodyguard, or it could mean both – I had no idea.

Rolf was surprisingly untalkative and for half an hour we sat in silence while the driver took us onto the San Bernadino freeway then off it again, heading up into some hills.

Then Rolf spoke to Manolo in English. 'I'm feeling very bottled up.'

'What does "bottled up" mean?' Manolo asked him, also speaking in English.

'It means there's something worrying me that I want to clear the air about. You know I'm the sort of person who doesn't understand how to plead and beg and cajole, I make agreements and I expect people to stick to them.'

Manolo looked pale. 'What agreement did we make?'

'You live with me and have what you want from the house. You have your own profession and your own money. If you want something more, you ask me. But you don't steal.'

'*Yo no hurté nada*,' Manolo said quickly. 'I never stole anything.'

Rolf shook his head and didn't speak.

We were now on a long straight road heading through scrubland towards more hills in the distance. Suddenly, in one combined movement, Rolf's bodyguard threw open the left-hand door of the car, grabbed Manolo firmly round the chest and projected him sideways out of the door so that the top of his body hung out of the side of the car. He then lay across Manolo's prone body and pressed his face towards the road until it was just six inches away from gravel and tarmac rushing past at seventy miles an hour.

My heart leapt as if it was me who'd been pushed out. The door was open, the wind was tearing at it, Manolo's body hung out of the car. Just one bump or ripple in the road would have torn the features from his face. Then he was back in the car.

He was back in a sitting position, the door shut, the countryside passing serenely by outside as if nothing had happened, his face contorted with terror, his mouth hanging open, saliva running out and dripping onto his trousers.

Outside, the scrub had given away to shrubs and palm trees. The distant hills had reached us and were now on our left – every hundred yards or so were billboards advertising new homes being built in the vicinity – normal everyday Southern California countryside.

'You're going to love Johnny Milano's,' Rolf told me. 'You too, Manolo. The food's simply wonderful.'

I could see Manolo's chest pounding in and out as he panted for breath. He touched his face gingerly and brushed his windswept hair with the palm of his hand, trying to flatten it. I couldn't imagine how hard his heart must be beating for mine was pounding almost as if it had been me who'd been held outside. He looked like jelly – collapsed in the seat – shocked beyond belief.

A sudden oasis of trees and greenery appeared on our left. 'Ahhh. Here we are,' Rolf announced calmly, pointing through the window. 'Look – there's Johnny waiting outside to say hello to us.'

It was a quarter to one; there was a large car park with plenty of cars parked in it. The place was attractive – big trees, outside tables, crisply pressed table cloths, vines growing on the terrace – a piece of Tuscany transported to Southern California.

Rolf opened the door and helped Manolo from the car, deathly white, still quivering; I wondered if he'd pissed himself. When I got out I found my legs buckling too.

Rolf greeted Johnny Milano with a hug and I was introduced effusively. 'This is one of my closest friends,' Rolf told him. 'The manager of Wham! – you know – the group who went to China. And of course this is Manolo, who you've met before.'

Manolo somehow managed to lift a limp hand which Johnny Milano crushed in his grip as he'd just done to mine. Then he led us to a large umbrella-covered table in the shade of a giant Californian oak, the edges of the white tablecloth flapping gently in the breeze. He seated us and beamed into my still shocked eyes. 'I'll cook you my special-est pasta – *fettucine marinara alla' arabiatta*. You're gonna love it. Now – what about wine?'

He snapped his fingers and the waiter brought a carafe of deliciously cold white Verdichio, then Johnny disappeared inside to the kitchen.

Manolo – ashen-faced, his body sagging, his breath coming fast – seemed unaware of where he was.

'Are you OK?' I asked.

'He's fine,' Rolf told me. 'No problem.'

The restaurant hummed quietly and efficiently like a good restaurant should. Over our heads the breeze shuffled the branches and a small acorn fell onto the umbrella above, then plopped onto the ground beside us. I began to think perhaps the incident in the car had never happened. I must have momentarily fallen asleep and had a nightmare.

Rolf sipped his wine. 'You know, Simon, sometimes people make me scared.'

My eyes flipped open. 'In what way?'

'Well you see, I'm not a person for expressing my feelings – not love, not hatred, not anger – so I have to show them instead. Like just now with Manolo. He made me so angry I couldn't talk about it – I just had to show him instead. Perhaps he hadn't realised how angry I was, but he does now. But it scares me what I sometimes have to do to let people know. Manolo could have got killed.'

'You mean – *you* could have killed him.'

'No, it would have been *him* who killed himself, by not doing what he agreed with me.'

'For God's sake, Rolf. If you were so damned angry, why didn't you shout at him, scream at him, hit him even.'

I was raising my voice and I paused to get it under control.

'How could I hit him?' Rolf protested. 'He's my boyfriend. We can't go hitting each other.'

'How can you be friends? You just pushed his head out of a car at seventy miles an hour and nearly killed him.'

'I didn't nearly kill him, all I did was let him know how angry I was inside. Now he knows, don't you, Manolo?'

Manolo, still lost in shock, appeared deaf to what was being said.

'I think you're mad,' I said.

'Mad?' Rolf's eyes opened wide with surprise. 'How can I be mad? It was perfect – I let him know, and now we're back friends again, having lunch – aren't we Manolo?'

The waiter arrived with three plates of Johnny Milano's 'special-est' pasta.

'Rolf – have you ever done that before?' I asked. 'I mean, what you did to Manolo.'

Rolf looked at Manolo and grinned. 'Not with Manolo I haven't. In Mexico the roads are too bumpy – it's not safe.'

It was a joke for Christ's sake. How could he joke about such a thing? I wasn't sure what to do – should I smile or sulk? Was it any of my business? Well yes, of course it was. Surely some part of what had just taken place was to do with Manolo teaching me tennis in Villahermosa, or swimming with me in Manila. Or maybe not?

Another waiter arrived with a three-foot long pepper mill, and then Johnny Milano with an open bottle of red wine. 'Barbaresco Sori San Lorenzo, 1952 – virtually unavailable anywhere else in the world. I think the last eleven bottles are in my cellar. This is one of them.'

He placed three vast wine glasses on the table and poured almost a third of the bottle into each, which hardly made a dent in them.

'Enjoy!' He smiled graciously. 'I'll come back and talk to you again over coffee.'

Rolf sat back and took a large gulp of the delicious Barbaresco. 'You know,' he said contentedly, 'life can be so good sometimes. Good food, good wine, good friends.' He lifted his glass to me.

'Listen,' I ventured. 'Since we're such good friends, if you ever felt angry with me would you please just tell me rather than doing what you did to Manolo.'

Rolf nodded. 'Sure! But I hope you understand, other people are in a position to express their anger with me in a similar way. Perhaps you should stay away from China for a while, then there would be no-one asking me for results.'

At that moment Manolo came back to life and pushed a fork into his plate of fettucine. Rolf and I followed suit, eating in complete silence.

Was this really about China? Or was it about Manolo? I couldn't decide. Suddenly the modest domestic strife of Donavon and Allan at 29 Bryanston Square looked positively enticing, as did the mundane trivialities of the pop business. Perhaps it was time to go back to London and find a new group to manage. But in my mind I was still trying to find a way that would make it possible to continue to know Rolf. After all, this was the same person I'd known and liked enormously for the last three years, it was just that there was a side to him I hadn't previously come across.

As I finished my pasta, I decided – no, after this meal there could be no more Professor Rolf. He'd given me a great deal of enjoyment but it was time to draw a line.

Rolf seemed to know what I was thinking. 'Simon – I think, after today, you'd be better off not seeing me again. I'm afraid in terms of your life and your world, I'm innately dangerous. So in respect of our good friendship which I've enjoyed so much, we should make this our goodbye lunch.' He nodded towards Manolo, now with a strange forlorn smile on his face. 'I think I've shown you why.'

I took a moment to take it in. Presumably Rolf had found what he'd just told me quite difficult to say and I felt strangely touched. I found myself smiling and raised my glass to him. But he didn't seem to notice.

When our eyes met I saw only seriousness. 'My driver will take you back to your hotel,' he said quietly. 'Manolo and I will stay for a while and talk with Johnny.'

43 AND THEN?

A couple of years later I'd neither given up the music business nor ditched my two ex-boyfriends. They were still in residence at Bryanston Square, still arguing, still running unprofitable businesses, still the people I cared about most.

Predictably, I had a new group to manage – Blue Mercedes. They'd had a song at Number One in the American dance charts for fourteen consecutive weeks and we'd just got back from a tour of the Far East.

Allan had made his trip to China, demonstrating chopstick hairstyles, arranged by Lew Mon Hung, including dinner after his show in Beijing with the wife of the new Prime Minister, Lee Peng. The trip had cost plenty, Lew Mon Hung having become as clever as Zhou at extracting money from people who wanted to do business in China and meet political celebrities.

Donavon had succeeded in pulling off his three-day Black Music Festival at Wembley with Chaka Kahn and Philip Bailey topping the bill. As was to be expected, the income hadn't quite matched the expenditure, but at least the loss had been borne by various departments of the GLC rather than by me.

Jazz, no longer connected with me, had secured a Number One hit for his girl-friend Yazz with 'The Only Way Is Up'.

CBS had been given the chance, and turned it down, of getting into China, Walter Yetnikof's boss, Tisch, saying it wasn't worth investing in anything which didn't show a profit within a year. 'In which case,' I told Walter, 'CBS might as well get out of the music business.' With which Walter agreed.

Connie, while still doing publicity for Allan, continued to do it for George too; and Andrew was said to be in Los Angeles, working hard at spending his money.

The Legacy, the amusing soap opera John Maclaren and I intended to make about London showbiz life, had spiralled out of control and we'd lost it. For Lynda La Plante, though, our idea of a London-based docu-drama had set her on the path to superstardom as a novelist.

And in Canton, I heard, there were six thousand army-issue bikes waiting for anyone who wanted to pick them up.

George had made *Faith*, a solo album that had gone to Number One in America, helping him to earn fifty million dollars from touring. Everyone said his mood had improved immeasurably, and I think I understood it. During his worst periods with Wham!, he'd been suffering from that worst of all ailments – infatuation.

To begin with he'd been in love – totally, head-over-heels, uncontrollably in love – with being a pop star. And the thing about being besotted in that way is that it insulates you from the rest of the world – other people's feelings become irrelevant, happenings around you become insignificant. You become over-focused.

Bit by bit his lust for success had cooled. He was left older and wiser and nicer. And one night I met a new George.

The night before, I'd been on *After Dark,* a late-night chat show on which another guest had been an aggressive young singer from a little-known Scottish pop group wearing a grass green jacket. Despite his fashionable jacket, he had an enormous chip on his shoulder about the glamorous and fashionable side of the music industry and said I represented everything he disliked most about it.

He continued with a flow of distasteful remarks which I attempted to parry with cutting replies. I was hoping a good one might pop out of my mouth just as the show ended, leaving him unable to respond as the titles rolled over his discomforted face, but this was a strange chat show – it had no cut-off time. It went on till it ran out of steam, sometimes till two in the morning or whenever the producer felt like going to bed. Every time I came out with a putdown that was perfect for ending the show, it just rambled on, as did Mr Greenjacket's abuse.

The next evening I was having dinner in the Caprice when George walked in with some friends. He saw me and came over. 'What a wanker, that guy on the chat show. I watched it to the end. I felt so sorry for you.'

George's friendliness – the lack of underlying distrust, of demanding eyes, of impending complaint – could this really be the same person? We chatted some more then rejoined our respective tables. Later, when I was leaving, he was leaving too. He took me to see the new stereo system in his Land Rover, still as charming as before dinner, almost flirtatious in his apparent enjoyment of my company.

It was nice. I mean, after three years managing him during which I'd never seen it, I felt pleased to have seen at last what his friends, his mum and dad, his sisters and cousins, Andrew, and David the ice-bucket thrower, must have seen all the time. It was extraordinary – the difference between being his manager and being completely independent of him. To say it was like knowing two different people was not enough. It *was* two different people.

Six months later I came into contact with Rolf again.

It was a Monday night at the Hippodrome when I was swirling and sweating on the dance floor, buzzing with booze, my eyes flicking around me grabbing images like strobes – a static dancer, a silver T-shirt, a frozen laugh and …

… the manager of the disco standing at the edge of the dance floor waving a cordless phone at me.

I stopped dancing and followed him through soundproof doors to his office, then put my ear to the phone.

'Simon? It's Manolo, in Mexico.'

'Good heavens, how did you find me?'

'I called you at home and they said you were at the Hippodrome. Rolf has died. Would you like to attend his funeral? It's tomorrow.'

Being given news like that in the middle of a fun night out rather spoilt the atmosphere. As for attending the funeral – I've never been a great fan of funerals but this one felt worth going to. My friendship with Rolf had been left hanging in the air and being at his funeral might help tie up the loose ends. I presumed it would take place in Mexico, though it was just as likely to be Shanghai or Tokyo or Timbuctoo. I wondered if I could get there in time.

'Where will it be?'

'Bournemouth crematorium. Two o'clock tomorrow afternoon.'

I was shocked. It was quite hurtful to think that Rolf had been in England and not called me. But of course, we'd decided there should be no more contact between us.

Manolo had a problem with his visa and couldn't go, but I wanted to. So the next morning I drove down to Bournemouth, arriving at the crematorium just before two.

Inside, a funeral service was in progress. Outside, a dozen or so people were waiting around for the next one. They looked an ordinary bunch – men, women and teenagers.

I decided I must be at the wrong place and walked over to check the notice board. Sure enough, it stated: '2 p.m. – Mr. Rolf Nueber'.

I walked back to the group of waiting people and spoke to a plumpish woman in her forties. 'I'm a friend of Rolf Nueber. I'm here for his funeral. Are you anything to do with him?'

'It's a friend of Uncle Rolfy,' she shouted to the others, and they all came over.

I couldn't believe it! He had children, grandchildren, nephews and nieces. During the twenty years he'd been in Bournemouth he'd apparently lived a life of absolute normality – married with three daughters, all of them now in their late thirties with children in their early teens, as English and ordinary as could be imagined.

One of his daughters told me, 'Mummy died nearly twenty years ago. We children were almost grown up at the time so Daddy left home and went off travelling round the world. He sent us money every month and came back once or twice a year to visit.'

'Where did he die?'

'Right here in Bournemouth. He came last week for my fortieth birthday but as soon as he got here he had a heart attack.'

It was unbelievable that Rolf could have fathered such normality. Like everything else about him, it just didn't add up.

Except. When he'd talked to me in Manila two years earlier he'd spoken about 'his kite being anchored'. At the time I'd presumed he meant 'to his murky business life'. Now I understood better. It wasn't his business life that anchored him, nor was it his two boyfriends, it was *this* – a completely commonplace life – a regular family in Bournemouth.

I was introduced all round and went with them into the small non-denominational chapel, clean and bare and smelling slightly of Dettol. I decided I would duck out of joining them for drinks afterwards; I felt too uncomfortable. The homely father and uncle these people remembered must have been so completely different from the person I'd known. I doubted there could be a single thing in common between *their* Rolf and *mine*. But I was proved wrong.

The service was a humanist one with no religious connotations. The short pieces of music the family had chosen were all from *Sketches of*

Spain by Miles Davis. As we came out of the church one of Rolf's daughters asked me if I'd enjoyed them.

'Very much,' I told her. 'In fact I once sat with Rolf in Mexico listening to those very same pieces of music.'

She giggled. 'I bet he was smoking a joint. He always did when he listened to jazz.' Her eyes were full of amusement. 'Are you going to tell us a little of what he got up to? He was always so secretive. Who was the woman he lived with in Mexico? When he got ill he told us to call someone called Manolo. Is that his son?'

'I never once saw him with a woman,' I told her truthfully. 'And I can promise you Manolo is not his son.'

She pouted – surprised – puzzling over what I'd said and perhaps not wanting to put two and two together. 'After mummy died and daddy left home we all thought he'd gone off with another woman. Mummy always accused him of being a womaniser – always disappearing off to London. She presumed he had a lady-friend there.'

'Mostly, he took photographs and collected wine,' I said. 'And of course, he travelled endlessly.'

'Why?' She raised her eyebrows questioningly. 'Why was he always travelling? He was such a mystery. What on earth did he actually do?'

'I never really found out. Except for his language school in Germany.'

'But that didn't exist,' she said abruptly. 'I went looking for it once when I was on a weekend trip to Berlin. It was just one of those serviced offices – you know, the type you rent by the month with a phone number and someone to answer your calls.'

I shouldn't have asked the next question but I couldn't stop myself. 'But he *did* teach when he was here in Bournemouth, didn't he? When you were all children, he *was* a professor of languages, wasn't he?'

She shook her head, puzzled at the question. 'He was a businessman. I'm not sure what sort exactly. Like I told you, he was always off in London. I don't think he was ever a teacher.'

It was strange – as a pop manager I'd often had to promote a public persona not strictly in line with its owner's true self; moreover I'd always known Rolf was a rogue. I shouldn't have been upset but I was. That he was a professor of languages had been central to my perception of him.

A few minutes later, when no-one was looking, I sneaked back to my car and set off for London. I wanted to hear nothing else about Rolf that could make him different from the person I'd known. Nor, I felt, did his family. We'd both known our own version of him and for my part I'd enjoyed it enormously.

The truth seemed so unnecessary.